# KOREA'S HERITAGE

*A Regional and Social Geography*

## ABOUT THE AUTHOR

Shannon McCune was born in Sonchon, Korea in 1913, the son of the renowned American scholar-missionary family. After receiving his B. A. from the College of Wooster in 1935, he did graduate work at Syracuse University and Clark University, receiving his Ph. D. from the latter in 1939 in the field of geography. His doctoral thesis was entitled "Climatic Regions of Tyosen (Korea)."

He joined the faculty of Ohio State University in 1939 to teach geography, taking leave during World War II to serve the U. S. goverment in intelligence work. In 1946 he was awarded a Presidential Decoration, the Medal of Freedom, for his work in China. From 1947 to 1955, he was Professor of Geography at Colgate University. During 1953–54 he was on sabbatical leave from Colgate as Fulbright Visiting Professor at the Institute of Geography, of Tokyo University.

Professor McCune returned to Korea on two separate occasions to do field work, once in 1938–39 as a William Libbey Fellow from Clark University, and again in 1954.

He has contributed over eighty articles to various geographical, educational, and international affairs journals and has been actively associated with various scholarly organizations concerned with geography and international affairs. The present work, his first full-length book, consolidates and organizes the material collected over many years of intensive research into Korean geography.

# Korea's Heritage

## A Regional &

## Social Geography

by | Shannon McCune

*Provost, University of Massachusetts*

published by | CHARLES E. TUTTLE COMPANY

Rutland, Vermont

with the cooperation of | Tokyo, Japan
the International Secretariat
Institute of Pacific Relations

DS
902
M 23

*Published by the Charles E.*
*Tuttle Company, Inc.*
*of Rutland, Vermont & Tokyo, Japan*
*with editorial offices at*
*Suido 1-chome, 2-6, Bunkyo-ku, Tokyo*

*Printed in Japan*

TO
EDITH

# Preface

Korea, 85,000 square miles in area, is only a small segment of this world's surface. The thirty million Koreans are only a small portion of this world's people. Yet this peninsula is of great importance in these days of international tension. Knowledge of Korea's geographic position, character, and diversity is needed if sound decisions are to be made concerning this strategic area. It is the aim of this book to present this geographic knowledge—the heritage of Korea.

Naturally, as one who was born in Korea and who spent his boyhood there, I have certain prejudices; to me, Korea is a land of beauty and the Korean people are likeable and have many fine qualities. Field research in Korea and study of available literature has convinced me that the role of geography, though a silent role, is extremely important in the lives of the Koreans, living as they do close to their land. This book may reveal my prejudices; it purposely stresses the geographic factors which are too often neglected. In the discussion of Korea a regional approach is employed, for by understanding the parts a person can better understand the whole of Korea's geographic character.

I am greatly indebted to many people who have kindly aided me in the preparation of this book; naturally I am solely responsible for the material I have presented. Jonathan Kistler, Associate Professor of English at Colgate, painstakingly went over an early draft and corrected much of the text. Lilo Rudas efficiently typed the manuscripts in various stages. Numerous Colgate students aided in the research and in assembling the material; Charles F. Steffens, Dan Scanlon, and Alec Frost have been most helpful. My colleagues on the Colgate faculty, officers in the University administration, and students (particularly an Area Studies class who used parts of the manuscript as a text) have been a source of aid on various occasions. I am indebted to the continued personal interest of William L. Holland of the Institute of Pacific Relations; the formal acknowledgement of their support appears elsewhere in this book. Roger F. Evans of the Rockefeller Foundation supported phases of the project; I am thankful to the Foundation for a grant and its extension. The maps were skillfully drafted by E. P. Magaha, Jr. The pictures were generously furnished from a number of sources. Numerous persons interested in Korean studies in the United States, Canada, Japan, and Korea have been kind enough to go over parts of the manuscript and I am grateful for their suggestions. During my trip to Korea in May of 1954, my sister-in-law, Evelyn McCune, and L. George Paik, who has been like an elder brother to me, were especially helpful, along with a host of Koreans and Americans who aided me in gathering material for the final revision of this book. My family has been most patient and helpful while I have been working on the research and its culmination in this book.

S. M.

# Contents

# List of Maps and Charts

# List of Plates

# KOREA'S HERITAGE

*A Regional and Social Geography*

| | The Korean Peninsula: |
|---|---|
| *Chapter 1* | Its Location and Diversity |

KOREA is located in the heart of the Far East. This fundamental fact of geographic location has always been a major factor in Korea's history. Surrounded by the major powers of Asia and the Pacific—each vitally interested in controlling the strategically located country—Korea has become many times a battleground in a struggle for power. To the southeast, only 120 miles distant, lies Honshu, the principal island of Japan. To the west, at about the same distance, lies the Shantung peninsula of China. Manchuria, the northeastern province of China, shares most of Korea's northern boundary. Finally, in the northeast, for eleven miles along the Tumen River, lies Russia. Not only Korea's strategic location in the Far East, but its geographic character as a peninsula has been a key factor in its history. As a peninsula it has served as a bridge between powers on the continent of Asia and powers in the Pacific. However, the narrow peninsula is no easy highway; rather, it has often become a blind and tortuous alley in which aggressors have spent themselves. This fundamental aspect of Korea—its peninsular location in the heart of the Far East—needs stress.[1]*

* For bibliographic references and notes, referred to by superior numbers, see Appendix A.

3

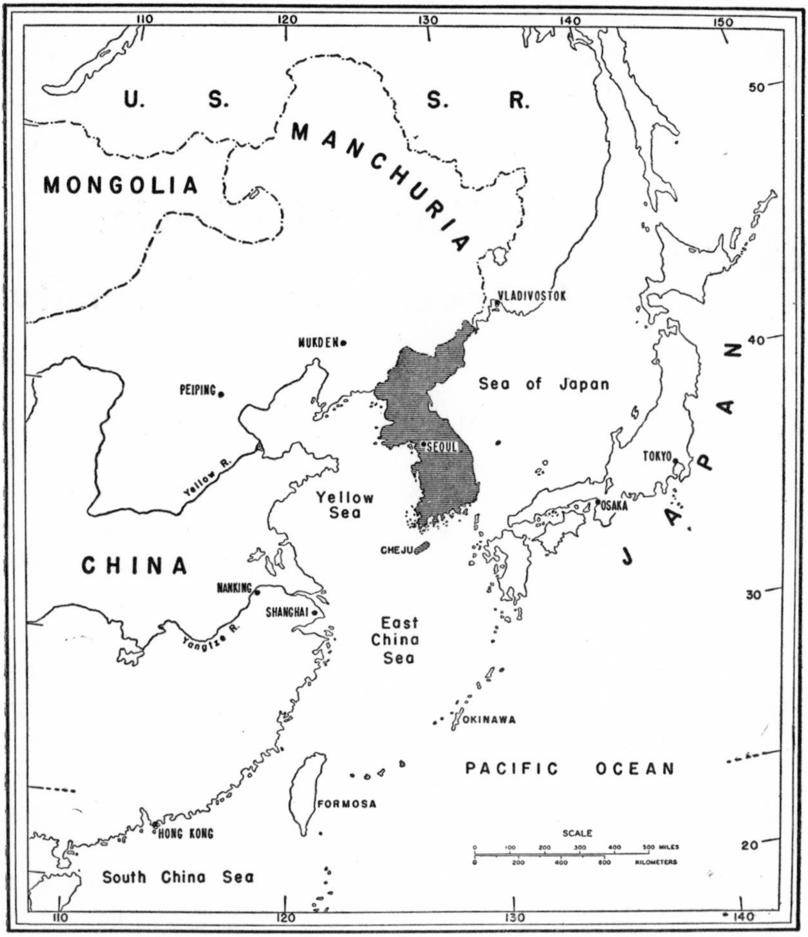

FIG. 1.—The location of Korea in the heart of the Far East.

The Korean peninsula is not large; with its adjacent islands
it comprises 85,285 square miles, roughly the area of Minnesota.
Elongated and irregular in shape, it stretches about six hundred
miles between latitude 43° N. and latitude 34° N., though the
island of Cheju off the southwest coast extends to latitude 33°

06′.[2] Thus, the northeastern section of the country is in the same latitude as New England, and the southern section is in the latitude of South Carolina. Just as a cross section from Boston to Atlanta shows geographic diversity, so Korea has marked differences because of its latitudinal spread.

The peninsula is not of uniform width; from a broad base on the Manchurian border it narrows down to a waist of 120 miles between Wonsan and Pyongyang and then widens at the Hwanghae peninsula. It narrows again and extends to the southeast with a rather uniform width of some 160 miles. The exact longitudinal limits of the peninsula are 124° 11′ to 130° 56′, a width very slightly greater than that of New York State. The shape and location of the peninsula have often been likened to "a dagger pointed at the heart of Japan." This figure may be exaggerated, but it does suggest that the close proximity of Korea to Japan has been an important factor in the politics of the Far East.

The Sea of Japan, to the east, is relatively deep. The continental shelf is narrow and etched by occasional submarine canyons. There are few islands, few broad expanses of beach, and few natural harbors; lagoons blocked by bars at the mouths of narrow bays are notable features of the eastern coast. The tidal ranges are small, two or three feet at the most. Off shore some eighty miles from southeastern Korea is Ullung (Dagelet) Island,* a small, volcanic island which has been under Korean suzerainty for many decades.

In contrast to the Sea of Japan, the Yellow Sea, on the west coast of Korea, is very shallow and has extensive tidal flats. Some rivers flowing into it have fairly deep estuaries. Harbors have been developed with difficulty because the tidal range is as much as thirty feet in places. Many islands, sometimes separated from the shore only by tidal flats, dot the coast.

* The use of two such different names for the same island may seem strange. A note on Korean place names is given in Appendix B.

The south coast, along the Korean Strait, has many islands, small bays, and peninsulas. It is a typical ria coast line, a coastal zone which has been submerged. Fifty miles off the southwest coast of Korea is the large volcanic island of Cheju (Quelpart), which had a semi-independent status at times in the past, but which has been under firm Korean control during recent centuries. The Tsushima Islands in the straits between Japan and Korea, though sometimes claimed on very tenuous grounds by nationalistic Koreans, are definitely Japanese.

The domination of the Korean peninsula by other Far Eastern powers seems to have been its peculiar fate. For most of its history Korea had a special relationship to China. Under the Confucian scheme of international relations, Korea was the "younger brother" nation to the "elder brother" nation, and the smaller nation adopted, perforce, much of the culture and many religious, political, and social ideas of its neighboring "teacher." For centuries Korean kings received symbols of investiture from the Chinese emperors. When China was subjected to invasions by the Tartars, Mongols, and Manchus, Korea too had to accept alien political domination.[3]

But during the period of Japanese military power, great pressure was exerted upon Korea from the other direction. About 360 years ago, the Japanese dictator, Hideyoshi, dreamt of conquering China, but these dreams were shattered on the Korean land bridge, partly because of the attacks by Koreans on the Japanese communication lines. However, by the end of the nineteenth century, when Japan was developing into a modern power, the political, economic, and military pressure was renewed, and Japan got its first foothold on the continent of Asia by taking over Korea. Some of the battles of the Sino-Japanese war of 1894–95 were fought on the plains of Korea. Ten years later Japan came into conflict with Russia, and again the Korean peninsula was the scene of battle between its aggressive neighbors. After a short protectorate, Japan annexed

Korea outright in 1910, and for the next thirty-five years Korea was a Japanese possession.

In June, 1950 the importance of Korea's geographical location became a matter of world interest. The "international frontier" between the Communist-dominated world and the Free World had been sharply drawn at the thirty-eighth parallel in mid-Korea following the defeat of Japan in 1945. The thirty-eighth parallel was initially designated to serve simply as a line of demarkation for the acceptance of Japanese surrender by Soviet and American troops. But the line—a line of convenience—had soon hardened into a solid boundary. It was the violation of this frontier by armies from the north that turned Korea once more into a battlefield. Korea suffered the fate of a small nation located in close proximity to great and competing powers. The simple fact of geographical location once more became fundamental in Korea's history.

In a consideration of Korea today as equally significant as the fact of geographic location is the fact of geographic diversity. The differences from place to place within the peninsula have been of fundamental importance during the long past as well as in the tumultuous present of Korea. When diverse areas, such as northern and southern Korea, which could profit from unity and which have so much in common, are separated by artificial barriers, only tensions and chaos result, as we have learned to our sorrow. The existence of geographic diversity in Korea must not be forgotten or glossed over; in order to be successful, any plans which are made for Korea's future must take this factor of geographic diversity into account.

Korea's geographic diversity is due to various facts. One of the basic factors is the contrast within the peninsula of plains and mountain lands. Only one-fifth of Korea can be cultivated, largely because of difficulties imposed by terrain. The mountain areas which make up the bulk of Korea are sparsely populated. The farmers live in dispersed farmsteads rather than in compact

villages. With the abundance of wood in these forested mountains, the farmers often shingle their log houses. Thus these
mountain areas are quite different from the plains, where most
of the Koreans live in closely-packed villages of thatch-roofed,
mud-walled houses. The rugged terrain throughout Korea
isolates individual river basins and valleys, so some plain-
dwellers live quite differently from their near neighbors.
Northern Korea is more mountainous and has less extensive
plains than southern Korea; within these two divisions there
is even more diversity in relief.

Although all of Korea has the general characteristics of a
humid, mid-latitude, monsoonal climate, yet here also are geographic diversities, particularly in the length of the cold winter
season. The mountainous northern interior has bitterly cold
winters, the southern coast has mild temperatures with monthly
averages above freezing; naturally there are gradations between
these two extremes. These climatic differences, especially between north and south, affect crop production and hence population densities. In the south a crop of barley may follow a crop
of rice, cotton, or some other cereal; in the north only a single
crop of rice, millet, wheat, or other grains can be grown. Soil
and vegetation differences also reflect these climatic diversities.

Successive waves of migration into the peninsula were
followed by contrasting regional developments and by a series
of invasions, which affected different parts of Korea in different
ways. Thus the cultural history of Korea varied from place to
place and from province to province within Korea. Social
stratifications developed among the Korean people and in recent
decades there have arisen sharp contrasts between rural and
urban life. However, despite these diversities in historical
development, the Koreans are of one race, with one language
and culture, and deeply conscious of their common heritage.

Naturally, in the economy of Korea there are some significant
regional diversities. When the country was under Japanese

control, southern Korea, with its better physical base for agri- culture, was forced to specialize in commercial rice for export to Japan. Northern Korea, blessed with mineral resources and potential hydroelectric power, was exploited thoroughly by the Japanese as a raw material supply base for their war industries. However, the cliché which has been used to describe these two divisions of Korea as "the Agricultural South and the Industrial North" is an over-simplification. In spite of recent development of mineral resources and hydroelectric power plants and the consequent growth of huge industrial complexes, the people of northern Korea are still predominantly farmers. In the south, on the other hand, there has been a considerable development of manufacturing and some resource development, so that it is not a purely agricultural land. Certainly with the effective aerial bombardment of industrial facilities in the north and the destruction during the war of many manufacturing facilities in the Seoul area and elsewhere in the south, the distinction between north and south from the standpoint of modern economy is no longer so valid. All of Korea is now agricultural for the most part, though, if real peace comes, there are possibilities for the re- development of many industries. The differences of agricultural production, due to differences of climate and terrain, naturally result in differences in population density. Thus the five political provinces of northern Korea, with an area of 43,631 square miles, had a population of 8,223,477 in 1940, a density of 188.47 persons per square mile, whereas the eight provinces of southern Korea with an area slightly less, 41,654 square miles, had a population almost double that of the north: 16,101,558 and a density of 386.55 persons per square mile. In view of the war's destruction and the waves of refugees, this disparity in population is today even greater than two to one.

The weakening effects of geographic diversities within Korea were magnified by the imposition of the thirty-eighth parallel as a rigid barrier between North and South Korea after the surrender of the Japanese in 1945. The continuance of such a barrier, on each side of which divergent developments take place, could only serve to intensify these effects. Provided there is the opportunity for a healthy interchange of products, geographic diversity can give strength to a country—witness the case of the United States. But if areas are separated by curtains of iron or bamboo they are certain to become individually weaker, unless supported by large and continuing quantities of outside aid. If the framework which is developed in the future does not allow for peaceful intercourse, preferably under a unified, democratic, and independent Korea, then tension may continue and war again break out. Thus, the fact of geographic diversity is a very real one in the situation of Korea today.

Because of the importance of the fact of geographic diversity, either for strength or for weakness, the major theme of this book is to describe and analyze the differences and similarities from place to place in Korea. Special stress is given to the varied activities of the Korean people as they are carried on under different physical conditions. In the latter part of the book the peninsula is divided into two divisions, ten regions, and numerous sections, so that the geographic diversity which makes up Korea may be better understood. Geography is the silent factor amid the turmoil of Korea today, a heritage that needs to be known by thoughtful citizens of the United States and the world who are concerned with this strategically located peninsula.

# *Chapter 2* | The Land of Korea

THE casual tourist of prewar days, riding on fast trains past the slums of large Korean cities, by badly eroded and deforested hillsides, along muddy paddy fields, catching fleeting glimpses of hastily erected mud-walled houses clinging precariously to. hill slopes, would hardly consider Korea a land of beauty. And the American G.I. who served with the occupation troops in Korean cities or who fought up and down the Korean hills understandably found little to admire in all the devastation wrought by bomb and shell. But those who in the peaceful days before the war or during periods of calm in the fighting went out into the countryside, leisurely climbed the hills, rested on the slopes near old grave mounds and looked out over tree-clad mountains, knew a Korea which was quiet, timeless, and beautiful in its diversity. They saw the Korea that the Koreans know and love.

The observer with an eye to geographic phenomena sees Korea above all as a peninsula ribbed with mountains. French Catholic fathers, who were among the earliest visitors from the Western world, said the land resembled "a sea in a heavy gale." The mountains seem numberless—range after range extend as far as the eye can see. No plain is so extensive that the mountains encircling it cannot be seen on a clear day. In

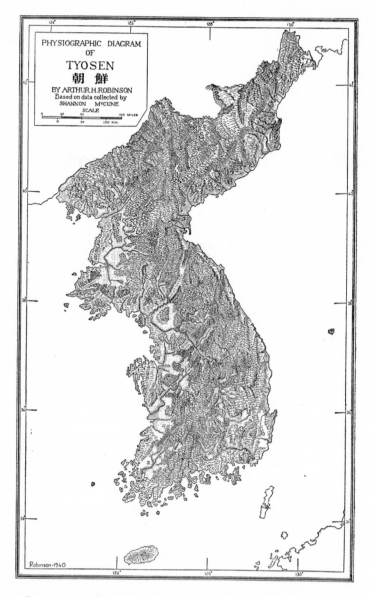

FIG. 2.—A physiographic diagram of Korea. This pictorial presentation of the relief of Korea by Arthur H. Robinson reveals some of the relief of the peninsula.

most cases the Korean mountains are the upthrown edges of structural blocks which have been subsequently eroded by streams. A few areas exist where volcanic activity and lava flows formed a hard capping.[4]

The Korean plains, which constitute only about one-fifth of this largely mountainous country, are found in pockets along the coast, more extensively on the west side of the peninsula than on the east. These areas, and some narrow ribbons of flood plains found along the upper reaches of the streams which have cut back into the mountains, are the only parts of the country suitable for cultivation. Stream erosion on diverse geologic material has been the major cause for the details of the present relief of Korea. In the interior some rivers have been deeply entrenched in winding valleys; in their lower courses these same rivers have extensive plains on which they deposit material when in flood stage.*

These mountains and streams are dominant in the terrain of Korea. The name Korea, which is used by Westerners for the peninsula, is derived from the name of an old kingdom, Koryo, which may be poetically translated as "The Land of High Mountains and Sparkling Streams," an apt epitomization of Korea. As a consequence of the distribution of the mountains and rivers, there is a considerable diversity of land forms in the peninsula. The northern interior, furnishing a solid continental base, is a mountainous land, dominated by volcanic Paektu-san and associated mountain ranges, in which the Yalu and Tumen Rivers and their tributaries are deeply entrenched. Around the margins of this land are plains and hill lands, a relatively narrow ribbon along the Sea of Japan, a broader expanse on the west, drained by the Chongchon and Taedong Rivers. South of a distinctive valley or depression which trends across the peninsula northeastward from Seoul is the Taebaek

---

* In Appendix C there is a table of the major rivers of Korea giving their length and the area of their drainage basins.

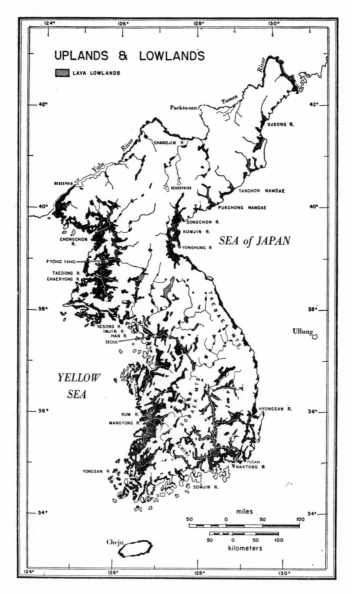

FIG. 3.—Uplands and lowlands in Korea. The lowlands are in black. The major rivers are named; see Appendix C for data on their length and drainage basin areas.

Range which parallels the east coast, squeezing a narrow strip
of plains and hills along the Sea of Japan. West of the Taebaek
Range are the drainage basins of the Han and Kum Rivers;
these rivers have developed extensive and fertile plains along
their lower courses. Trending southwest from the Taebaek Range
is another range, the Sobaek, which culminates in massive
Chiri-san. The Naktong River basin is thus segregated in
southeastern Korea.[5]

Both a close relation and a sharp contrast exist between the
uplands and lowlands of Korea. The sharpness of detail and
the lack of a solid vegetation cover on many hills give them an
exaggerated appearance of height and ruggedness, an effect
accentuated by the characteristics of the narrow, flat-bottomed
valleys beside them. It is out of the uplands that most of the
plains have been carved; it is from the uplands that the alluvial
material which covers some of the plains has been derived. The
map of uplands and lowlands which accompanies this chapter
appears to make their differences as sharp as black and white,
though in actuality they do grade into each other since they are
the result of a common geologic history.

The terrain of Korea naturally has a profound influence on
the daily lives of the Korean people. It has played a significant
role throughout their history. Certainly in the recent hostilities
in Korea the bitterly contested struggles for significant hill
summits and ridge crests have emphasized the importance of
terrain.[6] It was on the strategic hill crests overlooking the
southward trending corridors in central Korea that some of
the most severe fighting took place. Though in times of war
the terrain appears as a dramatic factor, in times of peace it
is no less important a factor, for it controls the distribution and
types of fields, the location of villages, and it handicaps or aids
the development of transportation between centers of economic
activity. This unusual diversity of land forms in Korea thus
constitutes a permanent stage on which is played the Korean

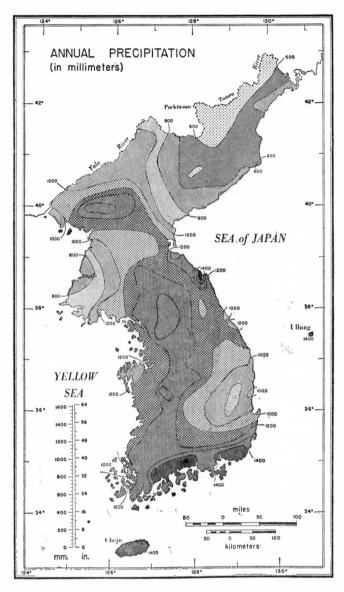

Fig. 4.—The annual precipitation of Korea. The data given in millimeters may be converted to inches by use of the scale.

drama, whether in peace or war, in prosperity or adversity.

The climate of Korea is a quiet and eternal dictator over the lives of the people. The Korean's choice of crops, his round of labor, and his daily activities are influenced by the weather of the peninsula. The natural vegetation, soil characteristics, many of the regional diversities, as well as the population distribution and the number of people who can live off the land are conditioned as much by the climate as by the terrain.[7]

Korea has a humid, mid-latitude, monsoonal climate. In the winter the average monthly temperature generally is below freezing. The summers are hot. The range of temperature is much greater in the north and in the interior than in the south and along the coasts. The average annual precipitation varies from twenty inches in the northern interior to more than sixty inches on the south coast, most of the rainfall coming in the summer months, when cyclonic storms, convectional activity, and occasional late summer typhoons cause disturbances in the warm, moist air drifting inland from the ocean. In winter the cold, dry air masses drifting outward over the Korean peninsula from the interior of the continent of Asia yield little precipitation. These seasonal climatic differences are due to the continentally-induced monsoon system. The passage of cyclonic storms gives diversity to the daily weather. Significant climatic variations are caused by differences in elevation and by proximity to the coastal waters as well as by latitudinal differences in Korea.

The most distinctive climatic season in Korea is the summer. In July all of the lowland areas, particularly the western plains and the Naktong River basin, are hot. Average monthly temperatures are in the 70°'s and 80°'s. The temperatures in the high elevations of the mountain areas and along the northeast coast where the cool Liman Current prevails are slightly lower. Warm, moist air moves across Korea from the maritime regions to the south toward the interior of the continent. When these air drifts blow steadily, large amounts of rainfall do not occur, but if they are forced to rise over colder air masses, or if convectional updrafts (due to the heating of the land surface and the subsequent heating and rising of the air) are strong, heavy rains fall. Hence in Korea the summer season is marked by many rainy days. In addition, convectional storms, characterized by thunder and lightning, bring heavy downpours, and passing cyclonic storms add still more. The pattern is one of clear and less cloudy days interspersed with rainy days.

As the season progresses into August, the rainfall lessens, except in the northern interior and northeastern coast, where the peak of the rainy season lags into August. During the summer "rainy season," throughout Korea the rivers and streams are filled with run-off water, often causing floods, and roads and courtyards turn into seas of mud, and the rice thrives under such circumstances. Occasionally, however, when the rainfall is limited or late, or when it is concentrated in only a few very heavy downpours, the crops may fail and the Korean farmer faces famine.

September is marked for most of Korea by a less steady flow of warm moist air and less humidity, though the southern coastal regions may be struck by typhoons, with their heavy rains and violent winds. These storms may cause great damage to the crops, for during this month, which is generally drier there, the rice fields are usually drained and the harvest begun.

October brings a decided shift in air mass movements; the dry, continental air beginning to move in more steadily, brings clearer weather. Nights are cool, particularly in the north, where frost commonly occurs. These clear fall days are the most pleasant of the year. By November winter has begun in the north, with occasional light snowfalls in the interior. In the south the days are still warm, and farmers may plant winter crops. By December there is little precipitation, though cyclonic storms may bring enough snowfall to provide a snow

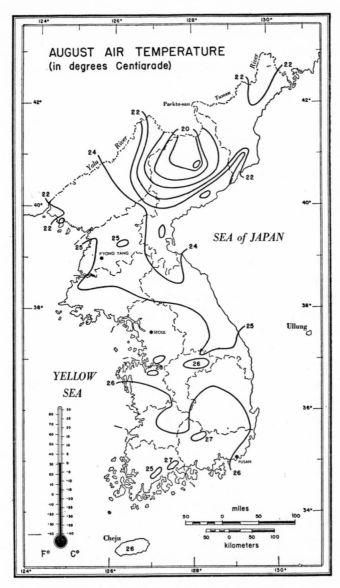

FIG. 5.—August air temperatures in Korea.

cover throughout North Korea. The northern rivers begin to freeze over.

It is during the winter season that the climatic contrast between northern and southern Korea is most apparent. For in the south, though nights may be cool, the days are still warm and the farmers can work in the fields and their children can gather twigs and leaves on the hillsides. By January, the dry, cold air from the continental interior brings severe cold waves, particularly in the north and in the interior. Precipitation is slight. The winds are usually not severe in velocity but are severely cold. The temperatures average below freezing during the month in all but the extreme southern coast, where the temperature is only slightly above freezing. In the northern interior and in the northwest part of Korea the temperatures are bitterly cold. This severe winter continues on into February, though that month is slightly warmer.

In March, the dry continental air drifts begin to abate, temperatures rise, and in the south, when maritime air begins to drift in, warm days are common. By April, thaws set in, particularly in central and northern Korea. The streams swell as the ice breaks up, and travel becomes difficult. In southern Korea there may be a slight increase in rainfall. This is very beneficial for the preparing of the rice seedbeds and paddy fields. The farmers begin their busy season. The flowering shrubs and trees add bright colors. Occasionally, though, the winds are gusty and variable in direction, and cyclonic storms add variety to the daily weather.

By May the approach of summer is evident. Warm, moist air begins to drift in from the south with more regularity, and rainy days occur frequently. Hot days are common in June, when the whole country is green and the growing rice takes on a vivid emerald shade. Convectional thunderstorms come often —the precursors of the heavy rainy season of summer. The warm, moist, tropical maritime air masses now dominate the

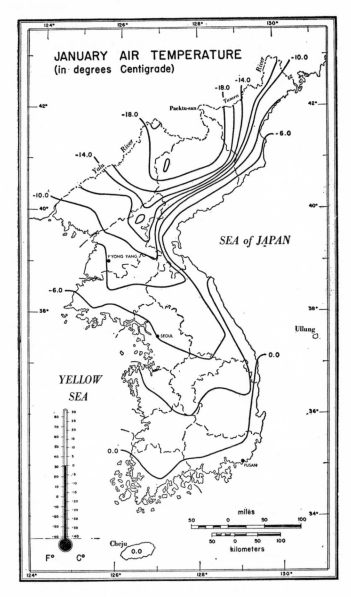

FIG. 6.—January air temperatures in Korea.

weather and the Koreans forget winter's cold blasts, though an occasional north wind still blows with mild force. Summer has arrived.

The variation of climate from place to place plays a dominant role in the geography of Korea. In winter the fields of southern Korea are green with barley, while among the spruces and larches of the northern interior the snow lies deep. In summer the farmer in the far north goes out on a mild sunny day from his isolated, shingle-roofed log cabin to work the field he has cleared by fire on a steep mountain slope; in contrast, his southern countryman leads his cow out from his thatch-roofed, mud-walled farmhouse in the village to plow his water-soaked paddy field in a falling rain.

The winter temperatures are very important to the agriculture and economy of Korea and constitute a dominant climate characteristic. If the cold is not overly severe, two crops may be grown in a year. Therefore, winter temperature differences are of obvious importance in characterizing climatic contrasts. The northern interior is extremely cold, having five months (November to April) with average temperatures below 32° F. In contrast, southern Korea, including a fringe northward along the Sea of Japan, has mild winter temperatures, January temperatures averaging above 26.6 F. (−3° C.). Southern Korea, therefore, should be set aside as a major climatic area; local differences are, however, important, and thus this area may be logically subdivided. The central and northern areas of Korea have considerable climatic contrasts from the two areas already delineated: the bitterly cold northern interior and the mild-wintered south. Maritime influence is especially strong in the northeast along the deep Sea of Japan, so this area may be set off as a separate area distinguished from western Korea by a milder winter, January temperatures averaging above 17.6°. The western part of central and northern Korea has cold winters, though not so cold as the

interior, and hot summers. Within this area are variations in
the degree of winter cold, and it may therefore be logically
subdivided on the basis of average January temperatures.

Because of its humid continental climate, Korea has conditions
favorable to the growth of extensive forests. Three-fourths of
the total area of the peninsula is classified as forest land. However, in 1940, of this forest land only seventy per cent was
classified as standing trees. In recent years this ratio of non-
forested land to forest land has increased. Three factors have
done much to change this phase of the geography of Korea.
The first is man, who, in his need for fuel, building material,
and arable land, has thoughtlessly destroyed much of his heritage.
The second is an insect, a pine bug, which has wrought havoc
on the pine forests. The third is forest fires which have gotten
out of control. Today the only true natural forests to be found
are in the far north and on the higher mountains or around a
few temples. Many of the forested areas are really second
growth stands, some areas having been carefully reforested,
sometimes with imported species of trees. Though a complete
and detailed study of the natural vegetation is not possible,
certain general plant associations can be noted.[8] For example,
in the cold north are extensive areas of larch and spruce; in
the central part of Korea are oaks and elders, along with some
conifers; in the warmer south are scattered patches of bamboo
and pine, though the vegetation here is generally deciduous.

The soils of Korea, which furnish the bases for most of
the human life in the peninsula, are not true soils; they are
immature soils which have been greatly changed by man's
activities through the centuries. Because of the diverse geologic
structure of Korea, a great variety of physical types of soils
prevails.[9] The eroded, alluvial materials in the lowlands of
Korea can be more easily cultivated than the residual weathered
rocks of the uplands, so on the lowlands are found most of
the productive agricultural lands of Korea. As the map of low-

lands shows, they fringe the coast line and go deep into the interior up some of the river valleys.  In general the soils of Korea are not too fertile.  In the densely settled portions of Korea, where farm boys rake leaves and brush, no opportunity is given for humus to develop.  The working and reworking of the soils of the land used for crop cultivation has produced man-made, rather than natural soils.

The climate, vegetation, and soils give distinctive character to the land of Korea.  They are factors which both aid and limit the activities of the Korean farmer.  They, along with the terrain, should be thought of as an integral part of Korea's heritage.

# Chapter 3 | The Historical Development of Korea

THROUGH the centuries the Koreans have emerged as a distinct people. Isolated by the mountains in the north and by the seas to the east, south and west, the Koreans have been able to modify the cultural heritage and ideas they acquired (or had forced upon them by invasion) from their neighbors, the Chinese and Japanese, and mold their own peculiar culture and economy. George M. McCune has summarized the matter thus:

The long historical continuity, during which Korean cultural and social patterns became firmly fixed, has left a unique heritage to the Koreans. They became a nation of one race, one language, one culture, and one proud past. The homogeneity of the Korean people is a significant factor in an evaluation of Korean political problems. Whatever disunity and diversity appear on the Korean political stage are not products of fundamental differences in race or culture within the Korean community, but are consequences of less substantial causes.[10]

This essential unity of the Korean people has been the result, in part, of the geographic factors.

The origin of the Korean people is shrouded in the distant past. According to Korean tradition, the founder of the country was a spirit king of divine origin, Tan'gun, who ruled for a thousand years. Even today in official documents published in South Korea, the year 1955 is referred to as the 4288th year after Tan'gun.  The little knowledge we have of the culture of the earliest peoples of the peninsula, based on the slim evidence of shell mounds and graves, would seem to indicate that these people lived in a neolithic culture and were grouped into tribes. It is believed that they came into the peninsula in waves from the plains of Manchuria or central Asia, where similar Tungus and proto-Caucasian peoples had their development.

In 1122 B.C., again according to tradition, a Chinese sage, Kija, came from China with five thousand followers and settled among the tribes in northwestern Korea in the area of the present-day city of Pyongyang.  The kingdom which tradition says he founded was called Choson.  There was undoubtedly some Chinese influence in Korea in the millenium before Christ, but perhaps it would be better characterized as the product of an amalgamation of groups of Chinese refugees or migrants— such as the reputed Kija—and of local tribes.  Southern Korea during this time, according to Chinese records, was controlled by three major tribes, the Sam Han (or Three Han).  In addition, in northeastern Korea there were other tribes, but at this period they were of little political significance.

In 108 B.C., according to firm historical evidence, the Han dynasty of China established colonies in northwestern Korea. One of these colonies, the Nangnang, had its capital in the vicinity of Pyongyang.  The tombs of this colony, which lasted until 313 A.D., give evidence of the very strong Chinese influence on Korean culture.  Bronze mirrors, baskets of lacquer work, headdresses, and many other artifacts are some of the finest examples of Han dynasty workmanship.  The influence of these colonies spread over the Yalu River into adjacent Manchuria and to southern Korea.

Eventually most of northern Korea was dominated by a strongly organized kingdom, Koguryo, which absorbed the areas colonized by the Chinese settlers and exercised control even beyond the Yalu River far into Manchuria. In the south, at the same time (57 B.C. to 668 A.D.), were two kingdoms, Silla and Paekche. Hence this period of Korean history is known as the Period of the Three Kingdoms. Silla had its core area in southeastern Korea, mainly in the Naktong River basin. Its capital was located at Kyongju. Paekche, the weakest of the kingdoms, had its center in southwestern Korea. Rivalries were sharp between these kingdoms. Smaller tribes and a lesser kingdom, Karak, which had connections with Japan, were caught between this rivalry and gradually absorbed.

During this period of consolidation, Chinese influence took new and important forms. Rice, introduced from China, became the dominant crop, and an intensive hand-tillage culture was evolved. The agricultural village became the dominant settlement form. In addition, Confucianism, with its emphasis upon the family, and Buddhism largely displaced the primitive religions. The northern kingdom, Koguryo, adopted Buddhism in 371 A.D., shortly after which schools and temples were founded. The ruling classes of Paekche, one of the two southern kingdoms, welcomed the Buddhist priests fourteen years later, and eventually Silla did the same. From Paekche and Silla, Buddhism passed on to Japan. As the T'ang dynasty, the successor to the Han dynasty in China, gradually acquired power, the Koguryo kingdom in northern Korea and adjacent Manchuria declined in power. Koguryo had fought a successful war against the T'ang invaders in 613 A.D., but was defeated in 668, when the armies of Silla joined with the T'ang forces to mount a two-way attack. At about the same time the Paekche kingdom was absorbed into Silla. The Japanese ties with Paekche had been closer than their ties with Silla; with the defeat of Paekche many of the Paekche leaders, according to Japanese tradition, migrated to Japan.

As a result of these developments Silla controlled most of the Korean peninsula from 668 to 935. However, the extreme

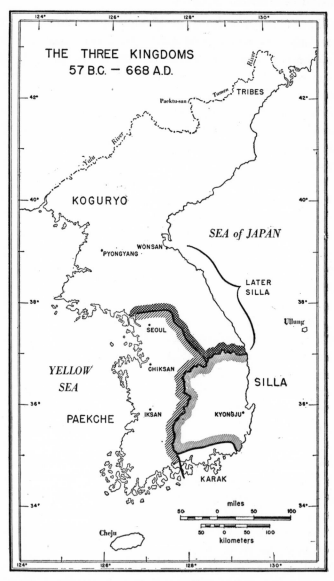

FIG. 7.—The three kingdoms which flourished in Korea from 57 B.C. to 668 A.D., when Silla, which had already expanded from its small area in southeastern Korea, gained control of almost the entire peninsula.

northeastern part of the peninsula was in the hands of tribes who did not acknowledge Silla's suzerainty, and northwest Korea remained a no man's land between Silla and T'ang-controlled China. Partly because Silla had been able to gain ascendancy in Korea by help from the T'ang dynasty, it was a nominal vassal to T'ang China; but in reality it was independent. This was the golden period of early Korean civilization. In Kyongju, the capital of Silla, Buddhism and the arts flourished.

Eventually, however, the court became decadent and the kingdom fell before a rebel from the north. The conqueror, Wang Gun, established his capital at Songdo, the present city of Kaesong. His kingdom, called Koryo—which has been perpetuated in the word Korea—lasted until 1392. Buddhism continued to be strong, though the Confucian ideas of government, including the examination system for civil servants, became deeply entrenched. Close ties between China and Korea were still maintained, and the exchange of envoys was accepted as a common practice. It was in this period that all of Korea was united for the first time under one ruler, though the tribes of the northeast still had only a quasi-official relationship with the unified kingdom. The state was well organized under a centralized system of government. Provinces were established to facilitate regional control of administration.

Predominant in the Korean history of these early periods was the struggle for power on the part of different core areas. The Taedong River basin, centered around Pyongyang, always occupied an important place. The Naktong basin of southeast Korea, and particularly the small but fertile area in the nearby basin surrounding the city of Kyongju, was significant. The valleys in southwestern Korea were not so important nor were the isolated northern mountain areas. As time passed and as the peninsula began to be an identity, neither the northwest nor the southeast core area was able to control the whole peninsula; the real "capital" of Korea came to be the plains of west central Korea.

Korea's location on the fringe of China and its accessibility to Japan were responsible for many of the troubles of the following centuries. Japanese pirates, who constantly harried the southern coast with hit-and-run raids, were hard to stop. The central government did not have sufficient power to protect itself fully. One interesting result geographically was that the Koreans located many of their towns up-river, in valleys five or ten miles from the seacoast. When pirates landed and went in search of loot, the Koreans organized defenses and burned the boats, isolating the raiders on the land.

However, the major outside forces affecting Korea during this period were the Chi-tans, or Tartars, and later the Mongols. These tribes rose to power on the dry plains of Manchuria and Central Asia. With their superior organization and weapons they were able to conquer China at different periods. Korea was naturally affected, and the latter half of the Koryo dynasty was marked by a succession of invasions from the north. The Tartars invaded the peninsula in 1011 A.D. and burnt the capital city. But their influence in Korea, as in China where they established the Liao dynasty (907-1119), was limited, compared to the influence of the Mongol invaders who came a hundred years later. When the Mongol horsemen approached the capital of Koryo, the king fled to the island of Kanghwa. A few years later when the entire peninsula had been overrun, the Korean king submitted himself to the Mongols. The Korean kings took Mongol princesses for their wives and court life followed the pattern established by the conqueror. In 1274, and again in 1279, Kublai Khan ordered invasions of Japan, and the Koreans were forced to join in these disastrous enterprises by furnishing ships and many men.

Despite the invasions of the Tartars and Mongols, Korean culture managed to survive and even flourish. Letters and

Buddhist-inspired art had a high development.  A number of Korean scholars writing in Chinese were recognized by their Chinese colleagues as equals.

In time the Koryo kingdom failed to meet the needs of the Korean people and was much beset by court intrigue and outside pressure.  Finally, in 1392, when the Ming dynasty ruled in China, one of the Korean generals, Yi Taejo, overthrew the Koryo kingdom and seized the throne.  The name for the country was changed to the very ancient one, Choson, and the capital was moved forty miles southeast from Songdo to what is now the city of Seoul.  The Yi dynasty lasted until its absorption by the Japanese in 1910.  Yi Taejo's early successors were men equally as able as he, and the nation's prosperity was broken only by the occasional ravages of Japanese pirates.  In the early years of the Yi dynasty momentous cultural advances were made when the Korean alphabet was formulated and metal movable type, replacing earlier types, was developed for printing.  At about the same time that the government was firmly established on Confucian principles, Buddhism ceased to be the state religion.  As a consequence, certain features of cultural life, notably the arts, declined.

From the geographical standpoint, one of the most interesting developments in the history of the early Yi dynasty was the recognition on the part of the government of the regional diversities within Korea. The provincial system was reorganized giving the governors of the provinces considerable authority; in the succeeding centuries the extent of their power was great or small depending on the political initiative of the central government.  These provinces were organized on the basis of location and used, in a number of cases, the same boundaries that had existed in the previous dynasty.  For some administrative purposes the capital city, Seoul (or Kyongsong), which lay in the province of Kyonggi, was considered a separate unit. Other provinces were formed out from the capital in each direction:

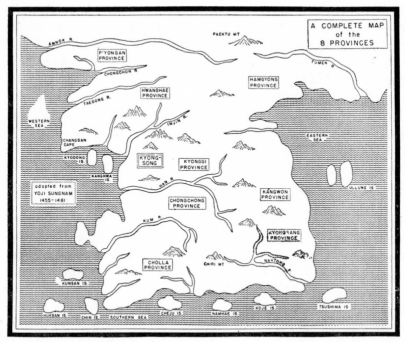

FIG. 8.—The eight provinces of Korea. This map, adapted from that in the *Yoji Sungnam* published in the early days of the Yi dynasty, has been used in its original form in the end papers of this book.

northwest, northeast, west, east, south, southwest, and southeast. Each province was intended to be a geographic and economic region. Each had major cities, from which the name of the province was derived. Each province had a coast line and generally was separated from its neighboring provinces by natural features: mountains, hills, or rivers. The development of this administrative system nurtured the growth of provincial loyalties—often quite strong—on the part of the common people. The provincial system enabled the government better to meet the problems caused by the regional diversities of the peninsula.

The first two hundred years of the Yi dynasty rule was a

relatively peaceful period.  However, in 1650 a party system developed which unfortunately weakened the central government.  For years this party struggle continued to be a dominant factor in Korean court life, and political intrigue supplanted political leadership among the noble class.  Gradually they became estranged from the common people.

Another consequence was that the military system fell into such a state of utter inefficiency that when the Japanese launched an invasion in 1592 they were met with little initial opposition. Hideyoshi, who had helped to unify and organize Japan, was attempting an invasion of China, but his forces were stopped eventually on Korean soil, for the topography of Korea was well suited to guerilla warfare, and the lengthened Japanese supply lines were easily cut.  Meanwhile the Korean navy, under the brilliant leadership of Admiral Yi Sumsin, operating off the coast of southern Korea, further reduced the flow of supplies needed for the operation.  The Japanese, additionally handicapped by the death of Hideyoshi in 1598, were forced to withdraw from the peninsula, leaving behind, however, the marks of their destruction.

The defeat of the Japanese was attributable in part to the intervention of the Chinese, upon whom the Koreans had called for assistance.  The price, however, which the Koreans paid was high, for the Chinese allies living off the land caused immeasurable hardships for the Korean people.  Famine, followed by plagues, decimated the population.  The major cities were plundered by the Japanese and then sacked by the Chinese. Many artisan industries were so severely affected that they never recovered.  The horrors of war and all the attendant miseries for the civilian population were not forgotten by the Korean people; through folk tales, legends, and paintings a bitter and traditional hatred of the Japanese was kept alive. The key geographical position of the Korean peninsula as a bridge between great maritime and continental powers revealed itself as of paramount importance.  Such seems to be historically Korea's fate.

The peace which followed the defeat of the Japanese was short-lived, for when the Manchus, from the plains of Manchuria, invaded China and overthrew the Ming dynasty, the Mings sought Korea's aid.  This was given loyally, though rather misguidedly, for in 1627 the Manchus invaded Korea to protect their flank.  They captured Seoul and placed a quasi-military government control over Korea.  The Korean king finally acknowledged allegiance to the Manchu cause, and the Korean crown prince was sent as a hostage to the Manchu court.

After these devastating invasions by both her neighbors, Korea wrapped herself in a cloak of isolation.  From 1609 on only tenuous ties were maintained with the Japanese, who were allowed to have a trading post in southeastern Korea.  The Manchu dynasty quite quickly became absorbed by Chinese customs and culture and adopted the Confucian scheme of international relations, a scheme in which China was the "elder brother" to her Korean "younger brother."[3]  This Confucian pattern of political geography was of great importance, particularly in the minds of the Korean court leaders.  Envoys were exchanged on a fairly regular basis, though in reality this exchange was a modified means of trade, for the envoys took with them products of their respective countries for exchange. When new kings ascended the Korean throne, notices of this action were sent to the Imperial court in Peking.  On occasion, seals as symbols of investiture were sent to the Korean kings. It was obvious that a small nation such as Korea would have to establish accord with its larger, more powerful neighbor. However, the Confucian system did allow Korea considerable independence and local autonomy.

Within Korea during this period there developed divisive tendencies detrimental to the vulnerable nation.  For one thing, the geographic differences between the north and the south accentuated political differences and fostered factionalism.

The south with its better agricultural land was much more densely populated, but over a period of at least four hundred years a noticeable northward shift of the center of population had taken place. Part of this is attributable to migration from the south to the north, though this is difficult to measure.

Northern Korea was perhaps more interested in isolation than was the south. In the north the natural isolation afforded by the mountains was increased at various times by the development of man-created barriers. At one time, it is reported, a wall was built all the way across northern Korea. This lacks confirmation; more likely it was a series of fortifications with intercommunications to guard the frontier. Later a "march" was established on both the Korean and the Manchurian sides of the Yalu River, and Korean settlements in the Yalu River basin were discouraged. On the Manchurian side a wall of stakes, the "Willow Palisade," delimited a zone some fifty miles from the Yalu River, and in this area Chinese farmers were prohibited from settling. As the pressure of population increased, however, both Korean and Chinese farmers moved into the area and eventually met at the river. In the northeast the tribes which had been nominally under Korean suzerainty were completely subdued, and Korean control was firmly exercised along the frontier zone up to the Tumen River and on occasion in areas across the river.

Unfortunately, Korean political leadership was often split by party factions, and a wide gulf existed between the court leaders and the people. Thus the Korean government was weak and venal when, a century ago, the Western powers and their Eastern counterpart, Japan, began to expand their interests in the Far East. Desiring peace and isolation and not realizing how tenuous was the tie with the "elder brother" China, the Koreans hoped to maintain their independence under the long-established Confucian scheme of world affairs, but these hopes were to be frustrated by subsequent events beyond her control.

This was the land, with all its political and geographical diversities, with its long and tortured history, which was opened to the outside world in the last quarter of the nineteenth century. As modern technical skills increased, and as political, economic, and military power became aggressive, Korea's isolation and independence of action were dealt shattering blows. The peninsula became a pawn in the struggle for power between other nations and groups of nations. Divorced from her hermit past Korea became a part of the total modern world.[11]

Looking back over the events of the last seventy-five years, it is easy to recognize that Japan has been the critical force influencing modern Korean history. Sporadically Japan had maintained trading bases in southeastern Korea, but the memory of Hideyoshi's invasion still rankled in the Koreans' hearts. However, in 1876 Korea was unable to deny the Japanese demand for recognition in a modern treaty. In the years that followed, Korea became recognized by other nations. The United States signed a treaty with Korea in 1882. Slowly the close relationship between China and Korea weakened as the "big brother" nation lost political importance and military strength.

The crisis came with the defeat of China by the Japanese in the war of 1894–95. One of the primary aims of the Japanese was to free Korea from Chinese suzerainty. Following the war, Korea's new independence was signalized by the changing of its name from Choson to Taehan and the building of a Temple of Heaven, a symbol of the highest sovereign position. Some internal reforms were instituted. In 1896, for example, the eight provinces were replaced by twenty-three administrative districts, a system which lasted for only a year. However, five of the original provinces, those at each corner plus the one to the south, were subdivided roughly in half, making of each a northern and a southern province. Despite some reforms, intrigue was still rife within the Korean court. Attempts at true liberal movements within Korean politics were rather short-lived. The king was not a strong leader, and the conservative and archaic character of the court was most difficult to change.

With the Russo-Japanese war, the Japanese struggle for power in Korea and the Far East reached another climax. Korean "independence" was one of the Japanese motives, but actually, of course, it was a struggle to keep Russian influence out of Korea. In 1904 a few skirmishes were held on Korean soil, and the sounds of naval engagements echoed off the coast. The Japanese used Korea mainly as a channel of access to Manchuria, where the large-scale engagements took place. In order to have this free access, the Japanese forced the Koreans to grant them some concessions. The Japanese developed several military ports, railroads, and other facilities to move their armies.

Thus with a court weakened by internal dissension and not clearly tied to the interests of the common people, and without backing from any other strong neighbors or from the outside world (though the government did make a fruitless appeal to the United States), Korea fell an easy prey to the Japanese. The king was forced to abdicate in favor of a son who was even weaker than he. A Japanese resident, Marquis Ito, really controlled the government through Japanese advisors in the various ministries. Ito's assassination by a Korean in 1909 led to further tightening of Japanese control. Finally Japan annexed Korea outright on August 29, 1910. Korea as a unified, independent country passed for a time from the international scene.

In their control of Korea the Japanese exercised slightly fluctuating policies.[12] Their basic aim was an integration of Korean economy with that of Japan. For example, during times of food shortages in Japan, Korean agricultural production was emphasized and the export of rice from Korea was stepped up. However, in other times, when the competition of Korean rice was harmful to the Japanese economy, rice production was retarded in Korea. This was done with little concern for the well-being of the Koreans. As Japan developed an industrial economy, particularly as it was developed to lead towards great military power, raw materials and primary processing facilities were widely developed. Changes occurred rapidly on the peninsula. The Korean population virtually doubled from an estimated 13,313,017 persons in 1910 to 25,900,142 in 1944. The increased pressure of people upon the resources of the land meant that though production was increased, living standards did not rise in proportion. This problem was magnified, of course, by the fact that the Japanese continued increasingly to exploit the country for their own benefit. In some years, for example, as much as half of the Korean rice crop was exported for Japanese use.

Within Korea significant political developments also took place as an aftermath of the Japanese conquest. The Korean royal family by edict and indirectly by marriage was amalgamated with the Japanese royal family. More important, the autocratic Japanese Government-General reached down into all facets of Korean life. Education along Japanese lines was introduced, and the Koreans were given little true political control of their own affairs. But despite the pressure of the Japanese the spark of Korean independence was kept alive. In 1919 a widespread independence agitation occurred, signalized by the signing of a declaration of independence by thirty-three patriots; this Mansei movement was brutally suppressed. During the late 1920's, under a more liberal Japanese regime, some Koreans, feeling that their political fate was sealed, practiced a form of collaboration with the hope that perhaps eventually a semi-autonomous regime could be achieved. However, Japanese activities in Manchuria in 1931 and their movement into north China in 1937 shattered such hope and showed that Japanese aggression had a definite pattern of political control.  In 1942 Korea became an integral part of Japan rather than a colony, though Koreans did not automatically receive Japanese citizenship.

By setting up an elaborate spy system and by playing upon factionalism within Korea, the Japanese succeeded in preventing the development of any strong political leadership.  Outside of Korea, wherever such activities were possible on the part of Koreans in exile, there were great political fervor and high hopes for independence.

The Japanese overlordship of Korea was dissolved at the end of World War II.  The period as a Japanese possession remains a bitter memory in the minds of many Koreans and accounts for the anti-Japanese feelings on the part of most Korean leaders.  Once again her hopes for peace and autonomy were frustrated as the peninsula became a battleground of clashing ideologies.  This time the contest in Korea was between the Soviet Union and the United States.  Actually, in no place in the world was a line more sharply drawn between these powers than along the thirty-eighth parallel in Korea.[13]  On each side of this line divergent political developments took place.  Immediately after taking the surrender of the Japanese forces, the Soviet army north of the thirty-eighth parallel set up a military occupation controlling the territory by indirection through so-called "Peoples' Committees."  In the south, American forces carried on direct military occupation, although they made increasing use of Korean leaders.  To resolve this unhappy situation after unsuccessfully attempting to negotiate with the Russians, the United States appealed to the United Nations.  Subsequently the United Nations supervised elections in South Korea, and from the government thus elected evolved the Republic of Korea, which had effective control south of the thirty-eighth parallel.

Ignoring the United Nations decision, the Russians fostered the growth and development of a so-called "People's Republic of Korea." This was organized along the usual Communist lines. Some Koreans made attempts to work out compromises between these two regimes, but their activities were never successful. Finally, on June 25, 1950 the North Korean forces crossed the thirty-eighth parallel. The United Nations Security Council labelled it aggression and the United States and other free nations came to the support of the Republic of Korea. The events of the succeeding years are well known: the retreat of the South Korean forces and the small number of American troops into the southeast corner of Korea; the counterattack and the landing at Inchon by the United Nations forces; and the advance across the thirty-eighth parallel and into North Korea, close to the Manchurian boundary. This was followed by the Chinese Communists' entrance into the war and eventually by the uneasy stabilization of the military forces in central Korea near the thirty-eighth parallel. Though a truce was declared on July 27, 1953, the exchange of prisoners did not take place until the winter of 1954, and the Geneva Conference discussed Korea at length in the summer of 1954. Obviously, the story is not finished as this is being written.

Too often ignored is the effect of all this warfare on the Korean people. The devastation of the land, the forced migrations of great masses of people, the continued tragic division of their country into varying halves have left scars which may not be healed for generations.

# Chapter 4 | The Political Pattern in Korea

THE political pattern in Korea today is a reflection of the past heritage and the geographic character of this peninsula that lies on the fringe of Asia. These factors are important, though they are often not recognized. Korea is caught in the mesh of world politics because it occupies a key strategic position on the international frontier between the Soviet World and the Free World. Strife in any part of the Far East has usually had its repercussions within Korea. Obviously, too, the long centuries of Chinese "superiority" and the various invasions to which the Korean peninsula has been subjected have had their effect on Korea's political geography.

In the distant past Korea had no set frontiers. Within the peninsula, various tribes, to whom new blood and ideas were added by waves of migration, eventually became kingdoms. Competition between kingdoms was severe at different periods. When finally in 668 A.D. most of Korea was united under the Silla kingdom, she had an unified political regime, protected by the surrounding seas and by the mountainous lands to the north. For many centuries, however, the northern interior and northeastern part of Korea were only loosely held and sparsely settled by Koreans. The Yalu River gradually became established between 500–1000 A.D. as the northwestern boundary, though the area was kept as a frontier zone rather than a rigid boundary. In northeast Korea after 1400, when the early founders of the Yi dynasty made agreements with the Jurchen tribes, the Tumen River became the boundary. However, Koreans and the tribes who became assimilated into the Korean cultural group have settled on both sides of the Tumen River, thus forming a significant group of Koreans in the adjacent area of Manchuria and Russia.[14]

Within the peninsula itself there was a continual contest for power between the different areas. The Silla kingdom (57 B.C. –935 A.D.) had its core in extreme southeast Korea; the Koryo kingdom (918–1392) had its core area in northwestern Korea, though its capital was in central Korea. Finally, the Choson kingdom (1392–1910) was established in central Korea, with its capital at Seoul; this capital was maintained as the administrative headquarters by the Japanese (1910–1945). These centers had difficulty controlling all of the peninsula with its geographic diversities and its geographic barriers to travel and communication. Thus evolved the political system patterned along Confucian lines. It allowed a considerable regional and local autonomy.

Essentially the government of Korea has been autocratic rather than democratic. The king was the symbol of government. The kingly successors, however, were not always the eldest sons, the crown sometimes shifting into collateral lines. Around the royal family was the royal court, which in reality ruled the country. Various ministries, some with classical names after the Chinese traditions, exercised much control. Through a system of censors, who reported directly to the king, checks on the activities of government officials were established. People could present petitions to the court, so that there was some popular appeal; however, since by custom the petitions had to be written in court language, i.e. classical Chinese, the common people had little recourse to them.

In the days of the Korean dynasties, the common people, of course, had contact with their government only on the local level. The provinces were divided into districts, or magistracies, usually the trading area of a large market town. The districts in turn were separated into smaller civil divisions, groups of villages. On the village level the common people had virtually their own self-government. But often the channels between these different levels of government administration were very poor, and a particularly wide gap existed between the village and the other levels.

Under Confucian doctrine the government of the country was carried on by moral precepts rather than by rigid law and the administrators were persons who, having been educated in the Confucian classics, would best know "the right." The services which the government provided were the usual ones of preserving law and order. It also fostered education through the examination system and the maintenance of libraries and study centers. Taxation to cover government costs consisted almost wholly of a primary tax in kind on agricultural production, but there were often extraordinary taxes to pay for the building of public edifices or maintenance of defenses. Most of the local public works—roads, bridges—and the care of the market places were paid by local taxes or by corvée—forced labor on behalf of the state.

Within their local area the village people had a form of democracy. The village elders were chosen by the position of respect in which they were held by their fellow villagers rather than by any kind of an election. These "informal leaders" guided the affairs of the village and usually acted as a cushion between the village and the official government. Because of the autocratic nature of the government most Koreans felt that the less they had to do with government, the better off they would be. To them the government provided only a very minimum of services, though it taxed relatively heavily. They also associated with the government a considerable amount of what appears to Westerners as graft and corruption, yet to Korean eyes was an accepted part of government. It became a serious problem only as it became excessive.

It was natural that when the Japanese came into Korea, they would continue the autocratic character of government. Though there was often marked opposition to the Japanese, armed resistance was actually slight. The Korean opposition expressed itself largely in the form of "non-violence" movements or non-cooperation with the Japanese.

The structure of the Japanese government in Korea was pyramidal. Though some advisory councils were set up, sometimes elected by taxpayers, the Korean people as a whole took almost no part in the government. Occasionally Koreans were appointed to the lower positions of government, and a few who had been educated in Japan achieved higher posts.

The Japanese kept military forces in Korea, in part for defense, and in part for training purposes. The head of the government, the Japanese Governor-General, always a military man, could call upon these forces if need be, though he usually depended upon the elaborate police system to maintain law and order. Consequently, Korea was essentially a police state. Japanese law was made the basis of government and was administered strictly and harshly. Old traditional forms of government were wiped out, as a new and alien force was imposed. The Korean people, losing their old traditions, felt little compulsion to adhere to the new. A rather lawless and very undemocratic political situation resulted.

The organization of government geographically by the Japanese followed the same pattern which had been previously established. Provinces, five of which had been subdivided into northern and southern provinces, kept their old boundaries. In some cases new capitals were established, either to centralize political authority more nearly with the economic centers of the provinces or to put the capitals on railroad lines. Several large cities were set up as municipalities with some independent governmental functions.

The Japanese reorganized the local government. Each county theoretically was to have an area of forty square *ri* (238.2 square miles) with an average population of ten thousand persons, and the towns or townships were to be four square *ri* (23.82 square miles) with an average of eight hundred families. Obviously this exactness was not possible. With the increase of population after 1910 these administrative districts inevitably grew disproportionately.

The organization of the counties allowed for flexible administration within some provinces where internal geographic conditions varied. For example, in South Hamgyong Province some county boundaries follow the crest of the drainage divide, separating the coastal areas from the isolated northern interior. At the lowest administrative level, of course, were fifty thousand villages which continued to maintain their informal governmental character, though they were subjected to more rigid control than had been the case in the past.

Though the services which the Japanese government provided were numerous, there were marked discriminatory features. For example, though the Japanese were a very small minority in the population, there were much better schools for Japanese children than for Korean children. Public health services, which had been virtually nonexistent, were particularly expanded by the Japanese. This, of course, resulted in a lowering of the death rate and a tremendous growth in population. Also the Japanese government entered much more directly into control and development of the economy of Korea. The state owned railroads, communication systems, savings banks, and rural cooperatives. Quasi-official companies were set up, for example, the Oriental Development Company. These companies owned great areas of farm land, operated various irrigation projects, and exploited Korea's mineral and hydroelectric resources.

The cost of the Japanese government services was heavy for the Korean farmers, and to make matters worse, taxes were collected in money rather than in kind. Assessments for irrigation services were often so heavy that the Koreans mortgaged and lost their land.

The Japanese administration lived relatively luxuriously within Korea and sent large profits back to Japan or invested heavily in Korea. The Korean share of Japanese military expenditures was disproportionate to the Korean concern with these matters. This drain and lack of opportunity naturally resulted in the gradual impoverishment of the Korean people. Certainly they did not profit equally by the increased productivity which was stimulated by the Japanese.

With the defeat of Japan in World War II Korean political patterns took on a decidedly different character. On December 1, 1943 at Cairo, two years before the end of the war, the Koreans had been told by the Allied leaders "that in due course Korea shall become free and independent." However, soon after liberation Korea found itself a divided nation under military occupation. Much can and has been written about the political events in the succeeding years. It will perhaps be more of value and to our purpose to assess a few factors from the standpoint of their relation to the geography of Korea.

A fundamental factor in the history of postwar Korea is the division of the nation by the thirty-eighth parallel into zones which were occupied by fundamentally opposed forces.[13] The thirty-eighth parallel was first chosen as a boundary between the Russian and American forces who were to accept the Japanese surrender. Its actual origin is veiled in military secrecy, which makes it impossible to ascertain just how and why it was chosen. A line to divide operational zones may have been discussed in a military staff conference between American and Russian officers at Potsdam in July, 1945, or possibly earlier at Yalta, in February, 1945. It seems likely, however, with the sudden collapse of Japan and the urgent need to form plans for surrender, that the decision to use the thirty-eighth parallel for this purpose was made in Washington by a small group of staff planners. Such persons could have decided to establish a simple line which was well marked on maps, which would roughly halve Korea yet leave the capital in American possession. The objective was to divide the responsibilities of accepting surrender rather than to set up zones of military occupation. Herein lies the tragedy of the thirty-eighth parallel: this line, created to serve limited military expediency was then maintained for other purposes; it meant the erection of an iron curtain destroying the national unity of Korea.

The thirty-eighth parallel, as would be expected of such a geodetic line, cut across land forms, political units, and transportation networks indiscriminately. For example, the Ongjin peninsula, south of the thirty-eighth parallel in western Korea, was cut off from the rest of southern Korea. The line went so close to the city of Kaesong that parts of the old city limits were included in the northern zone and the rest in the southern zone. The line cut across the grain of the land, for there were no mountain crests or rivers to divide areas and give physical validity to the boundary. It is obvious that the line had few advantages as an international boundary except for the ease with which it could be drawn on maps.

Most serious was the division of Korea into two economically disparate zones. To a considerable degree the two parts, north and south, were complementary to one another. The consumer-goods industries of the south depended heavily on the north for electric power and semi-finished raw materials; and the north depended heavily on the southern industries for consumer products. Secondly, the agricultural production of the south was greatly increased by the utilization of fertilizer, much of which was manufactured in the north. Lastly, the existence of the thirty-eighth parallel acted as an irritating force to make major and perhaps dangerous crises out of minor problems. As long as this barrier existed, widening the breach between the two sections, prospects for the establishment of a sound and stable Korea were dim.

The second fundamental factor in the history of postwar Korea was that the peninsula became one of the friction spots between the United States and the Soviet Union. Russian and American interests in Korea differed quite decidedly. Russia had for decades been concerned with Korean affairs. As Korea came out of its isolation at the end of the last century, Russia participated continuously in the intrigue and power politics which went on over the fate of its small neighbor. The first great test came in 1904–05, when Russia and Japan went to war. It is worthy of note that when Japan collapsed in 1945 the Communists demanded and received the same political position that Russia had desired under the Czar.

Russian interests in Korea were occasioned in part, of course, by the factor of geographic proximity. Korea and Russia border one another for some eleven miles along the Tumen River in northeastern Korea, and Vladivostok is only one hundred miles distant from North Korean ports. More important is the fact that with the industrialization of both northern Korea and southeastern Siberia, considerable potential existed for interchange of products—especially if Manchurian resources and industries were tied into one giant industrial complex. A rather significant group of Koreans, estimated by Russian sources as numbering 170,000 in 1937, lived in Siberia. Some of these had long been settled in the border region, and others were political exiles. In this group, especially among the younger generation, were a considerable number of Communists. There were in addition a relatively large number of Korean Communists in Japan, China, and Korea proper. The possession of all of Korea by a group friendly to the Soviet Union would be of no little strategic and political value to Moscow. Hence Russia's interest in Korea was easily understood.

In contrast, American interests in Korea were, originally, much less vital. Prior to the war, American concern was largely governed by humanitarian and, to a minor degree, economic factors. The United States was a long way away from Korea, and although a few hundred Koreans had been educated in America and some twelve thousand Koreans lived in Hawaii and California, Americans as a rule had little interest in the small Asian peninsula. Some Americans, to be sure, were quite aware of the highly successful work done by American missionaries. For instance, there were more Protestant Christians in Korea in relation to the total population than in any other Asian country. Some Americans knew that Korea had military importance. However, even during World War II, though logic and strategy would seem to have called for it, there was practically no training of Americans in the Korean language or in the background of Korean problems.

After the war, with the occupation of southern Korea and Japan by American troops the Far East assumed a new place in American thinking. To some degree it may be said that America inherited the Japanese position in that area of the globe. But as far as Korea was concerned, America was little prepared for the assumption of this position of power. There was still grave doubt in the minds of many Americans as to how vital Korea was for strategic, economic, or political reasons. It was at this time that America began to feel the first pressures of the "cold war." It soon became obvious that Korea was to be one of the "hottest" of the frontiers between the United States and the Soviet Union and that an American policy for Korea had to be formulated which would be part of the overall American strategy of meeting Communist aggression.

Resurgent Korean nationalism was a third factor of significance in this postwar period. The imposition of the thirty-eighth parallel and the subsequent rivalries and divergent actions of the occupying powers aggravated an already serious situation as far as the Korean people were concerned. With the liberation from Japan, Koreans had high hopes for complete independence. Though thirty-five years of Japanese control had strongly affected Korean customs and thought processes, a virile nationalism remained, but even so there was little in the way of well-organized Korean political action. In the short interim between the day that the armistice was announced and the day that the actual surrender of the Japanese troops took place, People's Committees were set up. These committees were not elected bodies. In some cases political prisoners released by the Japanese from jails or from surveillance (obviously some were Communists) plunged into political agitation and by mass meetings had themselves proclaimed as "people's representatives." In other cases, recognized Korean leaders—landlords, merchants, teachers, Christian pastors, etc.—were called in by Japanese officials and urged to set up committees to maintain order. Public opinion was the major force in giving authority to these groups.

In the north, these committees which were oriented toward the communist point of view were utilized by the Russian occupation forces, and those committees which represented the more middle-of-the-road or conservative elements were suppressed.* The committees which were allowed to function were also controlled by the process of grafting on native Korean Communists imported from Russia, Manchuria, and northern China. Through these committees a government, the People's Republic of Korea, was set up with a constitution based on the Soviet model. This organization claimed jurisdiction over all Korea. Accord-

---

* Information on the political developments in North Korea is difficult to obtain through normal research channels. The material given here must therefore be judged in that light.

ing to the constitution, the capital was Seoul, but Pyongyang was to serve as the capital city pending the formation of a unified government.

In the south, after an unfortunate period of some days while the Japanese were kept in control, an American military government was established. No recognition was given to an organization called (as in the north) the "People's Republic," though this likewise had been organized on the basis of local People's Committees. Immediately a number of Korean leaders, most of whom had lived outside Korea for many decades, returned from China and the United States to Seoul. Political factions and parties sprouted; intrigue was rife. Finally, in the autumn of 1947, after abortive efforts to consult with the Russians, the United States brought the question of Korean independence before the United Nations General Assembly. The Assembly voted on November 14, 1947, with the Soviet block abstaining, to set up a United Nations Temporary Commission on Korea. This Commission was to observe proportional elections in Korea of "representatives with whom the Commission may consult regarding the prompt attainment of the freedom and independence of the Korean people and which representation, constituting a National Assembly, may establish a National Government of Korea." However, when the U.N. Commission reached Korea early in 1948, it was not allowed by the Russians and their Korean puppets to go into northern Korea; consequently all of its subsequent work was restricted to the south.

Elections for a National Assembly were held in South Korea on May 10, 1948. Four-fifths of those eligible registered, and of those over ninety per cent voted. After some preliminary steps the Assembly promulgated a constitution for the Republic of Korea. The constitution set up a presidential system with the President elected by the National Assembly, the single legislative body. Dr. Syngman Rhee was elected President by an overwhelming majority of 180–16.  Theoretically, a system of checks and balances was provided among the three branches of the government, though the Prime Minister appointed by the President had to receive confirmation from the Assembly. The constitution called for guarantees of the fundamental rights and freedoms of the Korean people and gave the State a considerable degree of control over natural resources, transportation, finances, and education.

The following years were tumultuous ones in both North and South Korea.  Just as the two "governments" had been modelled on different political prototypes, so they developed in divergent directions in their internal administrations.  Some geographic changes in political units were made in both areas.  In North Korea a new province, Chagang, was made by grouping together a number of the counties of North Pyongan; some counties of South Hamgyong Province were amalgamated with those parts of Kangwon which were north of the thirty-eighth parallel.  In South Korea, the island of Cheju was given a provincial administration and the capital, Seoul, was given special status, equivalent to a province.

The two regimes carried on a considerable amount of counter-propaganda, attempting to undermine each other.  They were, of course, deeply involved in their own internal problems, which they tackled in quite different ways.  They were dependent upon outside aid, which was given by contrasting methods and in varying amounts.  The northern regime, as time went on, found its program of internal aggression against the southern Republic of Korea to be meeting with very limited success.  In the spring of 1950, for example, elections were held in South Korea in which eighty-six per cent of all eligible adults voted for members of a new National Assembly.  This was a notable symbol of the birth of democratic action.  The economy of southern Korea had been bolstered by large amounts of American aid and technical assistance.

The climax to this phase of Korean development took place on June 25, 1950, when, after a propaganda barrage calling for elections to unify the country, the North Korean troops moved across the thirty-eighth parallel.   This aggression was met by prompt action by the United Nations Security Council.   The

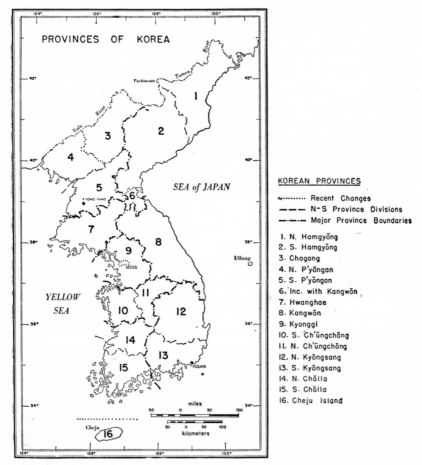

FIG. 9—The political divisions of Korea.   This map includes some of the latest political changes.   Figure 10 shows the population density by counties, so the minor political subdivisions appear on that map.

Council on June 27th recommended that such help be given the Republic of Korea "as might be necessary to repel the armed attack and to restore international peace and security in the area." Shortly thereafter American troops landed to support the forces of the Republic of Korea in meeting the North Korean challenge. The war was on.

During the hot Korean summer of 1950 the U.N. forces were fighting at odds which at times were as high as twenty to one. As General MacArthur said, the U.N. troops, largely Americans and South Koreans, "distinguished themselves in the most difficult of military operations—a delaying action." Within six weeks they had been pushed into a relatively small beachhead around Pusan. On September 15, the Allied landings at Inchon on the west coast and the breakout from the Pusan beachhead brought a drastic reversal in the fighting. By October, Republic of Korea forces moved across the thirty-eighth parallel and were followed a week later by Allied forces. By mid-November, some advance units had reached the Yalu River and much of North Korea was in the United Nations' possession. Then came a flood of Chinese Communist forces who, in General MacArthur's words, made of the Korean struggle "an entirely new war." The U.N. forces were pushed below the thirty-eighth parallel. After regrouping they were able to advance above the parallel in the east of Korea, though they did not advance so far in the west. Along a wavy north-east-southwest line which goes across Korea at a slight angle from the thirty-eighth parallel, the battle line was maintained for many months, though not without great sacrifice on each side. It was this line which became the truce zone set up on July 27, 1953.

The fighting was devastating to the economy of Korea. The major cities suffered immense destruction and the areas in which major military advances took place were severely damaged. Waves of migrants washed back and forth by the fighting have been, perhaps, the major sufferers.  In its gross strategy the war emphasized the importance of Korean geography, especially its character as a peninsula with two gateways— one the Pusan-Naktong River basin, the other the Sinuiju-Yalu River lowland. , The local strategy was guided by the diversity of the local terrain.  Thus, Korea once again became the devastated theater of a struggle between great powers, its strategic geographic position a severe handicap to peace and progress.

# Chapter 5

# The Korean Population Pattern

THE single most important map to illustrate a discussion of Korean geography is a map of population distribution. Such a map raises some interesting questions. What factors account for the patterns of distribution? What is the nature of the Korean people shown in these patterns? What are the local complexities of distribution that are glossed over in a generalized map of all of Korea?* It is obvious from a quick glance at such a map that the population distribution of Korea is very irregular. Many of the isolated parts of the northern interior have never been stepped on by the foot of man. In contrast, the agricultural lands of the south are densely crowded. But the density itself varies greatly within this highly populated area. In some places the contrast on the one hand between the relatively evenly settled plains and hill lands and on the other hand the densely packed cities located only a few miles away is very sharp.

One of the important features of the population of Korea is the relative absence of minority groups, though, of course, this was not the case when the Japanese controlled the peninsula. In 1944, for example, there were 708,448 civilian Japa-

---

* The answer to the first question is the theme of this chapter. The answers to the last two questions appear to be of a more subjective nature and are treated in the next chapter.

nese, mostly settled in the cities of Korea. At the end of the war, all of these were repatriated to Japan. In 1944 a small group of Chinese lived along the Manchurian border of Korea and in some of the larger cities, but these numbered only 71,400. In the same year Europeans and White Russians, engaged in missionary activities or in business, were an infinitesimal fraction of the population.

The high density of the population in Korea today is the result of a tremendous increase which has taken place in recent decades, a population "explosion" of serious consequence. The data for recent years, which is fairly reliable, shows that the population increased from 19,523,000 in 1925 to 25,900,142 in 1944.[15] Growth in recent decades has been estimated to be at the rate of 1.7 to 1.8 per cent a year. Using the more conservative figure, counting the migrations which have taken place in the postwar years, and taking into account the tremendous disruptive effects of the Korean war, it may be estimated that the Korean population in 1955 numbered 31,000,-000. A growth of this magnitude presents numerous problems which affect the geography of Korea.

During the Yi dynasty (1392–1910) some interesting data on the population of Korea was collected. These figures, obviously, should be used with caution, for the data were based on taxation records and it was to the advantage of the tax collector to report a low population. Also, since the figures were based upon the number of taxed families, omitting many who were landless, it has been judged that the census recorded perhaps only half the actual population. The first "census" figures were for the year 1395, at the start of the Yi dynasty but these are obviously inadequate, since they give the figures of 152,403 families and 322,746 persons. These same low figures were also used with slight increases for the years 1397 and 1404. Larger and perhaps better figures are given for the period starting in 1639. The data was reported on a three-year basis from that time to

1789. The figures in 1639 record a total of 441,827 families and 1,512,165 persons. Then occurs a rapid growth of population to 1693 when the number of households was 1,547,237, and the population 7,045,115. This was followed by a sharp drop in 1696 due to a famine, which in turn was followed by a gradual building-up to a little over seven million for the period from 1730 on. In 1789 the population was estimated at 7,403,606 and the households at 1,752,837. A more adequate census was taken in 1807, when data by province was recorded. At this time the total population stood at 7,561,403. There then came a decline in population; it is difficult to tell whether this was actual or whether the figures represented governmental ineffi- ciency or difficulty in collecting taxes.

From these historical materials it is seen that for some centuries the population of Korea was relatively stable. This was a period of self-sufficient, agricultural economy. To be sure, numerous historical records tell of draught, famine, and flood, which took their toll of lives. There was little knowledge of medicine to curb the epidemics which swept through the peninsula from time to time. Perhaps partly as a counter to this hazardous existence the Korean was oriented toward the maintenance of the population through a large birth rate. As one student of the problem, Irene Taeuber, has noted:

Early and almost universal marriage, the high prestige of the fertile wife, the aversion to abortion, and the supernatural sanction of a folk religion which demanded sons insured a human fertility adequate for the preservation of people and culture.

The opening of Korea to the outside world and its annexation to Japan was followed by a population growth of major con- sequences. The Japanese exercised a better control over epi- demics, and the food supply was regulated so that major famines did not occur. The death rate declined markedly, though by Western standards the death rate was still quite high. The expectation of life at birth in 1926–30 was 32.4 years for men and 34.9 for women; only sixty per cent of the boys lived to reach the age of six. As the death rate declined, however, there was no downward trend in the birth rate. Urbanization and industrialization, which took place under Japanese suzerainty, did not have much immediate effect on the birth rate, but the widening of the gap between death rates and birth rates had its obvious result in a tremendous growth of population.*

The growth of population is significant, but even more important geographically has been the movement of people. A study of the early records shows a decided northward trend of the population and during the Japanese period this trend continued. The north was the pioneer land. It is of some interest to note that much of the movement was from adjoining southern provinces; it was not a wholesale movement of people from the south of Korea to the north of Korea.

The disruption of the population patterns in the war and postwar period and especially during the years of hostilities has been tremendous. Immediately after World War II the Japanese were repatriated and an estimated 1,100,000 Koreans, many of whom had been working in war industries, came back from Japan; most of them settled in South Korea. In addition to this movement there were some significant changes within Korea. It has been estimated that as many as two million Koreans fled from Communist-dominated North Korea to South Korea. The military operations after June 25, 1950 set up waves of uncounted thousands, or millions, drifting back and forth. The population figure for Korea can only be at best a guess—considering the Korean prewar figures and taking into account the events since then—we might accept tentatively a figure of 31,000,000 for 1955.

After the war, when the repatriation of Koreans from Japan took place, an estimated six hundred thousand Koreans chose

---

* The growth of the populations by provinces from the year 1925 to 1944 and for South Korea in 1949 can be noted in a table given in Appendix D.

to remain in Japan, where, today, they constitute an important minority group, particularly in such cities as Osaka.[16] Though there was also a flow of Koreans back from Manchuria and northern China, it is estimated that a million Koreans now reside in Manchuria, most of them living in the Chien-tao region, across the Tumen River from northeastern Korea.

However, great as the migrations from Korea may have been, the major movement was within Korea itself. This is the movement from the villages into the cities and industrial areas, particularly into those of northern Korea. This trend was particularly marked in the later years of Japanese rule. In recent years the repatriates from Japan and the refugees from North Korea have further swollen the cities of South Korea.

These features of growth and movement have resulted in the present distribution of Korea's people. The map shows only the general pattern, for it is impossible on a map of this scale to indicate minute local differences. The distinction between the predominant village-settlement pattern of most of Korea and the dispersed settlements of the northern interior and the mountain lands is completely lost. One might assume that since Korea is predominantly an agricultural land a map of population would be practically equivalent to a map of crop land. However, the relative supporting power of crop land is an important factor. For example, infertile upland fields support only a meager population. In addition, dense populations are often supported by fishing, mining, commercial, governmental, and industrial activities.

The distribution of people in Korea has certain distinctive characteristics. First and foremost is the concentration of the population in the lowlands—along river plains—and the sparsity of habitation in the mountain lands of the interior. The Korean population thus appears to be pushed out to the edges of the peninsula, along the coasts. It is important, however, to realize that terrain and arable land are the dominant factors here,

rather than proximity to the sea; thus, for example, the upper
Han and Naktong River valleys, though far distant from the
sea, have dense populations.

Another dominant characteristic is the concentration of
population in the south, where there is a better physical base

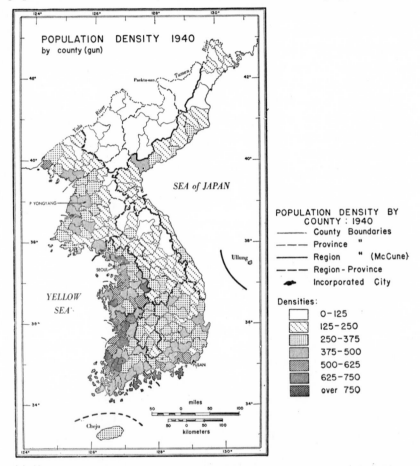

FIG. 10.—Population density in Korea. This map is drawn on the basis of
county data for 1940. Included on the map are the boundaries of the geographic
regions discussed later in this book. Densities are given in persons per square mile.

for agriculture. The density of population in Korea south of
the thirty-eighth parallel in 1949 was 556 persons per square
mile. (A comparable figure for the entire United States was
forty-nine persons per square mile.) In the prewar and World
War II period there was a greater relative growth in population
in the north, but the south still had the larger population. In
recent years, the trend northward has been reversed by the
migrations of repatriates and refugees to the south, so that
the preponderance of the south over the north in terms of population has been more accentuated.

The last important feature of the distribution of people in
Korea is the concentration in cities. Urbanization has been a
feature of Korean population trends since 1930. This has been
caused by numerous factors, but especially by the development
of a modern economy. It should be stressed, however, that
though the cities have had great growth, the dominant population group in Korea is still to be found in the rural village.
The relation between urban and rural population for all of
Korea from 1940 and for South Korea from 1949 has been shown
cartographically in Figures 11 and 12.

The character of the Korean population is of considerable
significance. It is perhaps useful to study a simple table
(Figure 13) of the age and sex distribution of the Korean
segment of the population, which in 1944 totalled 25,120,174.
(In that year there were in Korea 708,448 Japanese and
71,510 Chinese and other foreigners, but these are not considered
in the table). As may be noted, Korean women slightly
outnumbered the men 12,559,001 to 12,521,173. The preponderance of youths is shown on the chart of age groups.
Because of this the effective labor force was large and growing
at a fast rate.

The labor force (the gainfully employed or persons available
for gainful employment within the group from fifteen to fifty-
nine years of age) was estimated to be 8,928,000 in 1940,

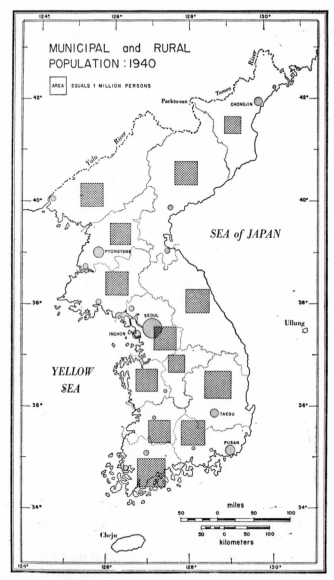

FIG. 11.—The municipal and rural population by provinces in 1940. The squares are the rural population; the circles with the same unit of area per number of persons are the cities, or municipalities.

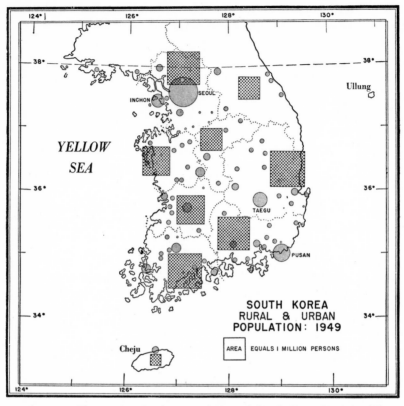

FIG. 12.—The rural and urban population of South Korea in 1949. The squares are the rural population; the circles are the cities and major towns as separated in the census returns for 1949.

9,173,000 in 1944, and 11,192,000 in 1950.  This labor force was adequate in skill and number for agricultural production, but it was decidedly deficient in the higher skills required for industry and transportation—employment skills formerly exercised by the Japanese.  In 1944, about seventy-one per cent of the Koreans were dependent on agriculture for a livelihood. Due to the great increase of mineral exploitation and industrialization because of the Japanese war economy, eleven per cent of the population was dependent on mining and industry. This is decidedly different from prior years when only two to three per cent were so dependent. Minor percentages were engaged in other occupations in 1944.

The educational status of Koreans was and is low, particularly in technical training. Under the Japanese, there was little emphasis given to advanced education for Koreans. In the words of one of the high officials of the Japanese Government-General: "Koreans should be taught to follow, not to know." After World War II there was a notably successful literacy

AGE GROUPS OF KOREANS 1944

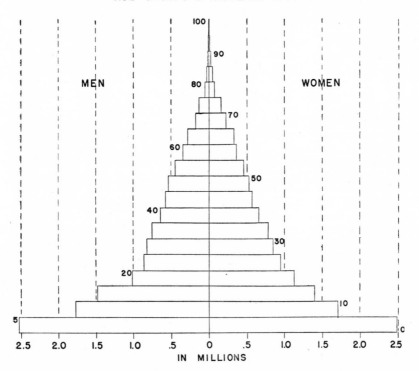

FIG. 13.—The age groups of the Korean segment of the population in 1944 grouped in five-year intervals and separated between men and women.

campaign and illiteracy decreased markedly. However, school facilities and teachers for more formal training were sadly lacking. Though these were being improved, with the fighting in Korea after 1950, the educational system received very heavy blows. Students were needed as soldiers, and their training was almost completely disrupted. As schools are able to be reconstituted, special emphasis is being given to technical training. It will be many years before Korea has an adequate technically trained labor force for non-agricultural economic activities. The present nucleus of trained people is small, but around them, through in-service training and special schools, much can be accomplished. The potential is there, but it needs development. In fact, the hard-working, virile, resilient Korean population is one of the major assets for the reconstruction of Korea.[17]

# Chapter 6 | The Korean People and Their Way of Life

THE Koreans are a mixture of Tungus and proto-Caucasian stock, generally similar to other peoples of the Far East. Their general character is the result of an amalgamation of strains introduced by a succession of waves of migration from the north. Some scholars believe, however, that consideration must be given to the possibility that migrants from the Malayan area and south China influenced the racial characteristics of the Koreans.

The Koreans are midway in height between the shorter Japanese and the taller north Chinese and Manchus; the average male stature, according to a recent study, is 5' 5", the average female stature is 5' 1".

The skin of the average Korean is a light yellow-brown, in some cases with a reddish tinge. The skin color appears darker among the farming and common people and lighter among the upper classes of society. The eyes of the Koreans are usually brown and marked by a slight Mongolian eye fold. Their hair is straight or slightly curly, and dark brown to black in color. The cheek bones are commonly high and relatively prominent; the nose is concave with a flattened bridge.

The Koreans have characteristics which set them off from their neighbors and make them a distinct "people." However, the greatest differentiation is a cultural one, embracing such varied but telling things as language, dress, diet.[18]

Despite the fact that the official written language of the Korean court through many centuries was Chinese, the Korean people developed their own unique language. The language is heavily loaded with borrowings, both in words and structure, from the tongues of their conquering neighbors, the Japanese and the Chinese. Dialectical differences throughout Korea are fewer than one might expect, considering the geographical diversity of the land.[19]

Before the fifteenth century scholars who wished to become government officials had to learn Chinese, the language in which the Confucian classics were written. However, under the aegis of the early Yi dynasty rulers, a simple and effective phonetic alphabet of twenty-five letters was invented. Because of its simplicity this script, *onmun*, or *hangul*, was disparaged by the scholars; fortunately, however, it was used for informal writing. If necessary, any Chinese characters which the writer felt were needed might be included in order to gain precision. Christian missionaries and Korean scholars kept *onmun* alive in recent decades even in the face of concerted opposition of the Japanese. At the end of World War II its use in the battle against illiteracy in both North and South Korea became a symbol of the nationalistic aspirations of the Korean people.

Although "modern dress"—the dress of the west—is often seen by the traveller in Korea, the fashions which were maintained for hundreds of years may still be considered the standard. Perhaps the most distinctive thing about Korean dress is that the apparel of both men and woman is white, though greys, blues and (particularly among the wealthy) pastels are not unusual. The men wear wide trousers bound tightly at the waist, and, on formal occasions, gathered at the ankles by colored bands. Their jackets are short and loose and are usually fastened by a tie with a single bow, though the "modern"

Koreans might prefer buttons. Over the jacket they may wear a large, pocketed vest. On formal occasions the Korean gentleman may wear, in addition, a long flowing coat which overlaps and is tied, on the right side—never the left—with, again, a single bow tied in a prescribed manner. The hats are equally distinctive: in the olden days, when his hair was tied in a topknot, the Korean wore a high-crowned hat made of lacquered horsehair; the modern Korean, of course, has no topknot and may wear a Western-style hat or cap. The taste in shoes varies according to the wealth, social position, and the amount of modernity which marks the man: the older style called for Chinese-style shoes. Poorer people wear rubber or straw shoes, with or without stockings. When they are working in the paddy fields, of course, the farmers usually go barefoot.

Women's dress is somewhat like the men's, except that in the old style they wear two pairs of trousers, one shorter than the other, the longer not reaching the ankle and never tied. In modern days, they wear slips as do their Western sisters. The Korean woman wears a pleated skirt, usually very long. Her inner jacket is short and tightly bound across her breast. The country woman may wear a cloth around her head, though headgear varies considerably according to regional customs and the style of the hair-do. Sometimes the hair is worn at a bun at the back of the head; or it may be braided and then looped around the head, particularly if the woman's household duties require her to transport a load on top of her head.

Children's clothing is similar in design to that of adults, but is often made of colored material—particularly the short jackets which boys wear on ceremonial occasions. The sleeves of these jackets are a riot of brilliant colors arranged in narrow stripes.

Like most people in the Far East, the Korean makes his clothing of cotton, though the wealthy may wear a silken jacket and outer coat. Winter clothing is usually quilted with cotton. Hemp is sometimes used, particularly when a son goes into mourning. Then he may wear a hempen coat of a distinctive design, and complete his costume with a large wicker hat.

It is only natural that in the past decades many of the features of dress for which the Koreans have been noted should pass. The impact of the West has been tremendous, and nowhere is this so clearly seen than in the dark uniforms worn by the Korean school boys and girls, or in the brilliant pastel colors which the girls and young women wear. Among the people who have not been touched by the hand of the West, many of the older customs and fashions still obtain. The resurgent nationalism has resulted in a revival in the wearing of the traditional dress, particularly among the women.

Like most of the peoples of the Far East, the Koreans have made rice the staple of their diet; in fact, in the Korean spoken language, the common word for food is "rice." Among the poorer people of northern Korea, however, rice is often a delicacy, something to be relished in place of the usual diet of cereals such as millet, barley, wheat, and grain sorghum.

Customarily, rice dishes are frequently supplemented with fish, vegetables—often soy beans—seasoned and cooked meats, such as beef or chicken, and soups. One food which is unique is *kimchi,* a variety of vegetable pickles, which, in its most delectable (to the Korean) form, is full of red peppers; it adds spice to the interminable diet of rice.

In modern Korea the food problem, aggravated for many by the hardships of war, is not an easy one, for cereal production has not kept pace with the tremendous growth in population. Many Koreans subsist on a starvation diet.

One of the most interesting aspects of Korean culture to the Westerner is the fact that there is little uniformity of religious belief or practice.[20] In a typical Korean family, the women may adhere to the Buddhist religion, which was introduced fifteen centuries ago; on the other hand, the men may be followers of the Confucian ethical system. Christianity, introduced only in recent decades, has a large number of devoted adherents and has had a profound effect on the culture and life of the people.

However, the only religion which one might call uniquely Korean is Chon-do-gyo. This is an extremely eclectic faith which its adherents believe has been able to combine the good features of Buddhism, Confucianism, Christianity—as well as Taoism. In the last decades of the nineteenth century Chun-do-gyo had a widespread vogue, in part because of its reformist nationalistic tone. Suppressed by the Japanese, who were unsuccessful in forcing Shintoism on the conquered Koreans, Chun-do-gyo has seen some revival since the freeing of the peninsula.

All-pervasive in the minds of the Koreans are varied forms of nature worship; the people's love for their native land has been transformed into a virtual religion. Good and evil spirits are often allied with natural objects. So-called "devil-posts" are still occasionally seen on guard at the outskirts of villages. Within the village an old tree with wide-spreading branches is often an object of veneration. On the tops of passes one finds piles of stones, tossed there one by one by travellers who hope for good luck on their journeys. Wisps of clothing taken from sick children are tied to trees some distance from the villages in the hope that the evil spirits will stay with the clothing and leave the children. The exorcising of evil spirits by women or by blind men is a common practice.

The Korean's nature piety is nowhere more apparant than in the choice he makes for burial sites, usually the most beautiful spot he can find. The ideal site is on the curve of a hill, looking out over a picturesque plain. There the families on festive occasions go to care for the graves and worship the spirits of their ancestors. Wealthy folk often build pavilions on hill summits so that the people may retire to worship and contemplate the peaceful beauty of the valley hills.

Often associated with religion and seasonal festivities are sports and games. One such game, now passed from the contemporary scene, was the stone fight, which was engaged in by all the men and boys of one village against those of another village. Tug-of-war, using heavy straw ropes, was also a common sport in the olden days. However, most of the sports and games were more dependent upon individual skill: wrestling, chess, kite flying, and many others common to people of all lands. Such typical Western sports as soccer and basketball have been widely introduced through the school system, and some Koreans are famous for their feats in marathon running and long distance skating.

The Korean social organization is perhaps the most important feature of the Korean way of life. On the whole it represents an adaptation of Chinese customs based on Confucian principles. The key to the social structure is Korean village life and the blood ties between the people there. The basic unit is the father-dominated family, and a number of families are often grouped together, in part by proximity of living arrangements in the village, into clans. The impact of Western ideas has shattered much of the strength of the family structure. In their attempts to change the Korean way of life the Communists have been especially effective: they have struck at the family system to undermine the importance of the elderly and the males, so that communist doctrines may have easier acceptance.[21] There is no doubt that the old family system has its weaknesses and that it is usually allied with a debilitating conservatism, but it does give Korea a remarkable stability.

The usual pattern of family life is founded on the Confucian concept of the correct relationship between people—the "five relationships." These revolve about the ideas of superiority and inferiority: thus, the wife is subordinate to the husband, the sons to the father, the younger brother to the older brother, the younger friend to the older friend, and finally the subject to the ruler. Hence the senior male member, usually the father and husband, holds the ruling position in the group. After his death, his influence, and that of his forebears continues under the common practice of ancestor worship.

The Korean village family unit very often occupies a single household. The sons' wives, who are from another clan, become a part of the family unit, and achieve something more than inferior status only if they give birth to males who will carry on the family line. A mother who has had sons—and ultimately grandsons—is able to exert strong behind-the-scene influence, which may be exercised indirectly through the daughters-in-law or through the father and husband. The younger sons, unless they succeed to the position of the eldest son by death of their older brother before he has a son, have an inferior status, though in recent years, they have been drifting away and establishing new homes outside the home village.

The patrilineal family is tied to other families by this process and it is these groups of interconnected families which make up the clans. Clan members usually have the same family name. It has been estimated that there are 1,072 clans in Korea, though there are only 326 surnames. Some ten family names are used by eighty per cent of the people. It seems as though one in every four or five Koreans is named Kim. Though each clan occupies villages or parts of villages, they may have connections with other branches of their clans, sometimes long distances away.

Within the village is an informal structure designed to benefit the allied families. The heads of the families act as leaders of the village. Among the family heads certain individuals may occupy a superior position as "informal leaders" or "village elders." These persons are called upon to arbitrate disputes, keep peace and order, stimulate public works, and act as liaison for higher political authorities.

This strong Korean clan, village, and family system would seem to be very autocratic. However, numerous safeguards exist—particularly the Confucian concept of proper conduct.

Thus if a family head, or an "informal leader," is too autocratic, he is considered as operating outside the bounds of propriety and will feel the strong weight of public opinion.

In general, then, the social organization is based on this family and clan loyalty. Of less strength are loyalties to the district or group of villages surrounding the market town. Even less strong are the loyalties to the province and to the nation. As could be expected, national loyalty is strongest when some outside power is challenging the country, since the nation is thought of as a defense, though a distant one, of the family system.

The impact of Japanese power had a profound influence on the Korean social structure. The Japanese system of government allowed little local autonomy in the family and village. But the structure has suffered even more with the advent of a modern mobility; families have broken up or individual members have moved to the cities. Many of the ties between families in the clan and village have been erased and above all, the postwar military occupations, and the war itself with its wholesale devastation, have shattered the family system perhaps beyond repair.

Parallel with the family system is a class system, also in part derived from Confucian ideas. According to the old concepts, the educated person occupied a special position in the community, for he was equipped to pass the government examinations and obtain an official position. As a government official he had the power to acquire wealth, usually in the form of paddy fields, and become a member of a strong minority—the landlord class. In Korea, there was a wide gulf between these landed aristocrats and the rest of the population. However, it was never absolutely impossible for people in the lower group, often with the help of their family and village to become educated, pass the examinations, and acquire positions in the upper class. In the parts of Korea dominated by the Communists, the technicians who

# THE LAND AND PEOPLE OF KOREA

1      The mountains are high everywhere in Korea;

...some are abrupt like the crest of Heartbreak Ridge.

The plains may be very small in the north...

2

...or more extensive in the south.

3

At the junction of plains and mountains villages are often clustered.

A flight across Korea from Seoul to the east shows...

5

...the bare, eroded hills and the flat plains along the
Han River,

...the winding channel of the upper Han entrenched in great loops,

6

7

...the even crest-line of the Taebaek Range, and...

...the flat plains and low hills along the east coast.

8

The seasons come and go and the clouds change with them, as these pictures from Pyongyang show.

9

In the fall there are often light clouds;

10

...in winter the skies may be clear, but the snow cover will last a long time in the north;

...in spring the cherry blossoms are out in all their beauty; and...

11

...in summer the heavy cumulus clouds bring rain.

12

The heritage of the past is still remembered, like the astronomical observatory of the Silla period in Kyongju,

13

...or the reputed grave of Kija in Pyongyang.    14

The Korean people have a distinctive dress,

...like those worn by these women spinning cotton,

15

...or this gentleman lighting his pipe.

16

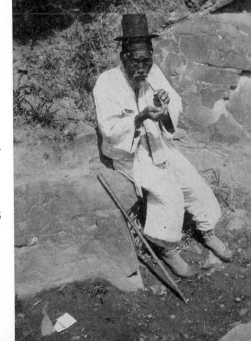

...people like these women washing clothes beside a wrecked Russian T-34 tank.

18

Men carry heavy loads on *chige*'s or A-frames...

...or use carts or sleds to carry their products, like this little pig on his way to market.

19

The thatching of a roof requires cooperation. 20

21       The houses are usually clustered together in villages.

Korean gentlemen keep their dignity, despite difficult times.

22

Korean women pay rapt attention to the *mudang,* or sorcerer, in a trance.

23

Above all, men and women alike have their work to do,

24    ...like this lady grinding grain in a discarded helmet, though...

...as families they are happy to worship their ancestors and then...

...have a picnic looking out over the valleys and hills which make 25 up their land.

had previously not had too high a social status, have experienced a dramatic upward rise in their social position.

Within the lower class, social stratifications were marked. At the top of the scale were the professional men. Next came the merchants, in part because of their better economic position. Then came the farmers, the bulk of the people, who occupied an honorable though not high position. Below them were the soldiers, recruited mostly from the farm families, and finally, at the bottom of the social scale, were the butchers, the beggars, and the sorcerers.

It is impossible, of course, to offer an absolute generalization about the "character" of 31,000,000 Koreans. What they are like depends on one's point of view. To the Japanese conqueror, the Koreans were a simple, lazy folk, who above all needed the whip and the spur. To the Christian missionary, the Koreans were a quiet, rural folk, whose basic good qualities needed only the further stimulation of a powerful faith. But to a Westerner who is inclined to take people as they are, the Koreans at their best are a likeable people, good-natured, shrewd, and kindly. He sees them as a people who have been conditioned by centuries of close village association, and whose habits of conduct often reflect the ideals expressed in the Confucian term "reciprocity." Sometimes—because of the rigidity of the formal family organization or because of the sufferings attendant upon poverty and subjection—they are an extremely volatile people, well deserving the not uncommon appellation "the Irish of the Far East." Though tied closely by bonds of blood, they are often inclined to argument and factionalism—particularly when it is fostered by those who calculate to gain at the Koreans' expense. In the face of "outside" opposition they can be extremely fierce in pride and in action. But in the end, the Korean knows there is work to do, and his strong, plodding diligence and his admirable forbearance in the face of troubles that would break lesser people, manage to help him exist and even flourish.

Perhaps the two things which best symbolize Korea to the unhypercritical Westerner are the thoroughly-worked paddy fields at the foot of the rounded hills and the graceful pavilion which graces the top, from whose steps the Korean can look out over a land cumbered with troublesome history, yet not without burgeoning hope.

Despite the fact that in the modern era the home life of many Koreans has to a great degree been revolutionized, the old styles of living and construction have been remarkably persistent— particularly in the villages, where the mud-walled, thatch-roofed houses seem eternally bound to the farm fields which surround them. These settlements vary considerably through-out Korea, particularly from one region to the next, but there is one type which might be considered as approximating the typical. This type of Korean home is a one-story, two or three room house with sheds adjoining for animals or farm imple-ments. There is a courtyard in front of the house and the whole home is surrounded by a stone wall.

The houses are constructed of materials readily at hand. Usually, the foundations are made of large stones put at each corner of the rooms, and sometimes at the mid-points. Then walls of earth, mixed with stones or broken tile, are built up to the height of the main foundation stones, or, often, two or three feet higher. Along this base of rock and earth, large timbers are laid, preferably of red pine. The uprights are then set, usually five or six feet high. At right angles to these are mortised other timbers, which run parallel to the base timbers. Between the wooden frameworks thus erected are fastened a crisscross of grain sorghum stalks or reeds roughly woven together; on this wicker-work is plastered mud which has been mixed with rice straw. Finer mud is plastered over the rough mud. Small wooden frames are set into these walls, usually a foot above the base timber and a foot below the top timber. In these frames latticed wooden doors are hung on hinges, and over the lattice is pasted white paper through which light can filter into the rooms. The doors between rooms may be sliding lattice screens, paper-covered.

The roof is usually covered with a thatch of rice straw, made in long rolls and laid so as to overlap and form a solid roof. The addition of new layers over the old—as time goes on—produces a heavy, solid, waterproof roof. The roof timbers are allowed to extend beyond the timber to form eaves. Sometimes they are supported by additional pillars so as to allow for a longer front eave. Extending under the front eaves is a verandah, often of boards.

At one end of the house is the kitchen, whose floor is usually made of pounded mud. A stove with a fireplace opening at floor level is along the inner wall of the kitchen. The flue from the kitchen stove leads under the floors of the adjoining room or rooms to a chimney erected at the other end of the house, producing a very effective radiant heating system. This is an ingenious way Koreans have of conserving fuel.

The floors of rooms other than the kitchen are usually made of pressed earth or smoothed stones and are covered with layers of oiled paper, which sometimes extend up the walls. In other cases, however, reed mats cover the dirt floors and the walls are not papered. There is little furniture: there may be small dining tables and wooden chests to hold bedding, and few if any chairs. Koreans usually sit on cushions on the floor. They do not wear shoes in the house.

For house construction local materials are used: stones, mud, wooden beams, grain sorghum stalks, and rice-straw thatch. As would be expected, there are variations; for example, in some areas split slate is used for roofing, and in some isolated areas, bark instead of thatch. In those parts of Korea where the wind is strong or snow is heavy, the roofs are held down with straw ropes or with logs tied by ropes. The type of roof may vary too, from a simple hip construction to a construction of a definite gable, and the amount of pitch will depend on the amount of rain and snow expected.

The greatest difference from the usual type of construction is found in the more isolated and heavily forested lands of the northern interior. There cabins are built with horizontally laid logs, which are coated with mud so that only at the corners of the buildings may the logs be seen, and the roofs are of rough-hewn shingles. A special type of construction is found in volcanic Cheju Island, where the walls of many houses are made of rock.

The houses of the landlords and the wealthy class are much more substantial with many more rooms and brick or white-washed walls. Such houses are built with numerous wooden beams and pillars and are covered with the distinctive tile roofs, the gently-curving tiles being laid with the concave sides up to form ridges. In modern times, particularly in the cities, galvanized roofing has been introduced for house construction.

Even among the houses of the non-wealthy there are variations. The smallest houses, mere huts—one room with a lean-to kitchen—may measure from ten to twenty feet in length, ten to fifteen feet in width, and seven or eight feet in height. But most houses have two rooms, each roughly ten or twelve feet square, with a kitchen. These rooms may be arranged in a straight line, or with one room at an angle to make an L-shaped structure. Other common shapes are U-shapes and a double L with the L's fitting together. The larger houses with five or six rooms, each about fifteen feet on the side, will have places for fires for the rooms which are distant from the kitchen.

Around a typical village house, and sometimes around town houses as well, is a vegetable garden. Climbing plants, such as gourds, are often planted near the house and extend over the

roof. Large jars for *kimchi*, small jars for soy sauce, or preserved foods are kept under the eaves of the houses, near the
kitchen; often the *kimchi* jars are buried in the courtyard.
Bags of rice are kept in sheds, storerooms, or under the eaves.
Sometimes a well is dug beside the garden.

The animal sheds, toilets, and woodsheds are often mere
thatch-roofed lean-tos. More commonly, however, these are
set off from the houses, on the side of the courtyard. A fence
of woven stalks usually surrounds the farmstead; but elaborate
homes, especially those which are in U or double-L shape, may
have solid walls and gateways. On dry sunny days the courtyards are much used and people often sleep outside in the
courtyards during the hot summer months. Again, there are
regional diversities in the shapes and character of the farmsteads.

A Korean village may comprise two or three houses or a
hundred or more grouped closely together.[22] The size of the
village varies with the terrain and productivity of the surrounding land. Usually they are located on the southern edges of the
hill slopes where the hills and valley floor meet and yet have a
water table which can be tapped for wells. In addition they
are protected by the hills from the strong cold winter winds.
The houses usually face south so that the courtyards get more
sunlight.

Living in a village means that the farmers must go out to
their fields, which sometimes may be a mile or more away.
Inconvenient as this may seem, it does afford better opportunities
to organize group work among the members of the village.

In the smaller villages life is markedly communal. Near the
center of many villages there may be a tree, surrounded by a
mound of earth, which serves as a meeting place for the men.
Another congregrating point may be the low, thatched building
which houses the communally operated grinding wheel. For
the women the traditional meeting places are the village wells

or along the streams, where they do the family washing. As a traveller approaches such a village one of the first things he may see is a pavilion built on the hillside, a traditional resting place. Near the outskirts of the village may stand a small building with a tiled roof, surrounded by mud and stone walls, which contains stone monuments erected in honor of meritorious citizens. If a wealthy landlord lives there, his house, with its tiled roof and courtyard dominates the rest of the dwellings. And occasionally the traveller may see a Christian church, with its belfry and cross, marking the impingement of the West on the East.

Market days in the villages are the exciting days teeming with life. A larger village usually has a well-defined market place with permanent stores surrounding it. In a small one it may be merely a wide place in the road or a courtyard. To enable the itinerant merchants to make their circuits of the villages and towns, market days are held in regular sequence, usually every five days. Surplus vegetables, eggs, and other produce are exchanged for things the local community cannot produce.

Many of the larger Korean villages are really towns, though it is difficult to make a clear distinction between the two. Because of its advantageous site, a village might develop into a commercial and administrative center. With the advent of Japanese control and better transportation facilities, numerous villages expanded into towns and were given a separate governmental status. Some such towns developed in virtually new sites, often at the outskirts of the old community, particularly when rail lines and depots were constructed and warehouses, police stations, schools, and post offices sprang up. These buildings, with their galvanized roofs and Japanese-Western style of architecture, stand in violent contrast with the more traditional Korean thatched or tile-roofed structures.

In old Korea the central capital and the provincial capitals and county seats were the only urban centers. These were ages old, and their narrow, crooked streets were lined with old houses and crowded with humanity. They were often enclosed by walls, whose imposing gates were located in each cardinal direction. The administrative buildings were set in parks, or had large courtyards enclosed by low walls.

With the modernization of Korea, some of these provincial capitals and many county seats were bypassed, and the administrative offices were moved to new centers, usually along railroad lines. Others were modernized on a tremendous scale: wide streets were run through the old congested areas; new subdivisions, usually on a utilitarian block pattern sprang up in the outskirts. The most noticeable new cities have been ports and railroad junction points and industrial centers.

In many ways the modern Korean city has little visible connection with its old past. Multiple-storied buildings have modified drastically the normally low skyline. The tempo is faster and the patterns of life are less stable. Except in the villages the old Korean way of life is fast disappearing.

*Chapter 7* | **The Basic Korean Economy**

THE economy of Korea is predominantly agricultural. The
Korean people live close to their soil. Thus, the resources of
agriculture, fishing, and forestry which provide for their food
and shelter are basic to their well-being now, just as they have
been for many hundreds of years. In modern times new
economic bases—mineral and hydroelectric resources—have
been developed; modern industrial plants, transportation and
communication facilities have been introduced. However, many
of these have been wrecked during the war, and much of Korea
is now dependent on its original resource base. It will be from
this base that the future economy will be erected.[23]

Korea affords an excellent example of "oriental agriculture."[24]
Usually, the holdings are small but intensively cultivated, and
the work is done almost exclusively by men, women, and children
using simple hand tools. Most of the fields average less than
half an acre in size, though a typical Korean farmer usually
cultivates several such fields located in different directions and
at varying distances from his village home. His total farm
averages from two to four acres. From this amount of land,
sometimes with the help of an animal to do the heavy plowing
but otherwise dependent on the painstaking efforts of himself
and his family, he tries to wrest a living. Pictures of him

trudging to his field with his farm implements, standing in his rice paddy, knee deep in water, or carrying a load of rice straw back to his home are truly representative of his way of life.

On the whole, the village in which he lives is self-sufficient and self-sustaining. His surplus farm products, at least those not siphoned off for taxes or for rent payments, he may barter for the small amount of consumer goods he himself cannot produce. Beyond that, he may aspire to increase his land holdings or improve his house and sheds.

If the farmer's land is suitably located, he will grow rice in preference to any other crop. The paddies, which surround the villages and cover the thousands of Korean valleys, are flooded by waters caught in catchment basins and distributed by primitive irrigation canals. If the farmer lives in southern Korea, he may double-crop his field with barley. Upland fields he uses for growing other cereals—wheat, barley, millet, grain sorghum, and sometimes cotton or tobacco.

With the coming of the Japanese, vast changes took place in the traditional Korean economy. Some of the change came at the direct instigation of the Japanese, but many of them were the simple result of the general impact of "modern ways" on Asian economic life. The widespread introduction of a money economy by the Japanese affected profoundly a people who, though not ignorant of the use of money, preferred a barter economy. Now, however, taxes and rent had to be paid in money, and this could be obtained only through the sale of farm products.

As the Japanese built new roads, spread a network of rail lines throughout the peninsula, and opened ports, a veritable revolution in the pattern of life was effected. The influx of manufactured goods caused the displacement of much of the village and home handicraft economy—the products of rural dyers, weavers, and potters. Men who had once been farm laborers now became part of a huge unskilled labor force, and with the managerial group almost exclusively Japanese, few Koreans were able to obtain commercial and professional status. The traditional economy of Korea—self-sufficient and exclusively rural in nature—was drastically modified.

To the Japanese, Korea was considered a source of two things: rice and raw materials. Though industry was to a degree increased, the major concern of the Japanese rulers was to increase the efficiency of the basic agricultural economy and to gear Korea's production to Japan's needs. In 1938, for example, agriculture accounted for 45.8 per cent of the gross value of national production, totally valued at a little over three billion yen.* On the other hand, industry, including the processing of agricultural products, accounted for 37.4 per cent, mining for 5.4 per cent, forestry for 5.4 per cent, and fisheries for 6.0 per cent.

The proportion of workers dependent for a livelihood on these varied economic activities also shows the importance of the emphasis on agriculture production. In 1938, 73.6 per cent of the total population (including Japanese) made a livelihood in agriculture, while only 7.0 per cent were associated with commercial activities, 3.9 per cent in the professions, 3.1 per cent with industry, and the remaining 12.4 per cent with other minor occupations. It should be noted that the per capita value of production of workers in agriculture in 1938 was much lower, eighty-three yen, than the average, 133 yen per capita, for all workers. Thus, agriculture did not have a highly preferred status, though it was the most important economic activity.

* At that time, the rough comparison with American values was three yen to one dollar. Data for the year 1938 is purposely used to illustrate this discussion for a number of reasons. After that year the Japanese moved into a very uneconomic war situation; some of the later economic data was falsified or suppressed: it is the nearest comparative situation to what might exist if Korea were once more at peace. Account must be taken, of course, in any projections, of the great growth of population (and its continuing growth at the rate of two per cent a year), the reorientation of the economy, and the devastation of the Korean war.

In their desire for increased agricultural output the Japanese made considerable effort to increase the amount of agricultural land.[25] However, the physical limitations of terrain, soil, and climate largely negated their attempts. In 1938 it was reported that the arable land was 4,957,730.7 *chungbo*.*

This was a small increase over the acreage of 1925 (4,571,546 *chungbo*), the first year for which fairly reliable data are available. (If, for comparison, one takes the inadequate, and probably inaccurate, data on cultivated land for 1910, 2,464,904 *chungbo*, it would show almost a doubling of the crop land from 1910 to 1938.) Of the 1938 acreage, 2,764,832.5 *chungbo* were in paddy fields, 1,750,843.6 *chungbo* in dry fields, and 442,044 *chungbo* in "fire-fields" (land cleared by fire on mountain slopes, often by squatters). Some twenty to twenty-one per cent of the total land area of Korea was cultivated in 1938.

It was, therefore, in intensifying the use of the existing fields that the greatest possibilities for increased agricultural production lay. One way was to reap two harvests from a field each season. The frequency of land utilization for 1938 was 135; in other words 6,109,991 *chungbo* were used during the year, though the total land cultivated was 4,526,758 *chungbo*. To accomplish more intense use of the land the Japanese sponsored irrigation and drainage projects. They were active, too, in introducing better varieties of seed and improved methods for controlling plant diseases and insect pests. They pressed improved farm practices—especially the use of commercial fertilizers.

By far their greatest emphasis was on rice production, for rice not only furnished the basic food for the Koreans, but—more important from the Japanese standpoint—provided an important food supply for the growing industrial and commercial cities of Japan. The agrarian policy, though couched

* The *chungbo* equals 2.45 acres. For the sake of comparison it may be noted that the average farm in Korea is about one *chungbo*.

in general terms of agricultural improvement for Korea, was Japanese centered.

The Japanese worried little about the repercussions which would be felt in the peninsula they controlled. Indeed, in normal times much of the rice sent to Japan was obtained by lowering the consumption of rice by Koreans and forcing them to substitute for their food millet imported from Manchuria. Thus, the increased rice production which took place in Korea did not benefit the people of the peninsula. For example, in 1938 the Koreans produced 24,138,874 *suk** of rice, but exported 9,521,000 *suk*; in other years as much as one-half of the production was exported.

These changes in the agricultural economy had other serious effects, perhaps the most important of which was the increase of farm tenancy. The holding of farm land by landlords had been a common practice in Korea before 1910. However, at that time the system was operated rather benevolently. By the force of public opinion tenant farmers were given virtual rights to control the land they rented and to renew their leases every year. Furthermore, landlords had the responsibility of helping their tenants in poor crop years. However, with the "commercialization" of agriculture under the Japanese much of this benevolence went by the board. Moreover, many small land-holders lost their fields because they could not pay for the land-reclamation and irrigation improvements which were virtually forced upon them. Thus, by 1938 only 18.1 per cent of the 3,052,392 farm families owned their own land; 23.9 per cent owned some of the land they cultivated and rented the rest; 51.8 per cent were tenant farmers; 3.8 per cent were farm laborers; and 2.4 per cent were squatters on fire-fields. In addition, farms became smaller in size; in 1938, only seventeen per cent of the farms were more than 2.5 chungbo (6.1 acres) in size, and 38.4 per cent were less than 0.5 chungbo (1.2 acres).

* One *suk* is approximately five bushels.

Speaking in general, the Japanese agricultural improvements were not universally effective, this being in part due to vagaries in government policy and inefficiencies in administration. The Korean farmer was not very eager to try out the new programs unless he could be clearly convinced of their value; and he was a hard person to convince. He was not easily won over, for example, by such a slogan as: "Cotton in the south, wool in the north," which the Japanese fostered to increase cotton production in southern Korea and sheep-raising in the north.

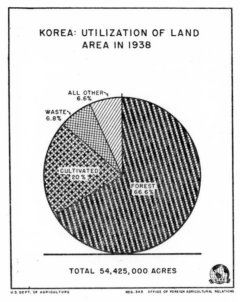

KOREA: UTILIZATION OF LAND AREA IN 1938

ALL OTHER 6.6%
WASTE 6.8%
CULTIVATED 20%
FOREST 66.6%

TOTAL 54,425,000 ACRES

U.S. DEPT. OF AGRICULTURE          NEG. 345   OFFICE OF FOREIGN AGRICULTURAL RELATIONS

FIG. 14.—Land utilization of Korea in 1938.

The most important physical resource in Korea is the land used for agricultural production. Many of the physical conditions—climate, soils, and terrain—which affect the productivity of the land and the general character of agricultural production have already been described. There are, however, considerable differences in agricultural activities, locally and regionally, which merit attention. For example, of the cultivated area about one-third is normally double-cropped, but such double-cropping can only be carried on in the favorable climatic areas of southern Korea. The crop distributions vary greatly from place to place and these distributions are significant. Also, farm practices carried on by the lowland and the upland farmers contrast radically, as do the practices of sedentary farmers, those

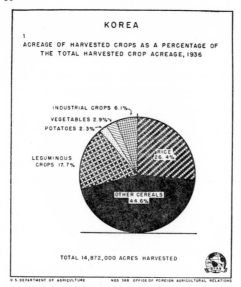

KOREA

ACREAGE OF HARVESTED CROPS AS A PERCENTAGE OF
THE TOTAL HARVESTED CROP ACREAGE, 1936

INDUSTRIAL CROPS 6.1%
VEGETABLES 2.9%
POTATOES 2.3%

LEGUMINOUS
CROPS 17.7%

RICE
26.4%

OTHER CEREALS
44.6%

TOTAL 14,872,000 ACRES HARVESTED

U. S. DEPARTMENT OF AGRICULTURE      NEG 368 OFFICE OF FOREIGN AGRICULTURAL RELATIONS

FIG. 15.—Types of crops grown in Korea.

who till the same field year after year, and the so-called "fire-field" folk, those who move from field to field. All these types of farming grade into each other, but it will be of value to characterize the three major types.

Normally, the upland sedentary farmers do not live in villages as do the dwellers in the plains.[26] Their fields— though generally larger —are poor, the soil very rocky and infertile, and yields are low. Rarely do the farmers attempt anything resembling contour plowing or terracing, though many of the fields are on steep slopes. On the whole, these upland farmers grow the hardier cereals— millet, barley, oats, buckwheat. Where soil conditions are better they may plant grain sorghum, corn, Irish potatoes (in the north), sweet potatoes (in the extreme south), soya beans, tobacco, and oil-seed plants.

Distinct from these sedentary upland farmers are the fire-field folk. These farmers are essentially squatters who have pre-empted the forested lands which are technically owned by the state. Partly because of the isolation afforded by the rugged terrain and lack of transportation facilities, the state has often been powerless to prevent the activities of these land-hungry people and has had to condone their practices. The earliest documented references show that fire-field agriculture occurred over one thousand years ago, during the Silla period

(57 B.C.–918 A.D.).  In the succeeding period a provision was made that pioneers who cleared the land would not be taxed until they had cultivated their land for five years.  It is perhaps as an outgrowth of this pioneering activity that the fire-field economy developed as a common practice in the isolated mountains of Korea.

The soil of many of the mountain areas is so poor that it cannot be tilled continuously.  The fire-field practice improves the soil fertility to a limited extent through the ash deposits from the fired vegetation.  Actually, all the vegetation is not burned; sometimes tall trees are "girdled," remaining as stark symbols of the destruction.  Ordinarily the fire-field farmer will use the land only two or more years before abandoning it and moving on to a new plot.  It is common, however, for him or a successor to return in ten or twenty years; thus, eventually, the fire-field may pass into a permanently cultivated field, though at best the field will never be very fertile.

During the period of Japanese control the acreage of fire-fields increased, according to official figures, though the increase may reflect somewhat the more accurate statistics that were gathered.  However, with the increase of population some actual increase cannot be denied.  The practice was perhaps even aided by the Japanese authorities, who were interested in raising production.  In 1938 almost one-tenth of the total cultivated land area of Korea was reported to be in fire-fields, 442,045 *chungbo*. On this land 277,648 families, or a population of 1,491,147 persons, were reported.  (The exactitude of these figures makes them somewhat questionable.)

These two types of agricultural activities—the upland sedentary farming and the fire-field farming—grade into each other.  On the whole, both are quite distinct from the procedures of the lowland farmers who occupy the largest cultivated area of the peninsula and whose method of farming is more truly representative of Korean agriculture.  The hand labor of the farmer and his family expended upon small intensively-worked plots located at various distances from the farm village is so great that Americans classify Korean farming as equivalent to vegetable or truck farming in the United States. Sowing rice in seedbeds in the spring, repairing the dikes, preparing the paddy fields, transplanting the rice shoots, weeding and re-weeding through the hot summer growing season, draining the paddy fields, harvesting the ripened rice by hand sickles in the fall, transporting the rice on the backs of farmers to the thresh-ing floors, flailing and winnowing the grain to separate the chaff and straw, hulling, cleaning, and polishing the rice grains —all these actions are accomplished through great expenditures of human labor with considerable skill acquired only through years of diligent practice. Naturally, some modern modifica-tions were introduced by the Japanese, especially in their large-scale commercial rice-production enterprises. More scientific seed selection and planting were fostered; strings laid across the fields guided those who transplanted the rice shoots along straight, well-spaced rows; chemical fertilizers were applied with care to the fields; small pumps or water wheels lifted the water from irrigation ditches or ponds; threshing was made more efficient by the use of simple treadle and blowing machines; carts or trucks took the grain to the market or the modern rice mill.

The lowland farmers are not exclusively rice growers. Around their farmsteads are small vegetable plots; over the thatched roofs grow gourds. In areas where the winters are not too cold, crops of barley are grown on the drained paddy fields. Usually on the land which cannot be made into paddy fields, but which can be cultivated, dry crops—cotton, tobacco, varied cereals, soya beans, and so on—are grown in the summer months; these dry fields, also, are double-cropped in the winter wherever possible. The lowland sedentary farmers are not on such a self-sufficient economic basis as the other farmers. In part, as a

26    The Korean people are predominantly farmers,

... living in small villages and cultivating flat alluvial plains and hill slopes.

They plow the hillsides for dry crops...

...and painstakingly flood the paddy fields.

29

Transplanting the rice shoots in straight rows...

...makes it easier to cut the grain and also gives a higher yield.

30

Rice may be thrashed by hand...

The results of a big harvest bring joy to everyone. 33

In the fall the family may winnow chaff on a windy day. 34

Farm women may grind grain at a community mill...

35

36    ...or work together to make *kimchi*, the Korean pickle.

37

Fishing villages dot the coast line, for...

...fish, dried or fresh, add needed animal protein to the diet.

38

## 39

Potteries make jars for *kimchi*, using primitive methods,

...though rice and grain may be milled with modern machines.

40

41

Fresh vegetables are sold on busy market days...

...along with hand-woven silk from a mountain village.

42

43

Stalls, more permanent, will sell cooking utensils...

...and rubber shoes.

44

Modern factories, like the chemical works at Hungnam, have been hit from the air during the Korean war...

46     ...and from the ground give only the impression of twisted junk.

Many of the bridges
have been damaged,

47

...making people revert to their old ferries.

48

49      Modern railroad facilities have also been smashed.

The farmhouse with its full harvest of grain, however, has been little damaged by the Korean war and is the hope for the future.

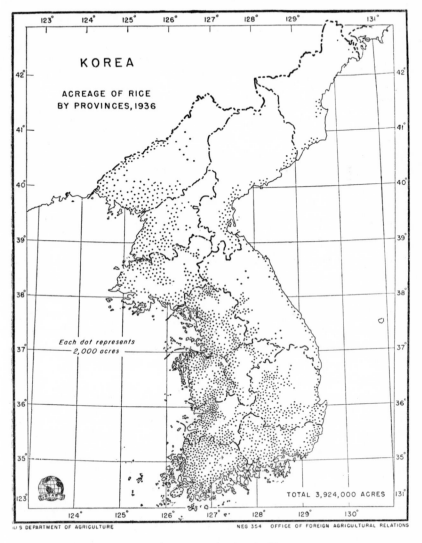

FIG. 16.—Rice production in Korea.

consequence of the commercialization of their agriculture, many of the lowland farmers were tenants rather than landowners, especially during the latter part of the period of Japanese control. In the postwar period in both North and South Korea land reform programs of varying types and with varying success have been put into operation, so that more of the lowland farmers now own the land they till.[27]

Considerable regional differences in farm practices and types of crops are found in Korea.[28]  In the northern interior and in the mountain lands of central and southern Korea fire-field and sedentary upland farming predominate; most of the crop land is devoted to hardy cereals; standards of living are low in this pioneer land.  In the coastal areas of northern Korea paddy fields are extensive, but dry-field crops occupy most of the agricultural land cultivated by sedentary farmers. In southern Korea rice is the basic crop of the farmers, densely crowded on the good agricultural land.  In the southern coastal areas where the growing season is long rice may be double-cropped with barley.  In the interior valleys and hill lands of the south, paddy fields are terraced far up the slopes, and dry field crops—cereals, cotton, and vegetables—are widespread; these fields may also be double-cropped to provide a food crop for the farmers who use their main crop for sale to pay their taxes or their rents.

It is on this resource base of regional diversity that future Korean agriculture development must take place.  It should be stressed that the really important method of increasing agricultural production is in making the lands already in use more productive by the increased use of commercial fertilizer.  During the war years when fertilizers were not available production dropped immediately.  It continued to do so until 1948, when the United States shipped in over 450,000 tons of fertilizer for South Korea.  One of the many great benefits to be derived from a unification of Korea is that commercial fertilizer

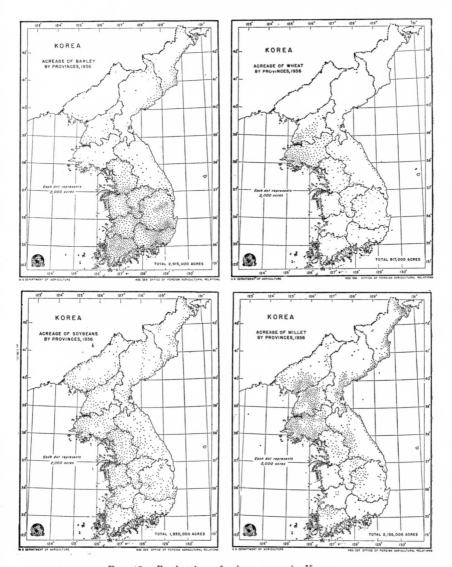

Fig. 17.—Production of minor crops in Korea.

that could be produced in northeastern Korea might again be distributed in the south. In recent decades fertilizer has been used almost exclusively in the rice fields; a considerable increase in production might result if more of it were used on the barley and wheat fields, which are not normally fertilized by Korean farmers.

There are other possibilities, such as those which were given an impetus under the Japanese: better seed selection, improved farm practices, and more modern irrigation. In addition, greater emphasis might well be given to double-cropping and to increasing the variety of crops; beans, peas, and other legumes could be planted more extensively. Some of these changes have already been put into practice on an experimental basis and have shown remarkable results.

The possibility of expanding the amount of the agricultural land should not be thought of very optimistically. Some swamp and tidal flats might be reclaimed and more upland farming is possible; however, such developments require considerable capital expenditure. The recent pioneering of the fire-field folk has been, in reality, a rather inefficient and wasteful development. Uncontrolled fire-field agriculture, without adequate safeguards against forest fires and erosion, is essentially un-economic from the standpoint of the total Korean economy.

The Korean farmers have an insufficient animal economy. Livestock, in 1938, accounted for only six per cent of the gross value of agricultural production. In that year there were 1,-717,063 head of work cattle, 1,506,628 pigs, 27,405 sheep, 44,-431 goats, 49,076 horses, and 7,165,166 chickens. The postwar years were marked by a serious decline in the number of cattle and other animals, and the recent hostilities in Korea have drastically reduced the number of farm animals. Korean animal husbandry has never been well coordinated with its agriculture. Too much of the farm work is done by hand labor, and the farmers do not get an efficient return from the farm animals they do have.  Further, animal feed production and grazing lands have not been well developed.  The Japanese plan for sheep production in Korea was notably unsuccessful.  Dairying is not well developed except near some of the largest cities; in 1938 there were only 2,306 dairy cattle in Korea.  It is obvious that any main development in animal husbandry in Korea would have to be preceded by some fairly basic changes in economic thinking; but with a well-directed and coordinated program this might be accomplished.

The basic agricultural activity, though seriously affected by the recent fighting in Korea, has not been subject to the same staggering dislocations as have other parts of the economy. Its continued health and development should have first priority in any post-hostilities programs.  By building gradually and by introducing new methods and new crops through agricultural extension services, by establishing and regulating equitable controls over farm tenancy, and by holding disastrous inflation in check, Korean agriculture can be transformed and serve as a basis for a solid economy.

Fishing has long been an important subsidiary occupation for individual farm families.  By trapping in the mountain streams and by netting and seining irrigation ditches, rivers, and ponds they have gathered unmeasured amounts of fish, which in the aggregate are significant.

In the early days sea fishing was generally limited to areas close to shore.  Under Japanese auspices, with the introduction of power launches, better nets, refrigeration and drying facilities fishing grew into a commercialized, big-scale operation, concentrated in a few major fishing centers on the east coast where the mixing of the cool and warm currents in the Sea of Japan afforded excellent fishing grounds.  Fishing on the south and west coasts was handicapped by the high tides and shallow seas.

In 1938 334,000 persons, or 1.5 per cent of the population,

were dependent on fishing as a primary occupation. They operated 55,883 fishing boats, supplemented by 3,731 carrying vessels; most of these were small sailing boats, averaging three tons displacement. A few thousand power boats averaged fifteen tons displacement. In prewar years the fishing tonnage fluctuated radically; for example, in 1937 the total catch was 2,115,785 tons; the catch in 1938 totalled 1,759,100 tons, including 975,500 tons of sardines, 620,492 tons of other marine animals; and in 1939 it was 2,046,243 tons. In 1940 the sardine schools began to move away from the east Korean waters and there was a sudden drop in the normal one million ton sardine catch. After 1940 the sardine catch was negligible. The sardines were used largely for fish oil and glycerine rather than for food, so that this loss was mainly a blow to the highly commercialized fisheries.

During the war, fishing operations were naturally curtailed. The Japanese took most of the larger fishing boats to their home waters, and those that were left suffered from lack of upkeep; hence, at the end of the war the Korean fishing industry was in a sad state. Great efforts were made with American aid to revive the fishing industry in South Korean waters. These programs met with some success, though the outbreak of fighting in 1950 disrupted the efforts.

Korea's fishing industry is most important for food production; in addition it supplies an important commodity for foreign trade with Japan and Hong Kong. The fishing resources are relatively rich; before World War II Korea was actually the sixth most important fishing country in the world. It is possible for Korea to reestablish this important industry in the future and thus provide fish and other marine products in large amounts. These are extremely important sources of proteins necessary to supplement the rice-dominated diet of the Korean people.

The forest area in Korea covers about three-fourths of the

land.  As has been noted in the discussion of natural vegetation, the forests vary in their composition, depending on climatic and edaphic conditions.  In the old days of the Korean kingdoms most of the forest land was generally considered to be state owned.  A few forests around temples were given protection. Some forests were leased or deeded over to court officials and others for their use.  The state forest lands surrounding villages were often thought of as communally owned by the villagers for gathering firewood and brush.  Under Japanese control more stringent regulations were put into effect.  Some state land was deeded to Japanese companies for lumbering purposes. In 1942, of the 16,274,380 *chungbo** of forest land, 5,327,636 *chungbo* were state owned, 1,066,031 *chungbo* were publicly owned by provinces and other governmental units, 189,967 *chungbo* were owned by temples, and 9,690,746 *chungbo* were under private ownership.  Most of the state-owned land was in northern Korea.

The forest land varies in its character.  It has been estimated that not more than one-third of the forests can be considered merchantable timber.  Though some seventy per cent of the forest land is in standing trees, they are generally of poor quality.  In the past, serious devastations of pine bugs, called in Korean *songjong* (Gastropacha Pini. L.) affected the forests. The latest epidemic occurred toward the end of the last century and this natural havoc was augmented by the uncontrolled cutting of wood-hungry farmers.  In addition, forest fires have taken a severe toll.  It has been estimated that two-thirds of the forest land was entirely denuded.  By exercising stern control and by using modern reforestation practices, the Japanese did much to restore the forest land.  Cutting continued at a rapid rate, however, especially as the demand for timber for war industries increased.  Toward the end of World War II shipbuilding programs and industrial demands caused a sharp

* One *chungbo* equals 2.45 acres.

rise in cutting. It is estimated that in 1944 the Japanese were over-cutting by more than 130 per cent of the normal allowable production.

After the expulsion of the Japanese, with the relaxation of controls in the early period of military government, much severe and foolish cutting took place. This was especially the case in the reforested areas of southern Korea. Consequently, Korea's present forest lands are in very poor shape. A continual problem is that in their search for fuel the Korean farmers have stripped the forest lands near the villages. Women and children rake the ground for needles, leaves, and brush and break off twigs and branches as high as they can reach. As a consequence, in densely settled areas bare hillsides or slopes with only scrub growth are almost universally evident.

The importance of the part-time forestry carried on by the Korean farmers is difficult to measure.* In addition to cut wood, or lumber, firewood and brush are major items, as are leaves for green manure for compost piles (later to be used on the fields). Because of the lack of coal in South Korea there were great increases in both the demand and the prices for firewood and brush in the postwar period.

Forestry as a full-time occupation has not been carried on by many Koreans. However, in the mountain lands of northern and central Korea full-scale forestry has been an important type of land use. In recent decades the excellent stands of conifer forest were exploited by the Japanese. The Yalu, Tumen, and Taedong Rivers and their tributaries were used for rafting logs, and large-scale cutting operations developed. The government controlled this commercial forestry very rigidly, and the profits were an important source of revenue. The exploitation of the forests as a direct resource is therefore a significant feature of Korean economy.

* Appendix E contains tables of data on the character of forest land in Korea and the amount of forest production.

Associated with the forest economy are the hunting of wild animals and the gathering of special products. Among the products gathered from the forests is wild ginseng, a medicinal herb highly valued by the Chinese and Koreans. The number of people involved in this occupation, however, is very small.

The preservation of the forest resources and their proper management in the future is most important. North Korea is decidedly a surplus producing area, and South Korea a deficit area. If trade could be established, or if the peninsula were unified, it is obvious that the forestry production of the north could be developed on a solid basis for the total Korean economy. It is especially necessary that the ravages of erosion from the stripped hill lands be stopped. Well-regulated forests could provide a steady supply of firewood and lumber for the Korean economy.

# Chapter 8 | The Modern Industrial Economy of Korea

THE transformation of the Korean economy which has taken place in recent decades has been caused largely by the exploitation of the mineral and power resources of the peninsula.[29] This transition in parts of Korea from an "Oriental economy," dominated by rice production, to a modern industrial economy dependent upon hydroelectric and mineral resources has resulted in numerous anomalies, such as heavy cables of hydroelectric power lines swinging high over minute paddy fields.

In the early Korean economy little was done to develop mineral resources. Stone and clay products, of course, were used in building and in making tile and household wares, and brass was manufactured from native copper and zinc. Alluvial gold deposits were exploited. But at that time the Korean economy could not be termed in any sense one which was dependent upon minerals.

Under the impact of Western economy and technical skill, Korean mineral resources were exploited at a higher rate. Some of the earliest Western contacts with Korea were made for the purpose of mineral exploration. In the last part of the last century a number of concessions were granted to Western capitalists for the development of mineral properties, particularly gold mines. Some of the lode deposits which were developed had other minerals in association with gold. Modern dredges supplanted to some extent the simple alluvial washing devices for placer gold that the Koreans had utilized for centuries.

The most radical changes in the exploitation of the mineral resources of Korea took place, however, under the Japanese. Korea became an important source of industrial raw materials and a primary processing center for such materials. This effort was accentuated in the 1930's as Japan prepared its war machine for Asian conquest. The resources of Korea, located close to Japan and in an area over which firm control could be exerted, were well suited for exploitation. Various low-grade mineral deposits were utilized with the help of Japanese government subsidies. Especially significant was the production of anthracite and lignite coal, iron ore, copper, graphite, tungsten, magnesite, fluorspar, mica, gold, and silver. The peak of this production was reached in 1944.*

Concurrently, industrial facilities were developed for supplying consumer wants, for processing raw materials, and for manufacturing component parts for final assembly in Japan. Especially significant was the development of chemical industries, textile mills, and food processing plants. Since these developments required power, the Japanese began the construction of large-scale hydroelectric plants, particularly utilizing the Yalu River and its tributaries in northern Korea. Finally, the economy was knit together by a railroad and road system, and ports were built for ocean shipping.[30]

The development of the mineral and power resources of Korea has not been evenly spread for the very obvious reason that the geologic occurrence of the minerals and power resources is very scattered. Though often a number of minerals may

---

* Appendix F has a table of production of the major minerals in Korea in 1938 and 1944 and a discussion of each of the major mineral resources and the hydroelectric power sources.

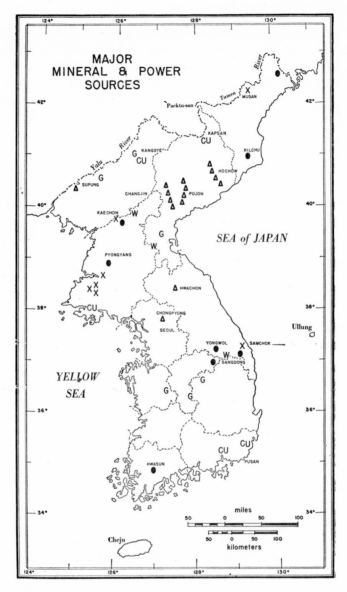

Fig. 18.—The major mineral and power sources in Korea.
△=hydroelectric power plants.  X=iron ore.  ●=coal.  G=gold.
CU=copper.  W=wolfram (tungsten).

occur in one complex ore body, there is no single well-integrated mineral area in Korea. For example, though iron ore is found in large deposits in northern Korea, good-grade coking coal has to be imported from Japan or China. This pattern of mineral occurrences necessitated the prior development of extensive transportation facilities and it also served to knit the economy of Korea closely to that of Japan and to the rest of the Far East.

The increase in agricultural production and the exploitation of the mineral and power resources of Korea opened the way in recent decades to the introduction of modern industrial enterprises. It is noteworthy that this industrialization did not grow as a natural development of the economy of Korea but was superimposed largely by the Japanese. They began by overhauling the system of processing the agricultural products of Korea to consolidate control and to cut down transportation costs. They constructed major industrial centers in the rice collection and exporting centers in south and west Korea to mechanize the rice hulling and polishing and to expedite the processing of other agricultural commodities.

Despite these developments, however, most of the processing of Korean agricultural products, especially those used locally for food, continued on the simple home or village basis of the past as part of the relatively self-sufficient village economy. Simple grinding wheels or pounders, run by animal power or occasionally by water, processed most of the food needed by the Koreans. Hand spinning wheels and looms continued to be used for making cloth. The farmers used their slack time for making farm utensils and straw ropes and bags. However, these simple cottage industries had to meet the increasingly severe competition of modern industrialization.

The impact of the growing industrialism was evident in the part of the economy concerned with timber and fishing products. Modern sawmills were built near the mouths of the major rivers of northern Korea to process the logs that were floated down in rafts from the virgin forests of the interior. Prior to the coming of the Japanese much of the fish caught along the shores of Korea was dried for use in Korea; this required a relatively small amount of processing since it could be done on a simple basis of salting and sun-drying. However, under the Japanese, the fishing grounds of the east coast were widely exploited in order to increase the production of glycerine, fish oils, and dried fish cake. The commercial fishing was particularly extensive when the sardine catches were high, but, as has been noted, the sardine catch practically vanished in 1940. Production decreased further in the postwar period because of a shortage of tin plate for canning the fish products and the deterioration of the industry.

The production of consumer goods was also revolutionized under the Japanese, and Korean capital, though small in comparison with Japanese capital, contributed significantly to this development, particularly in the textile industry. Some cotton was produced in Korea, but much had to be imported to meet the demands of the increasing population. In the later period of their control the Japanese erected rayon and other textile plants in the outskirts of Seoul and Pyongyang and at Inchon and Kwangju. But all of these industries suffered reverses from shortages of raw materials in the days after World War II, and the plants themselves both in North and South Korea have been severely damaged during the Korean war.

The rubber shoe industry can be used to illustrate some of the changes affecting the relatively simple and self-contained handicraft industries of Korea by the introduction of a new product. Normally the Koreans used straw or leather shoes, most of which were produced as a part-time occupation by the Korean farmers in the winter. When factories were built to manufacture the molded rubber shoes, which of course had numerous advantages, particularly in the rainy season, the rural handicraft economy was drastically upset. Thus, too, imported kerosene gradually supplanted vegetable oils in the simple lamps of Korean rural homes, and the five gallon tins in which the kerosene was imported supplanted the earthenware jars used for carrying water. The changes caused by industrialization were manifest in other ways: modern-style hats and caps replaced the quaint, lacquered, horsehair hats, and modern paper drove off the market the paper which for many centuries was a distinctive product of Korea. A natural—and revolutionary —effect of the innovations was that Korean agricultural workers needed payments in money so they could purchase the products of machines.

Korea was a decided asset to Japan in the years just prior to and during World War II.* It produced iron ore and other minerals that the Japanese needed for its ships and guns. With its advanced hydroelectric facilities, it helped develop the Japanese production of chemicals. The peninsula supplied rice in abundance, though as Korea itself became industrialized, the high export priority was modified. And not of least importance to the Japanese was the forced contribution Korea made in manpower; thousands of Korean laborers helped run Japan's mines, industrial plants, and shipyards. American forces who captured Japanese islands in the far-flung stretches of the Pacific almost invariably rounded up hosts of Korean laborers whose job had been to build fortifications and construct airfields. They had been unwilling allies at best.

Fortunately for the Koreans, their land was little touched by the ravages of World War II. Towards its end, when the Allies were in a position to strike Korea, the sinking of Japanese merchant ships and the mining of ports were so successful in interdicting trade from Korea to Japan that large-scale bombing of the peninsula was considered unnecessary. But the effects

* Appendix G has tables on the nature and growth of industrial establishments in Korea in 1938 and 1944 and a discussion of major industrial centers of Korea.

of the war were evident none the less. Much of the Korean industrial plant was run down and in poor repair. With the departure of the Japanese there was naturally a serious shortage of technicians. Further, by payment of excessive bonuses, the Japanese had set off an inflationary cycle. But the unified and dynamic industrial economy which the Japanese had created in Korea received its most shattering blow by the imposition of the thirty-eighth parallel as a gradually hardening barrier across the center of the peninsula. Subsequently, the fighting in Korea since June 25, 1950 devastated the industrial economy. The serious inflationary situation has made it very difficult to re-institute the industries after the cessation of hostilities.[31]

Korean economy has been greatly benefitted by an improved —a Westernized—transportation system. Most of the changes that have taken place in the peninsula in the last seventy-five years, changes that have destroyed forever the "hermit" and self-sufficient character of the country, derive, if indirectly, from the fact that railroads, highways, ports, and airfields enabled Korea's resources—particularly its mineral deposits— to be tapped, its agriculture to be commercialized, and its industrial potential to be developed. In the wake of these came hundreds of other developments so extensive in character that the whole fabric of life was revolutionized.

In the pre-modern days internal transportation was limited, on the whole, to mere trails which connected village with village and province with province. There was only one major road in the whole peninsula—the Imperial highway—which ran northeast from Seoul through Pyongyang to Uiju on the Yalu River. This was the road taken by the envoys who exchanged visits with the court of the emperor in China. Theoretically, additional roads connected each of the provincial capitals with Seoul, the seat of Korea's government. Other than that, the system included only short highways fanning out from the provincial capitals, and numerous winding and muddy trails, over which porters or tough Korean ponies carried the packs of itinerant merchants and government officials.

Korean farmers often used oxen to drag heavy loads on sleds or in carts, but most of the carrying was done on the backs of man with the aid of a device called the *chige*. This is a simple frame roughly in the form of an A, with two sticks fastened at right angles to the frame. The carrier puts his arms through braided-straw straps attached to the frame and rests the load on his back and shoulders. Another means of transportation in the early days was the sedan chair. These were used by court officials and at weddings, when the bride was carried to her new home.

In pre-modern days, the rivers of Korea were used for rafting lumber, the lower stretches of some of the major rivers being utilized for the movement of bulky commodities such as firewood, charcoal, and clay pots. The boats had shallow drafts and were equipped with sails. For the upstream movement the boats were towed by human beings, who dragged the boat against the current and through rapids. There was little seagoing traffic, though the islands offshore were visited by junks and fishing boats. However, coastwise traffic over long distances was very limited.

When the Japanese first came into Korea in 1904, the only railroad was the one built shortly before, under American direction, to connect Seoul with its seaport, Inchon (or as the foreigners then called it, Chemulpo). During the Sino-Japanese war, the Japanese had constructed a few ports and roads, but it was not until the Russo-Japanese war of 1904–05, and shortly thereafter, that the greatest railroad expansion took place. From the first, Japanese railroad construction was pushed with one eye on military advantage.

The main rail line built by the Japanese ran from Pusan northwest past Taegu, over a pass on the Sobaek range, to a new town, Taejon. From there it went north to Seoul. From

Seoul the main line followed the old "Imperial road" to the northwest and passed through Kaesong and Sariwon, to Pyongyang. From Pyongyang it continued north, crossing the Yalu River at Sinuiju where it connected with the Manchurian system. This railroad, which was of standard gauge, as are almost all the railroads of Korea, was double-tracked in later years for its entire length of 590.2 miles.

Branching off from this main line an important track was laid northeast from Seoul to Wonsan, utilizing a well-defined passageway. From there it was gradually extended along the east coast to Chongjin and then north to the northernmost bend of the Tumen River. There it connected with the Manchurian railroad system. (Part of this line in Korea was operated by the South Manchurian Railway.) This line was continued down the Tumen in a southeasterly direction to the port of Unggi and to the port of Najin a short distance away. Only part of this 674.8 mile railroad was double-tracked. Though a line was projected to go northeast along the coast connecting Chongjin directly with Najin and Unggi, it has not been built.

In southern Korea the Japanese built a railroad southwest from Taejon, on the main line, through Iri to the port of Mokpo, in the extreme southwest. From Iri a short line extended west to the port of Kunsan, and another line was later built directly south from Iri past Chonju and Sunchon to a new port, Yosu. From Sunchon a line went westward and then northward to Kwangju and from there to the Taejon-Mokpo line. A short branch line ran north of Kwangju. As a consequence, the important export rice-producing areas of southwest Korea were opened up.

Thus, the main northwest and southeast rail line, with its offshoots northeast and southwest, approximated, in design, a roughly offset X. From this basic pattern lines were later built as feeders or connections. In northwestern Korea an important line was built into the northern interior, going north from Pyongyang through Anju to Kanggye. Later this was extended to the Yalu River at Mampojin. Just before World War II, a line which had been gradually extended eastward into the interior from a point on the Pyongyang-Anju line was connected to a point on the east coast line north of Wonsan, thus giving an important connection across the peninsula in northern Korea.

A line was built from a point just south of Wonsan south along the Sea of Japan coast. It was expected that this line would be continued all the way along the coast, but it was only partially completed to a point just north of the thirty-eighth parallel. Further south, in the Naktong River basin, a line was built along the southern base of the Sobaek Range, extending from the main line eastward to Andong. (Later this line was taken up and the track used elsewhere.) Another similar line went east from Taegu to Kyongju and on to Pohang, a port on the east coast. Inland, south from this line, another line extended from Kyongju through Ulsan to Pusan. North from the Taegu-Pohang line a railroad was built just before the war to Andong and on, over rather difficult terrain, northwestward to Seoul.

On the whole, by 1944, at which time there were 5,012.5 km. (approximately 3,800 miles) of railroads, Korea had an adequate well-integrated railroad system. The total passenger kilometerage was 8,752,176,838, and the total ton kilometerage was 9,932,-661,868 tons. The construction of the rail lines had been costly; it has been estimated that the Japanese investments in Korean railroads were much greater than their total investments in business corporations. However, these investments must have been justified as a military measure, for Korea was an important bridge from Japan to Manchuria and north China. A Japanese mission could leave the island port of Shimonoseki by ferry and arrive at the Korean port of Pusan in seven hours; or from other ports in Japan it could go directly and quickly to Najin

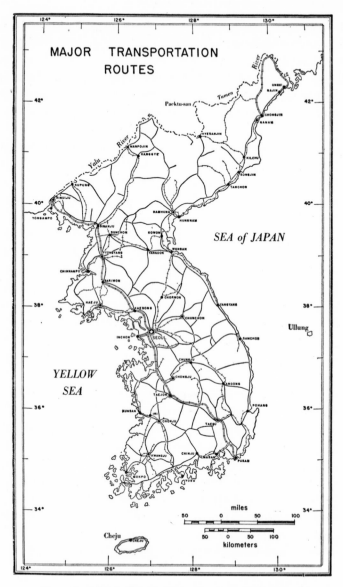

FIG. 19.—The major transportation routes of Korea.

or Chongjin; from these cities it could move rapidly over a through route northward to the fringes of the Japanese continental empire.

With the collapse of Japan and the imposition of the thirty-eighth parallel as a rigid boundary across the waist of the peninsula, the whole picture changed. South Korea was still connected with Japan by boat services; but northern Korea was isolated from the south as well as from Japan. Consequently, some lines in North Korea, like the newly constructed one east of Pyongyang to connect with the east coast line, assumed new importance, for they connected with northeastern Korea and the Vladivostok area of the Soviet Union.

Severed connections were serious enough, but on both sides of the parallel deterioration of equipment was even worse. Koreans had never been trained in large numbers for responsible technical positions on the railroads. Moreover, most of the railroads used bituminous coal, which had to be imported into Korea. The following figures illustrate the chaos of the rail system: though in 1947 South Korea had slightly more than half the total Korean rail mileage, the total passenger mileage in 1947 was less than one-third of that of 1944, and the freight mileage was only one-tenth of that for all Korea in 1944.

Great efforts were made to rehabilitate the major lines in both North and South Korea. Some new lines were reported under construction in North Korea, but this cannot be confirmed. In South Korea short lines were started into the coal regions of Yongwol, new locomotives, cars, and other equipment and supplies were imported from America by the U.S. Army or the ECA, and stockpiles of coal were built up by imports from Japan. However, the outbreak of hostilities in Korea in 1950 wrecked the hopes of rehabilitation and created tremendous damage. Major rail lines, bridges, marshalling yards, locomotives, and shop facilities were special targets for air attack.

During the early days of Japanese control, Korea's highway

system—if it could be called such—got little attention.  However, during and after the 1930's, the Japanese undertook the construction of dirt or gravel highways parallel to strategic rail lines and feeder highways to the major rail lines.  Regular bus and truck schedules were established.  In addition, highways— particularly in the northeastern provinces—were built for obviously military purposes.

Once more the Japanese supplied the technical skill and the Koreans the labor—largely forced labor, though in some areas the Koreans were allowed to pay their taxes by contributing their labor.  By 1944 great advances had been made; highway mileage totalled 19,000 miles, of which 7,800 miles—those of military or commercial importance—were maintained by the state, and 11,200 by lesser political units for local benefit.

Though fishing ports along the Korean coast were common, it was not until the Japanese came that large modern ports were developed.  Of these the largest and best equipped was Pusan, on the southeast tip of Korea.  Sheltered in part by an island and possessing a deep harbor, Pusan became the main passenger and freight funnel into Korea.  The port of Wonsan midway up the east coast had an early growth just before the Japanese occupation and continued to be of considerable importance.  In later years numerous other ports were developed along the east coast.  Ulsan, Pohang, Samchok, Hungnam, Songjin, Chongjin, Najin, and Unggi, all relatively small villages, were transformed into busy ports, particularly suited for the specific commodities produced or needed in their hinterlands. The southern coast of Korea with its numerous islands and bays also provided excellent harbors, and the Japanese soon expanded the facilities of Masan, Yosu, and Mokpo.

Unlike the east coast of Korea, the west coast suffers from very high tides, and the numerous rivers flowing down to the shallow Yellow Sea are handicapped by broad, tidal estuaries and extensive marshy flats.  The few major ports developed by the Japanese on this coast—particularly for the rice trade —were located near the mouths of rivers in areas where some protection could be obtained from severe winds and storms. At Inchon, the port for Seoul, the Japanese built a tidal basin to overcome the handicap of the high, thirty-eight foot tide. Their other major Yellow Sea ports were Kunsan in the southwest, Haeju in southern Hwanghae Province, Chinnampo, at the mouth of the Taedong, and Sinuiju (and a new port nearby) at the mouth of the Yalu.

The Japanese also undertook the construction of airfields, most of them, of course, for military purposes. However, one major commercial air route for passenger travel extended the length of Korea, parallel to the main railroad line, with an off-shoot to northeastern Korea. It linked the major cities, and made connections with Japan and Manchuria.

In the old days in Korea the news of an invasion or pirate raid was conveyed to the capital at Seoul by means of a chain of beacon fires lit on high hill crests. Not until the Japanese came were telegraph, telephone, public mail, and radio widely introduced. These were knit into an intricate and effective system. By 1944 the Japanese had opened ninety-three main post offices, and 1,010 local offices. In 1942 69,000 telephones organized in 921 exchanges were in use, mostly in the larger cities. Half the number were in Seoul. In 1944 there were 1,087 telegraph stations, mostly in post offices or in railroad stations, and a total linage of 6,000 miles. A major radio station was constructed at Seoul, and by 1944 there was a total of eleven radio stations in Korea, with 181,679 listening sets licensed to Koreans and 131,101 licensed to Japanese. Thus, Korea had a relatively good communication system, though the market place as a place for exchange of rumor and information was still the commonplace for most Koreans.

It is fairly obvious that the resources of Korea in human labor and skills, in agricultural production, in minerals and hydroelectric power, knit together by an adequate transportation and communication system, were tremendously exploited and developed by the Japanese. In the years following World War II, the strangulating effects of the thirty-eighth parallel as an economic barrier were most severe. The Communist aggression in Korea and the subsequent war devastated the Korean economy. It is difficult to make any predictions for the future. Certainly from the standpoint of economic potential, as indicated by economic development already accomplished, the future possibilities are great, but such developments can occur best if Korea is unified and able to carry on trade with the outside world. Even then the possibilities can be realized only if great efforts are put forward. Economic rehabilitation alone will likely require foreign aid in varied forms and large amounts. In recent decades many economic ties were made with Japan and much of Korea's economic development was consummated on the basis of providing some of the needs of Japan's war economy. Thus, new patterns will need to be established, though it is obvious that trade to the mutual benefit of Japan and a unified Korea should be reconstituted.[31]

Any future economy for Korea should be built on a sound, expanding, agricultural base. Associated with agricultural improvement should be the rehabilitation of the transportation and communication facilities and renewed development of cottage industries. As the basic economy becomes stabilized and as personnel are trained, consumer goods and heavy-scale industries could be expanded. Foreign trade, particularly in the Far Eastern sphere, would need to be developed, for Korea is deficient in certain raw materials. Her most significant products, particularly rice, could be produced in surplus. The total task of economic rehabilitation and development is no easy one, especially in the wake of the recent war.

A survey of Korea's economic potential may well be concluded by a rather simple illustration. In the days of their "hermit" existence, the Korean people illuminated their homes by candles or by simple oil lamps which used vegetable oils. With the opening of Korea to Western influence, foreign oil companies introduced more efficient kerosene lamps, which won popularity throughout the peninsula. Later, thermoelectric plants were built in the larger cities, and electric current was furnished for lighting the major urban areas. Just before World War II large hydroelectric power plants provided current not only for the cities but for many rural districts as well. After the war, these hydroelectric power plants, located mainly in North Korea, continued to supply power. However, with the development of tension between North and South Korea, this flow of power was cut off. More recently the warfare in Korea has seriously disrupted power production. Any attempt, now or in the future, to revert to candles or vegetable oil lamps would be a failure. For the future, then, Korea will need foreign supplies of kerosene and oil. More important, all of Korea will need the electric power which can be produced more efficiently in the north. This illustration of a simple economic need, light, shows the necessity of a Korea unified within itself and at peace with the outside world.

| Chapter 9 | # The Regions of North Korea |

THE geographic totality that is Korea is a combination of many diverse areas. In order to grasp the picture of the whole, one needs to consider the nature of the parts—the so-called "regions." What follows, therefore, consists of a study of the divisions, regions, and sections into which the peninsula may be classified. The procedure is in some respects a dangerous one, for it inevitably invites a certain amount of over-simplification of complex geographic phenomena and relationships. Nevertheless, over and above its utility as a method, it is supported by the precedent of history, for from early times Koreans themselves divided the peninsula into political provinces and districts according to patent geographic features such as mountain ranges, river basins, or even the physical accessibility of certain areas to cities. Further, certain provinces and districts were defined by political, social, or economic considerations, all of which to some degree were contingent upon geographic factors.

In modern days, geographers have divided Korea into geographic regions in a number of different ways. Three classifications of regions of Korea made by geographers which merit close consideration are those of Herman Lautensach, V. T. Zaichikov, and Pak No-sik.[32] Some writers have continued the traditional method based on provincial boundaries, sometimes grouping a number of provinces together, or considering each as a separate geographic region. The Japanese often made a distinction between the "interior" group of Korean provinces facing Japan, and the "exterior" group facing China. Another common method is to draw a distinction, based in part on climatic differences or land utilization, between northern and southern Korea. Thus, the six northern provinces including Kangwon in the north are sometimes differentiated from the seven southern provinces including Kyonggi. Still another method is to divide the provinces into three groups: south, central, and north. Numerous other regional schemes have been used, most of which are open to the criticism that they take into account only one aspect of the geography and not the geographic totality.

The classification of geographic regions used in this book has two principal features: it establishes three distinct categories of land area, progressively decreasing in size, and it stresses the details that make for geographic diversity. According to the first category the peninsula is separated into two large divisions—the North and the South—along a line partly determined by historical precedent since it follows provincial boundaries, but more significantly, by climatic differences between the north and south and the consequent contrasts in intensity of land utilization and population density. Although this geographic line—or more realistically, this zone—does not coincide with the now-famous thirty-eighth parallel or with the "truce line," it is close to them and therefore, perhaps, gains some additional sanction for use at this time.

The second category of land area includes three geographic regions north of the dividing line and seven to the south. The boundaries between the geographic regions embraced in this second category are drawn primarily on the basis of provincial or county borders. In part this is for convenience, but these borders on the whole mark climatic, terrain, and cultural

## Numerical Data on the Geographic Regions of Korea

| NUMBER ON MAP | GEOGRAPHIC REGION | AREA (square miles) | Population 1925 | | Population 1940 | |
|---|---|---|---|---|---|---|
| | | | TOTAL | DENSITY (per square mile) | TOTAL | DENSITY (per square mile) |
| 1. | Northern Interior | 15,789 | 781,068 | 49.4 | 1,049,744 | 66.4 |
| 2. | Northeastern Coast | 11,088 | 1,667,562 | 150.2 | 2,467,321 | 222.5 |
| 3. | Northwestern Korea | 16,754 | 3,707,646 | 221.2 | 4,707,412 | 280.9 |
| | North Korea | 43,631 | 6,156,276 | 141.06 | 8,223,477 | 188.47 |
| 4. | East Central Coast | 2,609 | 374,405 | 136.3 | 559,513 | 214.4 |
| 5. | Central and Southern Mountains | 13,776 | 2,485,319 | 180.9 | 2,770,951 | 200.8 |
| 6. | West Central Korea | 6,304 | 2,877,621 | 456.8 | 4,000,913 | 638.3 |
| 7. | Southwestern Korea | 7,430 | 3,404,283 | 460.5 | 4,175,838 | 563.3 |
| 8. | Southeastern Korea | 10,798 | 4,007,889 | 371.4 | 4,365,894 | 404.3 |
| 9. | Cheju Island | 718 | 205,194 | 285.8 | 213,947 | 297.6 |
| 10. | Ullung Island | 28 | 9,992 | 356.8 | 13,502 | 479.4 |
| | South Korea | 41,654 | 13,364,703 | 320.85 | 16,101,558 | 386.55 |
| | Total Korea | 85,285 | 19,520,969 | 237.23 | 24,325,035 | 285.22 |

Note: The figures are based on computed county data; hence, small discrepancies occur.

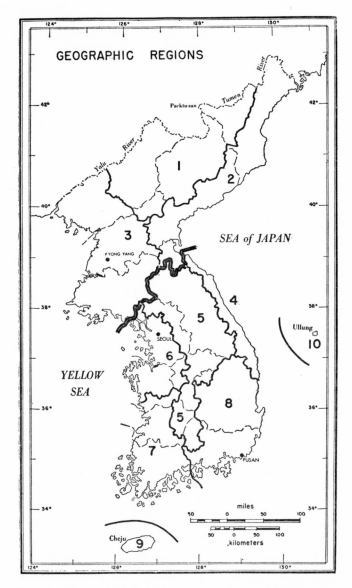

FIG. 20.—The geographic divisions and regions of Korea. See facing table for names of regions.

differences. The basic criteria for differentiating the geographic regions are mainly factors of physical geography—terrain and climate. Included also as a criterion in drawing the specific boundary lines is the important factor of differences in population density. The names chosen for the regions are purposely locational in character.

The third and last category of land area is concerned with the sections—the numerous parts into which the geographic regions may be divided. The criteria used for determining the sectional boundaries vary; the boundaries are drawn along traditional county lines; in some instances the realistic facts of physical geography or economic activity are considered while in others the existence of large cities with their environs are the determining factors.

The principal virtue of such a system of classification of land area into divisions, regions, and sections is that it enables one to give more precise and fruitful expression to the existing facts of geographic diversity. In short, it enables one to grasp more accurately the whole geographic complexity of Korea.

The principal geographic facts about the first primary division, North Korea, are that it lies adjacent to the continent of Asia and that its distinctive character is its mountainous base.[33] Though the Yellow Sea and the Sea of Japan influence the coastal areas of the division, northern Korea is essentially continental rather than maritime. Lofty Paektu-san, surrounding mountains, and lava-capped plateaus dominate the northern interior. The eastern escarpment of the mountain area is abrupt and the hills and offshoots of the interior mountains make the eastern coastal area rugged, with few valleys. In the west, the descent from the mountainous interior is less abrupt; consequently, hills and plains are more extensive along the coast. In their lower courses, the Yalu River and the Taedong River have created large flood plains, and in Hwanghae Province are rather extensive areas of low hills and broad valleys.

Extremely cold winters also are a factor one must consider in accounting for the low population density. Average winter temperatures in northern Korea measure well below freezing; for instance, Pyongyang, in the northwest, has an average January temperature of 17.6° F.; Wonsan, which is on the same latitude on the northeast coast, has an average January temperature of 25.2° F., and Chunggangjin, which is located at the bend of the Yalu River, deep in the northern interior, has an average January temperature of –6° F. One crucial consequence of this climatic fact is that northern Korea has a short growing season, which means that, with certain rare exceptions, northern Korean farmers are limited to one crop per year.

In its original state northern Korea was a densely forested land. However, human settlement slowly encroached upon these forested areas, and, more recently, commercial forestry has made further inroads. In the lower elevations much of the forest has been cut over, and growths of scrub oak and pine, and other less valuable trees have supplanted the natural vegetation. But large areas of virgin forest of spruce, fir, and larch still flourish in the drainage basin of the Yalu River.

In many respects northern Korea has been—and still is— what might be called a "pioneer land" dominated by a "frontier spirit." Factors of terrain and climate called for ruggedness, persistence, and individual initiative on the part of its settlers and later inhabitants. In fact, the people are more than often inclined to think of themselves as brave, energetic, virile—as "tiger hunters"—in distinction to the southern Koreans, whom they call effeminate, indecisive, and unaggressive. On the other hand, the southern Koreans consider their northern neighbors to be uncouth, barbaric, volatile, and quixotic and themselves to be stable, cultured, and hard-working. Both pictures, of course, are overdrawn, reflecting regional prejudice. Students of Korea would incline towards a view that the more essential facts are that the people of both areas speak the same language, follow the same cultural patterns, and possess a similar historical and ideological background.

In modern times, the industrialization of northern Korea and the development of its mineral deposits and hydroelectric power resources caused a tremendous increase in population, though the total is still much below that of southern Korea. In 1940 the total population for the five northern provinces was 8,223,-477, resulting in a density of 188.47 per square mile. By 1944 the population had grown to 8,859,710. But in the postwar years, as the political situation solidified and as many North Koreans moved south to escape Communist domination, the population decreased. However, new influxes from Manchuria, the normal growth of population, and other factors served to keep the total North Korean population at only slightly below the 1944 figure in the post-World War II period. Undoubtedly the Korean war has upset all calculations; the waves of refugees moving back and forth before the advancing armies, bombed-out cities, the presence of Chinese soldiers, and all the other effects of the military action have so confused the situation that it is impossible to give accurate population data for the present day.

In the historic past the population of northern Korea was largely centered in the valleys and plains along the north-western coast. The area around Pyongyang—where the Koguryo kingdom (77 B.C.–668 A.D.) had its capital—was the dominant political and economic center. On the other hand, the northeastern area was relatively isolated and undeveloped until recent decades when the Japanese developed hydroelectric and mineral potentialities to support their war economy. With the building of a railroad line between Pyongyang and the east coast in 1940 the northern realm was more closely knit together. However, the real integration of this area took place in the postwar years under the Russian-dominated regime.

What the future holds for North Korea is difficult to predict.

# NORTH KOREA

The recent changes have been great in North Korea,

...though the farmers still survive.

...the UN troops found cold and isolation...

...and devastation, like these scenes at Hyesanjin along the Yalu.    53

54       The farmhouses are often made of iogs and dispersed in their location, and...

55       ...roofed with shingles and bark.

Some of the valleys are broad, and on the valley floor rice can be
grown.

...was an old administrative and commercial center at the meeting of three rivers...

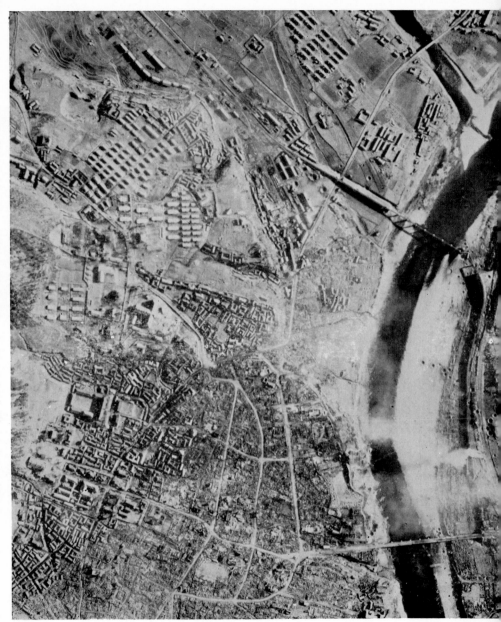

... but after air raids, the city was only ruins.

One of the key installations in North Korea was the Supung Dam on the Yalu,

...after successful air raids its power plant (in the lower right) was only a shell.

In Northwestern Korea, also, hydroelectric plants,

60          ...like this one at Pujon, were gutted.

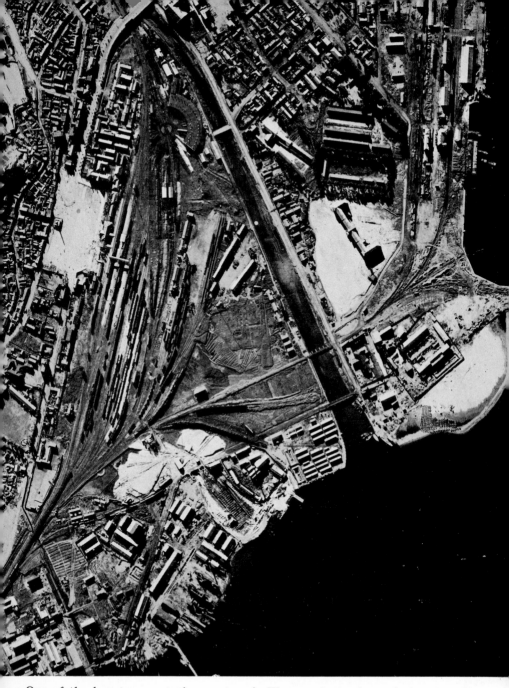

One of the key transportation centers is Wonsan, here shown before
the severe air raids.

These are the remains of the oil refinery at Wonsan after the war
had struck.

63

The transition from the Northeastern Coast to Northwestern Korea is not abrupt. This is the top of the pass between the two regions.

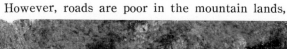

However, roads are poor in the mountain lands,

64

65 ...farms are isolated,

66 ...and fields are rocky; mountain streams yield few fish to diligent farmers.

In the hills there are few fields; 67

...on the plains rice fields dominate the landscape and the life of the people. 68

In older days in the courtyard of a farm home rice was
threshed,

...and in the market place all kinds of produce were exchanged.

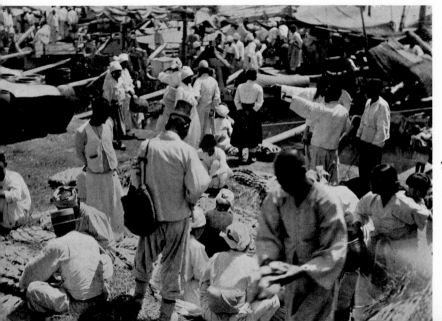

...even in the countryside, the devastation of war is evident.

The changes in the economy dictated by the Communist over-lords and certainly the aerial bombardment of its industrial facilities during the Korean war have modified the character of North Korean economy greatly. In a broadcast the North Korean radio on May 28, 1954 summarized the war damage which had been received: North Korea suffered more than one billion dollars worth of damage, lost eighty-seven hundred factory buildings and tens of thousands of men. The radio went on to say that as a result of the damage "production decreased to less than forty per cent of that of 1949, the year before the Korean war began, especially in vital production —chemical industries, electric power plants, fisheries and forestry industries—which are necessary to keep our economy stable."

North Korea's economic resources in the form of tillable land, coal and ore deposits, forests, and electric power potential still remain and could contribute significantly to the strength of a united Korea. However, according to recent reports, the North Korean regime has concluded an agreement with the Soviet Union for economic aid which is supposed to amount to one thousand million rubles (roughly two hundred and fifty million dollars) for a four-year period beginning in 1954. This is mainly for large-scale industrial equipment not only from the Soviet Union but also from eastern Europe. More signifi-cant is an aid agreement signed with Communist China for eight million million People's Bank Yuan (roughly three hundred and twenty million dollars) for a similar period. This is mainly for consumer goods and daily necessities. There are other indications which lead to the conclusion that North Korea is becoming more and more of an economic province of Communist China and, together with north China and Manchuria, closely linked with the Soviet Union.

## The Northern Interior

The Northern Interior of Korea is a mountainous land, cold, forest-covered, and forbidding. The mountains bind the peninsula to the continent of Asia and serve as a barrier between the two. In recent decades, as population pressures have increased and as modern technology has developed, the Northern Interior has gradually been opened to economic exploitation. Even so, the region is sparsely populated. Comprising 15,789 square miles, its 1940 population was 1,049,744—a density of 66.4 persons per square mile.

The Northern Interior is sharply segregated from the valleys of the Northeastern Coast—along the Sea of Japan—by a distinct though discontinuous escarpment. Naturally, the climate of the coastal region is less severe and human occupations there are quite different from those of the interior. The transition from the mountainous Northern Interior to the hill lands and plains of Northwestern Korea—bounded by the Yellow Sea—is moderate. Northwestern Korea is similar in many ways to the neighboring mountainous area; however, it is marked by less severe winter temperatures and a greater population density.

In many places in the Northern Interior, although the upper surface levels appear to be a gently-rolling surface, an uplifted peneplain or plateau, the terrain is generally rugged, marked by high mountains and isolated valleys. This is particularly true along the northern boundary, where the Yalu River and its tributaries and the upper Tumen River have entrenched themselves deeply. Volcanic Paektu-san appears as a long white massif on the skyline when observed from the summit levels. From this volcanic mass and from other volcanoes— particularly from those in the chain forming the boundary between North and South Hamgyong Provinces—lava flows have often capped the peneplain level creating a solid crusting. Other mountains, upthrown blocks, or older earth-folds add variation to the surface, particularly in the central and western portions of the region.

Cut off from the moderating influence of the Yellow Sea and the Sea of Japan, the Northern Interior has a distinctly continental climate, with relatively warm summers but with bitterly cold winters, particularly in the highlands. There are colder temperatures in the central part of the region than in the rest of the area. The data for Chunggangjin is fairly typical of the climate of the Northern Interior. There, the range of temperature is from an average of −6° F. in January to over 72° F. in July. The rainfall, averaging thirty-two inches a year, is concentrated in the summer, with fourteen inches coming in July and August. During the rigorous winters the rivers of the Northern Interior are tightly frozen, the snow lies deep in the forests, and the upland farmer stays close to his log cabin.

In general, forests and wooded slopes dominate the local landscapes. In some areas the forests have been virtually untouched by man and constitute the only extensive area of true natural vegetation in Korea. The forests are mainly conifers—spruce, fir, larch, and Korean pine. Commerical lumbering has been extensively developed in the last five decades. The logs cut in the interior forests are floated down the side streams, especially during the spring thaws, and then made up into large rafts which are floated down the Tumen River and, in much larger volume, down the Yalu River. The poor stands in the isolated slopes of Paektu-san and those on the poorly drained areas on the very steep slopes are still untouched. Where excessive cutting or forest fires have occurred, stands of aspen, birch, and spruce have developed, though these second-growths are not considered valuable timberlands.

Most of the forests of the interior were originally held as crown lands by the Korean kingdom. Later, under the control of the Japanese government, they were leased to Japanese companies, who practiced excessive cutting—particularly of the easily accessible and merchantable timber—despite the government's attempt to regulate lumbering practices. The fate of these forest resources subsequent to World War II is not known, but it is obvious that sound forestry needs to be instituted and maintained if this important natural resource of Korea is to be preserved.

One of the most important features of the Northern Interior is that it has served for centuries as an open frontier or pioneer land for the Korean people. Migrating into this virgin region, the land-hungry squatters often cleared the forest by fire—a procedure sometimes practiced elsewhere in the mountain areas of Korea but nowhere so extensively as in the far reaches of the north. From this method of clearing the land evolved a distinctive rural economy. A large proportion of these fire-field folk live in scattered, isolated units rather than in villages, as is common elsewhere in the peninsula. Their log cabins, plastered with mud and roofed with rough shingles, are unique in Korea. Another unique feature of the fire-field folk is that they are to a certain extent itinerant, abandoning fields as the mountain soil—initially fertilized by wood ash— becomes depleted and developing new fields.

For the most part the fire-field folk and those farmers who have become sedentary cultivate the hardy cereals. Handicapped by the bitterly cold winters, they work hard during the short summers to produce millet, grain sorghum, oats, rye, buckwheat, barley, wheat, and—in recent decades—potatoes. Those farmers who have been fortunate enough to obtain possession of suitable valley floors cultivate short-maturing varieties of rice. Naturally there are gradations between these two types of agriculture; some of the sedentary farmers who inhabit the river valleys still use fields initially cleared by fire high on steep mountain slopes.

It is not uncommon for farmers of the region to supplement their income by lumbering and fishing in the mountain streams. Specialized occupations, often carried on as part-time or seasonal activities by the farmers, are hunting wild animals and gathering ginseng, the medicinal herb. In general, the economy is self-sufficient, though the farmers obtain certain necessities in exchange for their cattle, pigs, or firewood. To a large degree such self-sufficiency is caused by the lack of transportation facilities in the mountainous interior, where dependence must be placed on trails or crude roads. Sleds, frames with curved runners, dragged by cows or oxen over the snow or the mud are a unique means of transportation.

Despite the paucity of well-developed commercial life, the Northern Interior is dotted with a few towns. These are usually located at valley junctions, where streams and trails meet. Such towns are often nothing more than military stations, established to maintain the appearance of control over a primitive no man's land of tiger hunters, bandits, and fire-field folk.

On the other hand, with the advent of Japanese control of the region, significant economic developments took place, constituting a veritable revolution in the economy of the mountainous interior. For one thing, the area was opened by truck roads and railroads—the latter penetrating the region from both east and west. Concurrently, extensive geologic exploration took place in search of mineral resources necessary for Japan's war economy. The development of these resources rapidly followed. The exploitation of the iron ore of Musan—though of low grade and requiring enriching processes—was of major importance. In addition, gold, copper and ferro-alloy metal deposits were mined, sometimes in areas of such extremely rugged terrain that spectacular overhead cable-ways had to be constructed.

Especially significant was the development of the hydroelectric power potential of the region. The Japanese dammed two of the headwater tributaries of the Yalu—the Changjin and the Pujon Rivers—and diverted the water southward, over the escarpment, through penstocks, and down to generators situated along the Northeastern Coast. Other projects were developed on other rivers and grandiose plans were made for further development of these power resources.

On the whole, the development of the resources of the interior by the Japanese profited the region only indirectly. Though a few primary processing and refining industries were established, the major effect on the region came through its being opened up to waves of migrants. The population increased appreciably—from 701,068 in 1925 to 1,049,744 in 1940. New towns such as Musan sprang up almost overnight, and older towns, such as Kanggye and Kapsan expanded.

Although the Northern Interior is a region with its own peculiar characteristics, one must realize that within the region itself are distinctive local areas. Three sections are worth distinguishing. The first, the drainage area of the Tumen River, is marked from the other sections of the interior because its forests have been extensively cut over. The present forests are of larch and oak, and do not constitute a very valuable resource. But perhaps the most distinctive feature of the Tumen section is the industrial complex created by the development of the Musan ore deposits.

The slopes of Paektu-san with their lava flows and other volcanic land forms are a second distinctive section. Here are spruce, fir, and larch forests relatively unexploited, though in many places the forest growth has been stunted by edaphic conditions, and in other places, which have been burnt over by forest fires, extensive second growths of birch and aspen, of little commercial value, flourish. The population of the section is virtually nil, consisting for the most part of a few bandit gangs, a few hunters, and an occasional fire-field farmer.

The third section which is distinctive lies in the western part of the region, where the Yalu River, with its deep entrenchments and meandering course, marks a sharp cultural boundary between China and Korea. On the Korean side of the river where the valley floor widens or where the intermediate slopes can be plowed, a considerable amount of permanent cultivation has taken place. Though dry cereals predominate in the total cultivation, rice is found in even the most isolated sections of the river valley. The section is also marked by numerous towns or villages which are located along the river or up tributary streams a short distance from the river. Among these are Hyesanjin, at the point where the Yalu turns west having flowed down the slopes of Paektu-san, and Chunggangjin, at the point where the Yalu makes a broad bend southwestward. A distinctive feature of many towns in this section are the waterfronts, where log rafts are assembled for their journeys downstream.

Little is known of the developments in this region, isolated as it is from the outside world, during the days of Russian occupation after World War II. Many of the economic developments had been carried out to fit the needs of Japan's economy; their continued development must have been curtailed or been modified to fit the new situation. Political changes were made in the western part of the region; a new province, Chagang, was made by dividing North Pyongan Province into two parts; the new boundary is identical with the western boundary of this geographic region.

The war in Korea had relatively little effect in terms
of direct war damage on this region. This is in large part
due to its isolated location and its physical geography. The
American marines and South Korean troops who advanced up a
narrow spearhead from the east coast were hurt almost as much
by the physical conditions as by the Chinese Communist counterattack. Aerial attacks have crippled the region's mineral,
hydroelectric power, and transportation facilities. Though
large in area, the Northern Interior will never be a region of
great importance to Korea because of its geographic limitations.

## The Northeastern Coast

Northeastern Korea is a region
of mountains and valleys lying between the Northern Interior and the
Sea of Japan. The maritime
influence, by moderating the climate
and modifying other geographic
characteristics, is a dominant factor
in this region's geography. In recent
times the construction of a railroad
line along the littoral and the
development of harbors for coastwise
shipping have tended to knit the
region together, though, because of
its terrain, it still has some diverse
and isolated sections.

During the last three decades the economy of the Northeastern Coast has been greatly transformed. Although the
basic agricultural activities of the bulk of the Korean people
in the region were widened and intensified, and although fishing
was commercialized, the major changes are attributable to

mineral exploitation, industrialization, and Japanese commercial activities. Inevitably such changes were accompanied by an increase in population. In 1925 the region had a population of 1,667,562; by 1940 it had increased to 2,467,321. Since the region has an area of 11,088 square miles, the population density in 1940 was therefore 222.5 persons per square mile. This is a somewhat misleading figure, for intensity of agricultural land use is not so pronounced as the figures for the region as a whole would lead one to infer. The data on which it is based includes the population of four large cities—Chongjin, Najin, Wonsan, and Hamhung—which had in 1940 an aggregate population of 390,877. It includes too a number of other industrial cities scattered in the coastal portions of the region.

The Northeastern Coast is blocked off from southern and western Korea by the southward extension of the mountains of the Northern Interior through the narrow waist of the peninsula. However, there is one all-important break though this barrier: the valley trending southeast from the port of Wonsan, across the "Iron Plain" into the Han River drainage basin, and from there to the capital city of Seoul. Throughout historic times this trough has been a major channel of communication between northeastern Korea and the rest of the peninsula. Also, in more recent times coastwise shipping has been of considerable importance in tying this region to the rest of Korea. Finally, just before the outbreak of World War II the Japanese completed a railroad line across the waist of the peninsula eastward to a point north of Wonsan.

Obviously, then, northeastern Korea, isolated as it may appear to be on the map, has been closely related to other parts of Korea. The Northeastern Coast, nevertheless, is a distinctive region, clearly delimited. The boundary between the Northeastern Coast and the Northern Interior is a relatively abrupt escarpment which forms the drainage divide between the Yalu River tributaries and the coastal rivers. It also coincides with climatic and, consequently, land utilization boundaries. The line which has been used for the southern sector of the region is the political boundary of South Hamgyong Province, which separates Hamgyong from Pyongan Province in the west and from Kangwon in the south.

The terrain of the region is made up of numerous mountain spurs and valleys extending from the Northern Interior to the Sea of Japan. Rugged inter-stream divides separate relatively deep valleys. Some of the valleys have wide flood plains in their lower courses; and along the coast rocky promontories separate the river plains.

Within the region a variety of terrain characteristics demark distinctive sections. In the north the region's western escarpment is neither so pronounced nor so high as in the rest of the region. The Tumen River, which marks the political boundary of Korea, drains an area of low hills and valleys. South of this area and inland from Chongjin is an extensive plain where a number of streams leading down from the mountain escarpment have coalesced. South of this plain is a region of complex geologic structure. A horst, or upthrown block, forms the peninsula which juts out into the Sea of Japan. Inland from this horst is a graben, or down-thrown block, which provides a natural route from north to south. Associated with the graben and horst structure are many volcanic features. South of this geologically complex region are a succession of hills and valleys. These vary in extent and character depending upon the size of the streams which are eating back into the escarpment of the Northern Interior and forming plains from the debris they carry. Around Wonsan is a relatively large basin caused by structural breaks and erosion. Hence, the Northeastern Coast is dominated by a basic pattern of narrow valleys and sharp divides.

The deep Sea of Japan provides an important moderating influence on the climate of the Northeastern Coast. At this northerly latitude one might expect to find very cold winters; but the winters are milder than they are in equivalent latitudinal locations in Northwestern Korea and much milder than they are in the Northern Interior. Winter temperatures in the region are still cold, going well below freezing; at least three months have average temperatures below 32° F. Unggi, in the northern part of the region, has an average January temperature of 15° F., and Wonsan, in the south, has an average January temperature of 25° F. At Songjin, in the center, the average temperature for January is 21.4° F.

The Sea of Japan has a cold current, the Liman, which drifts down from the north along this coastal region and moderates the summer temperature. Though the summer months are warm, they do not have the high temperatures found in Northwestern Korea. The warmest month in summer is usually August rather than July, which further indicates a maritime influence on the climate. The average August temperature at Songjin is 71.6° F.

Northeastern Korea receives abundant rainfall. The average annual rainfall at Songjin is 28.5 inches, over half of which occurs in July, August, and September. The funnel-shaped basin of Wonsan, which has high mountains directly behind it, experiences some of the heaviest rainfalls in Korea—an average of 53.5 inches per year. There are no climatic stations along the escarpment of the Northern Interior or on the mountain spurs, but judging from the vegetation and the stream flows one can infer that these areas receive heavier precipitation than do the valleys and coastal margins of the region. An important local condition, particularly in the northern and central parts of the region, are the coastal fogs, caused by the cool Liman Current. In some years the fogs may be so continuous as to cause crop failures.

The transition from the spruce, fir, larch, and pine forests of the Northern Interior into the semi-deciduous forest cover of the

Northeastern Coast is very abrupt. But many of the forests of the coastal region have been cut over, and much of the land is now covered with scrub oak and poor stands of pine. In some places the hills are almost barren, particularly in areas where firewood is gathered as a commercial product.

In no region of Korea is there a more marked duality of economy than in the northeast. The traditional self-sufficient agricultural economy strongly contrasts with the industrial and commercial economy dependent largely on outside sources for raw materials and on export markets. The agricultural economy is characterized by the cultivation of a single crop in the year with a minimum of commercialization; much of this agriculture is of a pioneer character. Rice is grown on paddy fields, located on the valley floors, on terraces on the lower elevations, and up the side valleys. Dry-field crops are grown on the natural levees and other sandy portions of the valley floors and on the slopes of the inter-stream divides. Though rice is the desired crop, proportionately it is less important than the dry-field crops —millets, grain sorghum, and other cereals. Wheat is rarely grown in the central and northern part of the region because of the cool summers. Large quantities of barley and oats are grown in the central area. Irish potatoes have been recently introduced throughout the region and their production has increased greatly. Different varieties of beans, and, in the northern part of the region, peas are commonly grown in large quantity.

The farmers along the Northeastern Coast live in villages located in the lee of the hill slopes along the edges of the valleys. Theirs is an isolated life, except for occasional trips to market towns located inland from the coast in the lower parts of the valleys. In exchange for their surplus grain and vegetables they obtain manufactured goods such as textiles, ironware, and kerosene. In recent decades, the lives of these farmers have been modified in several ways because of the increasing demands of the nearby industrial communities which sprang up in the wake of the Japanese exploitation of Korean resources. Some of the villagers were absorbed into industry as unskilled laborers. But the greatest change came in terms of an increased demand for food. Agriculture became intensified, types of crops were modified, the amount of tilled land was expanded, and the firewood cutting became increasingly important.

Along the coast itself, the Koreans met a different kind of fate. Fishermen, using small boats and antiquated types of nets and gear, were not able to compete with the power launches and mechanical equipment of the Japanese fishing industry. In the wake of this invasion, their only recourse was to serve as laborers in the fishing vessels and in the fish-drying and processing industries, or to turn to farming or factory employment.

Hence, the most important mark of the Japanese impact on the Northeastern Coast lies in the area of industry and commerce which the Japanese developed to support their war economy.

The basis of much of this industrialization hinged on the development of hydroelectric power. As mentioned earlier, the headwaters of the tributaries of the Yalu River were diverted to produce a concentrated flow of water down the escarpment to the coastal region, particularly in the southern part of the region, where a number of hydroelectric projects were established. The Changjin and Pujon projects, each of which had four hydroelectric power stations, provided a total installed capacity of 594,500 KW in 1944. Most of this power went into the industrial complex of the city of Hungnam. Another hydroelectric project in the middle section of the region was dependent upon the Hochon River, another tributary of the Yalu. Power from this installation, which had an installed capacity of 394,-000 KW, went mainly to the industrial areas in the central and northern part of the region. In addition there was a small

plant in the north at Puyung, with an installed capacity of 35,-
800 KW.   All of these projects were interlinked—not only with
each other but with the hydroelectric installations and industrial
areas across the peninsula in Northwestern Korea.

The fate of these hydroelectric plants in the post-World War
II period has not been well established.   According to reports
some of their equipment was taken away by the Russians as
"war reparations."   Some of the plants deteriorated, and
during the days of Russian control repair parts were shipped
in from Japan and the United States, via South Korea, in
exchange for electric power.   During the recent hostilities one
of the goals of the American marines and the South Korean
troops was to get control of these hydroelectric installations.
This control was very short-lived.   Subsequently the plants and
dams were bombed on numerous occasions and according to
reports were made inoperative.

Most of the industrial areas—the largest one being at
Hungnam—were processing centers for the mineral resources
shipped into the coastal region from the Northern Interior and
elsewhere.   Iron ore from Musan was smelted at Chongjin or
exported to Japan, and electric furnaces for high-grade steel
production were set up at Chongjin and at Songjin.   But the
industrial activity was not devoted to primary processing alone,
for soon manufacturing facilities were organized to produce
railroad and transportation equipment, construction materials,
and varied chemical products.

Perhaps the most important mineral resource of the Northeastern Coast itself is lignite coal.   This was mined near Kilchu,
in the central part of the region, and at Aoji in the lower
Tumen River basin.   Because of its low quality the lignite was
liquefied to produce fuel oil and kerosene for export to Japan.
Minor deposits of copper, gold, and ferro-alloys were also mined
in this region.

The Northeastern Coast became important as a corridor from

Japan and Korea to northern Manchuria. Rapid ferry service was provided from Najin to Japanese home ports, and coastal steamers touched at Najin and Chongjin. Unggi and Wonsan were military and naval ports. Wonsan, one of the first ports opened to foreign commerce in Korea in the previous century, became, under the Japanese, a focal point for trade between northeastern Korea and western and southern Korea. Because of its harbor facilities, an oil refining industry was established at Wonsan by foreign companies. Oil, imported from Southeast Asia and the United States, was refined and distributed from Wonsan in the ubiquitous five-gallon tins throughout Korea.

The development of industries, harbors, and military centers led eventually to a tremendous increase in road and railroad construction. The main rail line connecting with Seoul via Wonsan was extended north along the coast to Chongjin. From there it went directly north over a relatively easy pass into the Tumen River basin. The railroad paralleled the river to a point near its mouth before turning south along the coast to the ports of Unggi and Najin. There were branch railroads built, one going over difficult terrain all the way west to the Yalu. Supplementing the rail network was a highway and road system which further penetrated the isolation of northeastern Korea.

Although this coastal region may be divided into sections according to terrain and human occupation criteria, perhaps the most fruitful basis of subdivision is one relating to the economic changes which took place under the impact of Japanese exploitation. The northern section of the Northeastern Coast is an inhospitable land. Although the more or less self-sufficient farmers harvest rice and hardy cereals, as well as beans and vegetable crops, the extremely cold winters handicap any extensive agricultural development. Moreover, most of the forests have been cut over. In this section are certain valuable mineral resources—particularly the iron ore at Musan and the lignite coal at Aoji. It was for the purpose of exploiting the iron ore that a heavy-industry complex was developed at Chongjin, the leading city of this section. Access to the region (as well as to Manchuria to the west) was insured by the development of the harbor of Unggi, used largely as a naval base; of Najin, used mainly as a commercial port; and of Chongjin. The rate of population growth that succeeded these developments was among the highest in Korea.

South of this section, the combination of a horst, or upthrown block of the earth's crust, along the coast, and a graben, or down-thrown block, inland, makes another distinctive section. The hill lands—covered with second-growth forests—which make up the horst are relatively sparsely populated; a few fishing villages dot the coast line. Most of the people of the section live in the Kilchu-Myongchon graben, located between the horst and the extensions of the mountains of the Northern Interior. Associated with this graben are rather diverse geologic features. Volcanic cones, lava flows, and volcanic ash deposits have been etched out in varying patterns by the streams; but there are many patches of alluvial deposits useful for crops. Some of the section's minerals have been developed, notably the lignite near Kilchu. The industrial city of Songjin lies at the southern end of the section. The graben's major importance lies in its utility as a passageway, for the north-south railroad and highway follow it.

The southern part of the Northeastern Coast may be divided into a section extending from the Hamhung lowland north to the vicinity of Songjin and a section around Wonsan. Both are marked by isolated valleys supporting fairly dense rural populations who grow rice and dry-field crops on the hill slopes.

The section around Hamhung was drastically transformed by Japanese industrial expansion. The very small fishing village of Hungnam, near Hamhung, was developed into a major port by an artificial breakwater and harbor. On the basis of the hydroelectric power produced in this section chemical, notably nitrogen-fixation, and other industrial plants were built at Hungnam.

The section around Wonsan is rather different from the rest of Northeastern Korea. This is indicated by the fact that when the North Korean regime made its first changes in the internal political structure of the area under its control it amalgamated these three southern counties of South Hamgyong Province with that part of Kangwon Province extending north of the thirty-eighth parallel. The city of Wonsan has had a centralizing effect upon this section. Because of this factor, Lautensach, in his discussion of the regions of Korea, makes this a separate region. After Korea was opened to the outside world and during the early days of Japanese control, Wonsan served as an open port, a trading base for foreign commerce. Under the Japanese, Wonsan also became an important industrial and military center with an important oil refinery. It was a focal point for the trade of northeast Korea and for transportation connections between the northeast and the rest of the peninsula. A railroad built westward from this section to Pyongyang just before World War II became especially important when Korea was divided by the thirty-eighth parallel, for it provided the only significant east-west link. In addition to its strategic importance, the Wonsan section has the advantages of a milder winter and a hotter summer than any other section of northeastern Korea. Its heavy summer rainfall makes it the best section for rice cultivation.

At present the Northeastern Coast is under the control of the Communists. Even though the recent fighting severely wrecked its transportation facilities and industrial plants, the probability is that this region may again attain its position as one of the most economically dynamic in the peninsula. It is likely that it will be more and more closely knit with the adjacent areas of the Soviet Union and Manchuria.

## Northwestern Korea

Northwestern Korea has long been
an important region in the Far East.
According to legend, one of its first
rulers was a Chinese, Kija, who established his capital at what is now
the city of Pyongyang in 1122 B.C.
Centuries later—after 108 B.C.—the
Chinese again established settlements under the direct control of the
Han dynasty. One of these colonies,
the Lo-Lang (Nangnang in Korean)
had a highly advanced culture. By
57 B.C., however, control of Northwestern Korea, as well as parts of
adjacent Manchuria, began to pass to the control of a Korean
kingdom, the Koguryo, perhaps the strongest of the peninsula's
three kingdoms of that time. This kingdom held sway until
668 A.D., when it was succeeded by the Silla kingdom, which had
its center of power in southern Korea.

Hence, almost from the first, Northwestern Korea has been
subjected to pressures from outside, especially from its stronger
neighbor to the north and west, China. The region became a
veritable passageway into the peninsula proper, particularly as
the centuries-old tribute and diplomatic road ran from Uiju
through Pyongyang to Seoul. The Chinese influence was both
beneficial and harmful. The invasions, which naturally followed
the relatively easy coastal route through Northwestern Korea
to the heart of the peninsula, brought in their wake not only
superior civilization but devastation as well. One measure,
introduced at an early date to counteract the devastation

wrought by invaders, was the establishment of a frontier, or no man's land, along both sides of the Yalu River. In a sense, this was an attempt on the part of the Koreans, and the rulers of Korea, to isolate themselves. The history of Korea might well be written around the futility of this and similar attempts. Some of the battles of the Sino-Japanese war of 1894–95 were fought on the plains and hills of Northwestern Korea, as well as the skirmishes which marked the Russo-Japanese war of 1904–05. The most modern invasion, of course, is that of the Chinese Communists, under whose hand everything in North Korea now appears to rest. What is most surprising about Northwestern Korea, in view of its troubled history, is that it has been able to maintain a distinctively Korean culture.

Northwestern Korea is demarked from the Northern Interior by a drainage divide, for the most part, between the north-flowing tributaries of the middle Yalu River and the south- and west-flowing Chongchong and Taedong River systems. The southward extension of the mountains of the Northern Interior is the drainage divide between the Sea of Japan and the Yellow Sea and separates this region from the Northeastern Coast.

The region is dominated by mountains, both within the region and, more important, on its borders. From the mountainous Northern Interior a number of ranges extend into Northwestern Korea and provide a mountain backdrop to the region, particularly in the east. There a series of parallel ranges forms the backbone of the peninsula, effectively separating until recent times the eastern and western sides of the narrow waist of the Korean peninsula. The mountains within the region, associated geologically with the mountains of the Northern Interior, trend generally in a southwest-northeast direction. The mountains are made up of old earth-folds of varied granites and metamorphosed limestones which have been shattered into diverse blocks. Many of the mountains themselves are not particularly high, but where they rise abruptly out of the plains or where they occur in great profusion, they are impressive.

Of greater importance to the people of the region are the plains and river valleys. The lower reaches of the Yalu River, after it has left its deep mountain entrenchment, form a relatively extensive plain on the northern border. The southwestern slopes of the Northern Interior uplands are drained by tributaries of the Chongchong River, which forms a large plain extending from Anju to the sea. Along the coasts of North and South Pyongan Provinces are extensive tidal flats, some of which have been reclaimed by retaining walls and are used as fertile farm lands.

The most important river within the region is the Taedong, which flows past Pyongyang and empties into a large estuary, deeply indenting the coast line. The Taedong has a number of tributaries; the very name of the river means "confluent stream." It drains the largest interior basin in the peninsula. There are numerous small streams in Hwanghae Province, such as the south-flowing Yesong River, whose lower course marks the boundary of the province. More important, however, are the structural plains, particularly in the central part of Hwanghae Province. These are blocks down-faulted or down-folded between upthrown mountains and hills. On some of these interior basins a thick veneer of diluvial material has been laid.

The climate of Northwestern Korea is strongly conditioned by its proximity to the continental land mass. This continentality is reflected both in range of temperatures and in seasonal precipitation. Though not so bitterly cold as those of the Northern Interior, the dry, cold winters caused by the air drifts of the winter monsoon from the continental interior are a dominant characteristic of Northwestern Korea. However, there is some difference within the region between the warmer south and the colder north; the average January temperature at Haeju, on the south shores of Hwanghae, is 23° F.; at Pyongyang it is 17.6° F.; and at Sinuiju on the Yalu it is 15° F. On the whole the region has humid, continental climate, little modified by the Yellow Sea. Though the snows are sometimes heavy, most of the precipitation is concentrated in the summer months. For example, at Pyongyang over half of the average yearly rainfall of thirty-seven inches comes in the two months of July and August, when warm, moist air-drifts from the south are disturbed by convectional and cyclonic activity. Throughout the year non-periodic variations in the weather occur with the passage of cyclonic storms, or air-mass fronts.

Northwestern Korea was originally a forest land. At present, however, in the vicinity of the large cities and the densely populated agricultural areas along the coast, the hills are bare or covered with only scrubby second-growths. But in the mountains and hills away from the areas of dense settlement stand good forests of red and Korean pine mixed with deciduous trees—most commonly oaks and chestnuts. Although there is considerable commercial forestry along the upper reaches of the rivers, particularly the Taedong, most of the woodcutting is done as a part-time occupation by the farmers. Because of the severe winter temperatures, firewood, brush, and charcoal are much needed. Farm families work during the fall and winter cutting trees, lopping off branches, and gathering leaves. In many cases severe damage to the forests has resulted from such unregulated cutting.

Some of the earliest mineral resource developments in Korea took place in this region. Gold had long been panned from alluvial deposits and mined from small shafts. Some of the gold deposits were associated with complex ores containing copper, silver, and other minerals. New enterprises, some financed and managed by Westerners—Americans, French, and British, who held concessions from the Korean king—modernized these works by introducing drilling machinery and dredges. Later the Japanese squeezed or bought out the Westerners. A large refinery at Chinnampo was built to refine the complex gold ores.

Other mineral resources exploited by the Japanese were iron ore and coal. From scattered and complex anthracite deposits near Pyongyang the Japanese manufactured coal briquettes, some for the use of the Japanese navy and some sold commercially. The iron ore found in widely scattered deposits at Kaechon and other places north of Pyongyang and in northern Hwanghae Province was sent to the blast furnaces located at Kyomipo on the Taedong River estuary. Coking coal had to be imported, mostly from north China.

The industries first established by the Japanese were dependent almost wholly on thermal power derived from coal. Later, however, transmission lines were built over the mountains to draw upon the hydroelectric power produced along the Northeastern Coast. The real industrial expansion of the northwestern region however, came just before and during World War II, when the large Supung hydroelectric project on the Yalu was in operation. Sinuiju and Pyongyang became important centers for the production of such varied products as chemicals, textiles, aluminum, rubber shoes, bicycles, electrical equipment, and many varied consumer goods.

The Japanese were also responsible for the marked increase in agricultural production in Northwestern Korea. They introduced new crops, such as apples, provided better grades of tobacco and cotton, pushed the production of rice and soy beans, and expended great effort in reclaiming tidal flats and in constructing large-scale irrigation works. In view of subsequent events, it is important to note that much of the commercial production and agricultural improvement projects were under the control of Japanese companies.

The lands of these large Japanese-controlled companies, as well as those owned by absentee Korean landlords, were subjected to land redistribution when, after World War II, Northwestern Korea came under the dominance of the Soviet Union. Led by trained Korean Communists, the "People's Committees" appropriated the large holdings and turned over the use of them (though not their titles) to Korean farmers. However, the initial enthusiasm of the farmers was severely tempered when taxes and required service on public work projects put them in a worse economic position than they had been in before the "reforms." In addition, the farmers lost many of their very necessary farm animals, oxen and cows, to the Russian military commissariat. Without such animals they were unable to work their fields. One result of these developments was that many farmers—along with city folk—fled across the thirty-eighth parallel to find refuge in South Korea.

Northwestern Korea was the center of the Communist regime which dominated the northern part of Korea. Consequently it suffered especially when hostilities broke out in Korea in June, 1950. The United Nations forces wreaked havoc on the ground, the aerial bombardment wrecked mines, electric power plants, industrial centers, railroads, and bridges. Causing even more devastation, the Chinese Communist forces poured through this region and, it is reported, ruthlessly pillaged the rural areas.

Geographically, Northwestern Korea may be divided into two sections based upon the relatively sharp division, roughly paralleling the coast, between the plains and hill lands along the Yellow Sea and the section of mountains and isolated valleys of the interior. The interior section is an area of 9,472 miles, with a population in 1940 of 1,597,554 persons; or, in terms of density, 168.6 persons per square mile. The coastal section is slightly smaller—7,623 square miles—but contains the large cities and the richest agricultural land. There the total population numbered 3,109,858 in 1940, a density of 407.9 persons per square mile. The 1940 population of Pyongyang was 285,965, of Sinuiju 61,143, and of Chinnampo 68,658.

The interior section of Northwestern Korea is a transition

area bordering the Northern Interior. It, too, is dominated by mountains and hills, which have been etched out into sharp features by stream erosion in the areas of resistant rock and rounded features on the granite rocks. The section has very few broad valleys. The streams were entrenched in winding courses during a series of interrupted erosional cycles. The result of this complex geologic history is a maze of hills and mountains, none of them very high, and a limited amount of lowland suitable for cultivation.

Severe winter temperatures, particularly in the higher elevations, limit the growing season, so that farmers are restricted to growing fast-maturing varieties of rice and the hardier cereal crops. In this section a significant number of farmers practice fire-field agriculture: amid the ashes and stumps they plant a hardy cereal, like millet, for two or three years and then abandon the patch. However, most of the farmers are sedentary, living either in isolated, log-walled, shingle-roofed farmsteads, or, more commonly, in thatch-roofed, mud-walled houses clustered in small villages. Among the valley-dwellers rice is, of course, the desired crop. Usually, however, more of the crop land is devoted to millet, grain sorghum, barley, and buckwheat. Tobacco is sometimes grown on sandy soils derived from weathered granites. Like the farmers of the Northern Interior, they hew timbers for export, collect brushwood, and trap fish.

In recent years, of course, the isolation of this interior section was broken down to a degree by developments connected with mineral exploitation and commercial lumbering. The mines of the area drew power from the Supung hydroelectric plant on the Yalu River. A railroad running into the Northern Interior and another crossing the peninsula served to tie this hinterland more closely to the coastal section to the west.

The coastal lands, consisting largely of plains and hills, has a relatively milder climate than the interior section. Before

the great changes of recent decades, the people developed a
village economy based on rice and cereal production and fishing.
The section was largely self-sufficient with only the city of
Pyongyang having more than local importance. But few areas
were more thoroughly transformed by the industrial and commercial revolution introduced by the Japanese. The process
was the familiar one: agriculture became intensified and commercialized, mineral- and wood-processing industries were
introduced, transportation facilities were multiplied, and
seaports were built.

The two most important industrial areas which were developed
were at Sinuiju and Pyongyang, and these were connected by
rail with the cities of Manchuria. Sinuiju, a new city at the
bridge across the Yalu, became a major industrial center. The
industrial complex around Pyongyang was associated with the
iron and steel industry of Kyomipo. Further expansion of the
area was projected, in large part based on the importation of
Manchuria iron ore from the Tungpientao region across the
Yalu and of coal from north China. Apart from the heavy industry installations, plants producing a variety of consumer goods
were built at Pyongyang, especially in its fast-growing suburbs.
Further, some thirty miles to the southwest, on the estuary of
the Taedong River, a small fishing village, Chinnampo, was
developed into a major port and industrial center, notably for
rice-milling and copper and gold refining. To overcome the
twenty to thirty foot tidal range at this point of the coast,
special floating docks were constructed. Extensive salt pans,
dependent upon sea water and solar evaporation, were constructed north of Chinnampo to take advantage of the tidal range.
Finally, industrial developments near Haeju, on the south coast
of Hwanghae Province, included copper refining, chemical, and
other industries. A number of minor industries were situated
in towns along the major double-tracked railroad which knit
this section together.

Few areas of Korea suffered such devastation as the industrial section of Northwestern Korea, particularly the area around Pyongyang which at the conclusion of the armistice was said to be only rubble. Following hostilities, there can be little doubt that the region will again flourish, for it has within itself a balance of economic resources—fertile land, thick forests, hydroelectric power potentials, mineral resources, ports, and industrial sites—that can scarcely be matched anywhere else in the peninsula.

| Chapter 10 | The Regions of South Korea |

SOUTHERN Korea is much more peninsular and maritime in geographic character than is northern Korea.[34]   Though it, too, is a land of mountains and valleys, the difference lies in the fact that the mountains of the south are not massive or high and that the plains are much more extensive.   Consequently, the amount of cultivated land is greater, and the access from place to place is easier.   In central Korea the major range, the Taebaek, which runs north and south, parallel to the eastern coast, slopes abruptly down to the eastern coast; but in the west the headwaters of the Han River have etched out more gentle slopes.   Though there is a subdued extension of the Taebaek Range to the southeast tip of Korea, more important in the southern part of the area is the Sobaek Range.   This extends diagonally from the central Taebaek Range to the southwest, thus separating the Naktong River basin from the river basins of western Korea.   Old earth-folds, which have been truncated by erosion, and different levels of alluvium give variation to the western hill lands and plains.   The southwestern coast is a maze of islands and peninsulas, with structural lines going at cross angles.   The two volcanic islands which lie offshore at some distance, small Ullung to the east and large Cheju to the south-west, are grouped with southern Korea, though they are quite distinctive geographically and vary in certain other respects.

Southern Korea is fortunate in having a comparatively mild winter climate, though with respect to some of the interior locations the term "mild" can hardly be used. The average January temperature at Seoul is 24° F.; at Mokpo, in the southwest, it is 33.7° F.; and at Pusan, in the southeast, it is 35.6° F. The relatively mild winters are important, particularly in the lowland areas along or near the coast, for in those areas winter-cropping is possible. This means that two crops can be grown in a year, making possible higher population densities. This is perhaps the single most significant feature of the geography of southern Korea as compared to northern Korea.

The mountains and hills of southern Korea were at one time covered by heavy forests. However, farmers in search of wood and the ravages of uncontrolled insect pests have denuded many of the hills of their trees, so that barren hill slopes are now a common characteristic in the densely populated areas. The remnants of fine forest stands are found only in the mountains and in protected sites around monasteries or graves. The Japanese attempt to foster a large-scale reforestation program was frustrated in part by their own need for wood during World War II. In the chaotic postwar period, when the occupation authorities were unable to curtail the cutting of firewood and brush by the Korean farmers, more of the hill slopes were denuded, and again severe erosion set in.

The great increase in population in recent decades has become one of southern Korea's most pressing problems. In 1940, the eight provinces which make up southern Korea had a population of 16,101,558, and a population density of 386.55 per square mile. By 1944, the population had grown to 17,040,432 people. Though cities grew, as agriculture became increasingly commercialized, there were too few industries to supply outlets. As a consequence, many Korean men migrated to Japan to work. Manchuria too attracted many migrants, though hardly

as many as from northern Korea. Finally, there was a shift
to northern Korea itself as industrialization increased in the
north.

In the postwar period, when many Koreans—mostly unskilled
workers—returned from Japan, where they had been working
in mines and factories, the problem of population pressure in
South Korea became even more pronounced. Though the Japanese residents of Korea were sent home and thus gave slight
relief to this condition, the Japanese technical and administrative
skills were sorely needed in Korea. It was a difficult task to
replace them. The problem of population pressure was further
aggravated by the tremendous influx of refugees from North
Korea who, now landless, crowded into the southern cities.
Meanwhile the natural growth of population continued. To
top off the already desperate taxing of the economy, agricultural
yields fell from prewar levels because of a lack of fertilizer.
The situation was relieved by stopping the export of large
quantities of rice to Japan and by securing American economic
aid. On the whole, the splitting of the country by the thirty-
eighth parallel may have caused more suffering in the south
than in the north.

Most of the industries of southern Korea, unlike those of
northern Korea, where coal and iron ore deposits and hydroelectric power resources abound, were developed to meet consumer demands or to process agricultural products, particularly
rice. The major effect of this industrialization under the Japanese was practically to wipe out the traditional village handicraft economy, which for ages had produced the cloth, pottery,
shoes, tools, household utensils, and nearly everything else
needed by the rural population. It is, of course, almost impossible to assess definitely the effects the Korean war has had
on the economy of South Korea.* The devastation by bombing,

* Appendix H contains a table giving data on recent economic production in
South Korea.

by scorched-earth policies, and by disruption of law and order has been staggering. It has been estimated that five million of the twenty-one million South Koreans have been uprooted from their homes. At least 400,000 homes have been destroyed. Industrial and transportation facilities have been especially hard hit, and villages and cities in the line of battle have been severely damaged. The city of Seoul, for example, lost eighty-five per cent of its industry, transportation, and public utilities and half to three-quarters of its living and office space. Seventy-five to eighty per cent of the textile industry of the south, an important segment of industrial life, has been damaged by war and by partial dismantling on the part of the Communists. War damage in South Korea is estimated to have involved $1,500,000,-000 worth of productive goods. Internally, the crowding of people, the overloading of the transport lines by military traffic, the collapsing financial structure, and the inflationary chaos have caused tremendous economic havoc. It has been estimated that the level of total economic production in late 1952, estimated at $44 per capita, was one-third lower than that of the immediate pre-hostilities period; per capita consumption is probably one-fourth below that of the pre-invasion year. It is estimated that in order to raise the present South Korean standard of living by 1959 to the 1949 level, which was relatively low, $1,750,000,000 of outside relief and economic aid will be required—a stupendous sum to raise among the United Nations.

During the fighting in Korea, United Nations agencies, such as the Civilian Assistance Command and the Korean Reconstruction Agency have been striving valiantly with the social and economic problems of a nation swept by war. They have been working with agencies of the Republic of Korea in seeking solutions to some of these problems. The United States has been the heavy contributor to the United Nations relief work. Individual American and other United Nations troops, touched deeply by the suffering they have witnessed, have contributed generously. The expressed aim of the United Nations economic activities is to help the Koreans plan and build the solid economic foundation necessary for a unified, independent, and democratic Korea. At this moment, the possibilities of real peace during which reconstruction rather than destruction can take place —let alone the unification of Korea—seem remote.

## The East Central Coast

The East Central Coast of Korea is a narrow and irregularly shaped geographic region lying between the Sea of Japan and the Taebaek Range. Its length is approximately two hundred miles, and its width at its widest point is thirty miles. Though the mountains to the west bar easy access to east central Korea, there are outlets to the north, through the Wonsan section, and to the south, into the Naktong River basin. Some two thousand years ago, the region was the center of an independent kingdom, the Ye. But Ye was soon absorbed by its stronger neighbor, Silla, to the south. For many centuries the coastal region has been a part of Kangwon Province.

The Taebaek mountain range, which rises as a backdrop for the whole region, is the result of a series of crustal block movements. The coastal foothills are down-faulted sections flexed toward the Sea of Japan and arranged in an echelon pattern. Within the coastal region there are marked differences in geologic structure. Where biotite granite and similar rocks occur, erosion and weathering have produced rounded slopes and debris-clogged valleys. In areas where slate and other metamorphic rocks predominate—as in the central part of the region—the relief is sharp and angular, and the streams have been unable to develop flood plains. In recent geologic times, slight changes in the erosional level have entrenched the streams into winding courses, and elevated patches of sediments and alluvial materials. Many streams, blocked from the sea by sandy bay-mouth bars, empty into extensive lagoons. In general, the relief is characterized by valleys isolated by intervening headlands. The amount of arable land is small, and as a consequence the population is sparse.

Because of the northward-flowing warm currents of the Sea of Japan, the average winter temperatures for east central Korea, though a few degrees below freezing, are neither bitterly cold nor long in duration. The northern part of the region has an average January temperature of 27.5° F., while the southern part averages 31.5° F. August temperatures for the region average 77° F. The rainfall is quite heavy, forty to forty-five inches a year, with the maximum coming in the summer months. There are also some spring rains which are important as the farmers prepare their fields for the summer. This combination of relatively mild winters and relatively hot, wet summers has enabled the farmers of the region to practice winter-cropping in places where soil conditions are suitable.

The population of the East Central Coast is low in number, compared to that of its neighbors to the north, south, and west. The population increased from 374,405 persons in 1925 to 559,-513 in 1940. The population density of 214.4 persons per square mile in 1940 was relatively sparse in comparison to the densities of adjacent areas in southern Korea.

There are many reasons why the East Central Coast has not developed as rapidly as other regions in the peninsula. For one thing, it has no closely-knit railroad transportation system, though common access to the sea and a highway following the coast have tended to give it a certain amount of unity. The Japanese had planned to construct a rail line along the entire coast, but the project never fully developed. Train service was available only as far south as Yangyang, just north of the thirty-eighth parallel. Then, after World War II, when the parallel became a rigid dividing line bisecting the region, further development of a continuous rail link was abandoned.

The lack of arable land is another major reason why the region has not had great economic development. In general, its agriculture remains geared to the production of rice and cereals for home consumption. Though rice is grown on the valley floors—irrigated, occasionally, by primitive canals—a relatively high percentage of the arable land is given over to dry fields situated on the slopes of hills or in the areas of the bay-mouth bars. The amount of cereals and rice available for export is small. In fact, on occasion some of the fishing villages and larger towns have had to import rice from western and southern Korea.

Although the Japanese succeeded in commercializing the centuries-old, primitive fishing industry of the people of the coastal areas, the development was short-lived. For several years sardine catches were bountiful, thanks in part to new equipment; and the production of fish oil and fish cake, useful as fertilizer, boomed. But after 1940 the sardine schools left Korean waters, and commercial fishing slumped. Re-establishment of the fishing industry in post-World War II years has been difficult, and perhaps only 30,000 to 50,000 persons are now dependent on fishing as a major occupation.

Only slightly more successful were Japanese attempts to develop lumbering and industrial installations. They constructed sawmills along the coast to process the forest resources of the interior mountains—mixed hardwoods and conifers, and these woods were used extensively during the last years of World War II as part of a wooden-shipbuilding program. But the region's accessible forest resources were quickly depleted, and most of the slopes and inter-stream divides are today covered with a scrubby growth of pine and oak.

Industrial installations, near Samchok in the southern part of the region, were built for the production of cement, chemicals, carbide, and fertilizers. But most of this development depended on imported coal and electrical power from the mountains to the west. At present, the cement industry, with its capacity of 100,000 tons of annual production, operates at a low level because of the shortage of power; a similar situation prevails in the carbide plant. The chemical plant was damaged during World War II and is now nonoperative.

Thus, without major resources or cities (Kangnung, the largest, had a population in 1941 of only 30,278), handicapped by its inaccessibility, the East Central Coast remains one of the more primitive regions of Korea. Although the region attracts few travellers, it has much to offer anyone interested in scenic beauty—particularly along the coast, where pine-covered promontories pounded by the waves and sandy beaches protecting the lagoons from the rolling surf are particularly beautiful and it has much to offer anyone interested in the kind of life characteristic of most Korean villages before the era of modernization and industrialization.

Most of the villages are located a few miles from the coast, usually along the zone of contact between the hill slopes and the valleys. Such a location was particularly advantageous centuries ago, when the Japanese pirates made forays along the coast in search of plunder. The pirates would hesitate to attack inland villages for fear of being cut off from their boats. In recent days these isolated villages and the towns which dot the valleys continue the mode of life lived by their ancestors. The houses are thatch-covered, with the thatch held down by ropes or stones. The farmsteads are usually surrounded by low walls or wicker fences. The clustered storage buildings contain the year's crop of barley, wheat, vegetables, cotton, and hemp. Often in the center of the village is a single tree around which the villagers congregate in leisure times. At the village out-skirts stand small wayside shrines commemorating local events or individuals.

Fortunately, the recent fighting in Korea little touched the lives of these people, compared to the devastation it wrought in other parts of Korea. The region was not heavily bombarded, though one might assume that the indirect effects of the war were great indeed.

## The Central and Southern Mountains of Korea

The complex ranges of mountains and hills that extend through the central and southern parts of Korea are considered a distinctive geo-graphic region, despite the difficulty of clearly delimiting them. These mountains are neither so forbidding as the mountains of the north, nor are they grouped into easily defined ranges. However, from time im-memorial, they have served as barriers between the east and west of the peninsula and between south and central Korea. Because the change from mountain-dominated terrain to hill- and plain-dominated areas is often gradual in this part of Korea, secondary criteria, such as population densities and county or provincial borders, have been used, when necessary, to supplement terrain differences in establishing the boundary of the region. This is largely the case with respect to the western boundary. There the modifications in terrain are so gradual that the boundary drawn on the map must be considered as marking little more than a transition zone. The northern line runs along the provincial boundary and demarks, as well, the line between the divisions of North and South Korea. The eastern boundary is easily established: it generally follows the drainage divide which distinctly separates the interior mountains from the East Central Coast.

The mountains of central and southern Korea are the product of complicated geologic forces. In far distant geologic time old earth-folds between which troughs of sediments were deposited were contorted. This structure of folds and troughs had a general northeast-southwest trend. Subsequently, during a long period of erosion and crustal stability, the whole area was virtually levelled. Later this block of variegated structure was uplifted and tilted by diastrophic action, the upthrown edge of the block roughly paralleling the present coast of the Sea of Japan. The fault zone, however, was not simple or continuous, rather it was a series of faults. The high crests of the uptilted portion of the block are the present Taebaek Range, the drainage divide in central Korea.

Trending southwest from the Taebaek Range is the other major mountain range of southern Korea, the Sobaek. It has a somewhat similar geologic history as the Taebaek, being the result of an old earth-fold, resistant to erosion, which was then uplifted by a series of faultings of the earth's crust. The uplift of these blocks was not the result of one violent disruption of the earth's crust, but was accomplished by gradual stages of uplift. In West Central Korea the down-tilted portions of these blocks were covered by the Yellow Sea and by alluvial deposits brought down by rivers which were eroding the mountain areas. Some of these rivers, notably the Han and its tributaries, became deeply entrenched in winding courses.

Though the region as a whole is dominated by mountains,

there are considerable local and sectional differences in the relief. Some of the ancient earth-folds, which were further compressed in later geologic time, stand out as ridges of high terrain. In other areas molten rock welled up through breaks in the earth's crust to form small but distinctive lava sheets. Where the basic rock was easily eroded, rivers cut wide channels, creating interior basins. In areas of resistant rock the rivers were constricted to narrow channels, with only small areas of flood plains. Finally, certain basins are the result of structural deformation rather than of stream erosion and deposition. Surrounding these basins are hilly terrain and mountains.

Though a part of southern Korea, whose climate is generally considered mild, the region of Central and Southern Mountains has cold winters because of its high elevation and interior location. Of course, there is considerable variation from north to south and from crest to lowland within the region. The lowlands have average January temperatures of 18° F. in the north and 26° F. in the south. The western fringe has less severe winters than the interior parts of the region. Rainfall is plentiful throughout the region, though uneven in distribution. Sheltered valleys average about forty-five inches of rainfall annually compared to the southern flanks of the mountains, where the average is closer to fifty-five inches. Because of the mountainous terrain, heavy thunderstorms are common on hot summer days. Snow covers the mountain crests in the winter months, though there is a decided maximum of precipitation in the summer months.

The variation in climate in the region leads to vertical zonation in the natural vegetation. The crests of the highest mountains have true alpine flora, and most of the higher slopes are normally covered with coniferous forests. The lower slopes have mixed hardwoods and conifers, including Korean pines. One interesting local variation in natural vegetation distribution, dependent upon the angle and direction of the mountain slope, is found in the Diamond Mountains, in the northeastern part of the region, where the deciduous trees, which require more moisture, cover the northern slopes, while conifers predominate on the southern slopes.

Unfortunately, many of the virgin forests have been cut, and the remaining stands have been poorly protected. The second growths, mostly poor stands of scrub oak and pine, mixed with a variety of deciduous trees and shrubs, do not yield good timber. Even these relatively meager forest resources have been severely cut by the Korean farmers.

In this region, particularly, the Japanese instituted a vast reforestation program to reclothe the mountains and hills where severe erosion had set in. Their immediate aim was to prevent debris-laden streams from flooding valuable paddy fields along the valley floors. Additional damage to the forests may be laid at the door of the fire-field folk, though the extent of this method of clearing land by fire for the sake of obtaining what are at best sub-marginal fields is hardly as great in this region as in the Northern Interior and the mountainous areas of North-western Korea. At any rate, this practice—as well as, for example, the failure of the Japanese attempt to introduce sheep-raising in the uplands—is a reflection of the fact that the Korean people have a deeply ingrained tradition of crop cultivation.

It is not surprising that the bulk of the population is to be found in an area representing only one-tenth of the whole region, for it is the area of river valleys and basins that may best be cultivated. Taken as a whole, the region of the Central and Southern Mountains had a population of 2,770,951 in 1940, an overall density of 200.8 persons per square mile, but this figure hardly does justice to the facts regarding densities within the cultivable areas. Nowhere in the region are there any large cities. Chunchon, Wonju, and Chungju, which are located at the western margins of the region, have populations ranging from 15,000 to 25,000, but they represent little more than over-grown market towns, rice-processing centers, or administrative centers for the agricultural hinterland.

Most of the farmers are located in villages, nestled along the valleys. However, in the more mountainous areas the settlement pattern is dispersed, with the farmers living in individual separated farmsteads near their fields. As usual in Korea, the principal crop in the lowlands is rice; in the southern sections of the region double-cropping of the rice with winter barley is possible. The dry fields, which are usually located on the sandy soils of the flood plains or on the hill slopes, are used principally for winter wheat, cotton, and soy beans. Fields at higher elevations are used for millets, buckwheat, rye, and other hardy cereals.

For many years access to the farming villages in this isolated region was possible only by the use of pack ponies, porters, or cow-drawn sledges. Modern road construction was exceedingly difficult in the mountainous terrain and was attempted by the Japanese almost wholly for strategic purposes. The same in part is true of railroad construction. The main north-south railroad was constructed over the Sobaek Range at one of its narrowest points and was much later paralleled to the east by a line running northwest from Andong through the western part of the region to Seoul. In the northern part of the region the Japanese ran a line from Seoul northeast to Wonsan, through a relatively low pass, along a structural valley. At roughly the mid-point in this route a side line, noted for its spectacular switchbacks and tunnels, was extended to the borders of the Diamond Mountains.

One purpose which the rail lines served—particularly a side spur from the Andong-Seoul line—was to open the region's coal and other mineral deposits. The major coal deposits, a low-grade anthracite which disintegrates into powder and thus needs to be briquetted, are located principally in the Yongwol and

Samchok areas in the southeastern part of the region. In 1944 the Samchok area, which is the one most extensively developed, produced 944,000 tons of coal and the Yongwol area produced 275,000 tons. Other districts—Whasun and Kuam—in the southwestern part of the region also produced significant amounts of anthracite. Some of the coal was used for domestic use, some was used for the railroads, but its most valuable use was for the generation of electric power. A plant at Yongwol with an installed capacity of 100,000 KW consumed large quantities. This coal production slumped very badly after the end of World War II; it was gradually increased, almost reaching its peak production, but then was affected by the hostilities in Korea. However, in recent times production has again been increased. One of the major handicaps is imposed by the lack of adequate transportation in this area of mountainous terrain.

The anthracite coal is not the sole source of power, for the hydroelectric potentials of the rivers in the northern part of the region were partially developed by the Japanese. The largest projects were located on the northern branch of the Han River. At a dam at Chongpyong, south of the thirty-eighth parallel, one project had an installed capacity of 44,000 KW. Just north of the thirty-eighth parallel and recently under the control of the UN, at Hwachon, another large reservoir furnished water for a hydroelectric plant with an installed capacity of 90,000 KW. It is obvious that with the fighting raging for a relatively long period in this particular area these power facilities were greatly damaged, but they are now being rebuilt.

The exploitation of many of the other mineral and power resources of the Central and Southern Mountains decreased greatly or virtually ceased when the Japanese left the peninsula, for some of this exploitation was uneconomic and only fostered because of Japan's war-economy needs. Gold is still mined in the Kumjong area near Taebaek-san. Graphite is available in a number of localities in the Sobaek Range. Tungsten production has been fostered in order to provide an export earner of foreign exchange. In addition, lead, zinc, fluorite, cobalt, and molybdenum have been produced in minor quantities. Most of the mineral and power resources are developed for markets outside the region; in view of their nature it is doubtful that any major industrial area will be developed within the Central and Southern Mountains.

Sectional differences within the large area of the region are often sharp. The most famous section is the Diamond Mountains (in Korean, the Kumgang-san), located in the northeastern part of the region. Renowned for over five hundred years as the seat of Buddhist monasteries—at one time they numbered over 180—the section also boasts some of the most spectacular scenery in Korea. The mountain terrain is rugged, with myriad peaks of peculiar and striking form, swift-flowing streams, numerous waterfalls, and luxurious growths of virgin timber. In recent decades the Japanese developed the section into a more accessible tourist haven.

To the modern historian, particularly to one interested in military action, one of the most important sections of the Central and Southern Mountains is a strategically-situated corridor running from southwestern to northeastern Korea—in other words the natural passageway controlled from the south by the Seoul area and from the north by the Wonsan section. This corridor and the heights dominating it have been the scene of some of the severest fighting in the entire Korean war. Many decades ago the Japanese geomorphologist, Koto, identified the area as a graben, a down-faulted portion of the earth's crust. However, the passage has been more correctly described as a stream-eroded valley covered by outpourings of lava. The largest of these sterile lava patches, one located north of Chorwon, has the distinctive and appropriate name "The Iron Plain."

As indicated earlier, the southeastern area of the central mountains around Taebaek-san is a significantly different section because of its varied mineral resources, notably anthracite coal.

Far south in the southern mountains is a sparsely-populated section, the Chiri-san massif. This mountainous area is the result of an uplift of an old earth-fold. The section is dominated by Chiri Mountain, 6,283 feet in elevation, and associated mountains which form the boundary between Southeastern and Southwestern Korea. Like the Diamond Mountains, this section has some ancient Buddhist monasteries, but for centuries it has also served as a haven for bandits who found refuge in the lonely valleys and forest-covered slopes. In recent fighting, Communist guerillas secreted themselves in this isolated section.

On the whole, the major characteristic of the Central and Southern Mountains is its isolated location and lack of real potential for economic development. The farmers living in small valleys and basins are almost cut off from their countrymen to the east and west. In recent times the silence of some of these mountain fastnesses and narrow, winding river valleys has been violated by the sound of shell and plane, and the primitive economy of the people has been disrupted by floods of refugees from the north and from the plains looking for shelter.

# West Central Korea

The factors that contribute to the importance of the West Central region of Korea are a combination of the geographical, in the widest sense of the word, and the historical. Climate and terrain have made it an extremely rich agricultural land; it is a vital commercial region; and its population exceeds four million, or 638.3 persons per square mile, the highest density of any region in Korea. Further, the region occupies a central

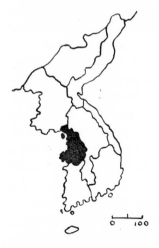

location in the peninsula, with easy access by road and rail line to the industrialized and resource-rich northwest, to the highly developed Wonsan and Hamhung sections to the northeast, to central Korea, and to the agricultural lowlands of the south. But perhaps the most important factor of all is that it is the seat of the capital and the largest city in the country—Seoul.

The boundaries of this region of 6,304 square miles have been established on the bases of comparative population densities and of county and provincial lines, which, it must be remembered, are themselves often based on minor terrain features. Thus in the northwest the Yesong River, which forms in this area the boundary between Hwanghae and Kyonggi Provinces, is used to demark West Central Korea from Northwestern Korea. The southern boundary and the line demarking West Central Korea from the Central and Southern Mountain region are likewise based on population densities, in combination with provincial boundaries.

The region as a whole is best described, physiographically, as plain and hill land. Geologically, it is the western and down-tilted portion of the complex block whose eastern extension comprises the central mountains, culminating in the Taebaek Range. During the recent geologic past eroded materials from the Han River and its tributaries have built up extensive plains in their lower courses. The process is a continuous one; when the main stream is in flood it develops natural levees, blocking the tributaries and these in turn form temporary lakes in which alluvial material is deposited. In recent historical times such erosion has increased appreciably because of the deforestation of the headwater areas. However, on some of the plains the remnants of old earth-folds or structural blocks stand up as islands in this sea of alluvium; elsewhere, rising out of the plains are hills and mountains, whose trend is generally northeast-southwest. The most noticeable range, an old earth-fold of complex structure, roughly parallels the Sobaek Range.

The climate of West Central Korea favors intensive crop cultivation. Summer rainfall is plentiful, over half the yearly average coming in July and August. In Seoul, for instance, in the six months from October through March less than eight inches of the average annual rainfall of fifty inches are registered. As for temperature, the region is a transitional belt between the cold-wintered north and the mild-wintered south. For three months most of the region has average monthly temperatures below freezing; January temperatures in the north average 22°F. and in the south average 30°F. Consequently, winter cropping of the dry fields is a common practice in this region.

On the whole, West Central Korea is marked by its poverty of natural resources other than tillable soil. Its forests of conifers and deciduous trees have virtually disappeared due to the urban demand for firewood, charcoal, and construction timber. Mineral resources are limited to minor deposits of tungsten and gold. Coal and hydroelectric resources are meager and unexploited.

Despite the lack of these resources, the region became Korea's first important modern commercial area. In olden times there was a concentration of economic power in the city of Kaesong, located almost on the thirty-eighth parallel, thirty-five miles northwest of Seoul. Kaesong was the capital of the Koryo kingdom, which governed Korea from 918 to 1392 A.D. The city, noted as a banking center and as the residence of landowning classes, was a busy exporting center; varied products, such as ginseng, paper, silk, and furs found their way from its warehouses to other regions of Korea, and to China—often as political tribute.

But following the fall of Koryo, the capital was shifted to Kyongsong (also called Hanyang), the present city of Seoul. (The word "Seoul" means, literally, "the capital.") When the Japanese seized control of the peninsula, Seoul was the natural site for their headquarters. The Government-General offices and bureaus, banks, schools, and various other institutions soon made it the "capital" in something more than name. Concurrently Seoul became one of the most important commercial centers of Korea. Milling industries and both large and small manufacturing plants flourished in the city and its rapidly-expanding suburbs. Using the power from a thermoelectric plant, supplemented by power brought in from the north, the industrial complex produced a large percentage of Korea's textiles, rubber shoes, electrical fixtures, farm implements, and other consumer products.

Already important as a transportation center, straddling as it did Korea's main north-south rail line, and lying only twenty miles from the port of Inchon, it became a rail hub when the Japanese ran lines from Seoul to the Wonsan section on the northeast coast and into central Korea. All roads led to Seoul.

Naturally the presence of large urban markets affected the agricultural production of the immediate hinterland. Rice, vegetables, ginseng, tobacco, grains, found a ready market. As the industrial areas expanded, land was reclaimed from flood plains along the rivers and tidal flats. The use of fertilizer and modern farm practices was encouraged, the leadership for these new developments being supplied by the agricultural experiment station at Suwon.

Although there are numerous towns and villages throughout the densely packed agricultural lands of West Central Korea, the city of Seoul is so important that it warrants special consideration. The city was chosen as the capital of the Choson kingdom by Yi Taejo, the founder of the Yi dynasty. Previously it had been a small market town of local importance situated three or four miles north of the Han River, where a circle of hills afforded natural protection to a cup-shaped basin. A wall was constructed on these surrounding hills to protect the city further. In subsequent centuries, the configuration of these walls changed, depending on the development of the urban center. At some distance from the city in each cardinal direction subsidiary castle towns were developed; these centers, particularly the one on Kanghwa Island, were used for refuge by the royal court in times of invasion. A large city of refuge for use in times of emergency by the populace was built north of Seoul near Pukhan-san, a mountain 2,750 feet high whose cockscomb peak dominates the skyline.

Seoul itself was laid out on a grand scale based, generally, upon a square pattern similar to that used for Chinese cities of the same period. In each cardinal direction large gates were built, and between them were set smaller gates. At night and during times of turmoil these eight gates were closed. The royal court was built in the north end of the city, facing south, close to the highest of the surrounding hills, but the bulk of the city proper was packed closely with one-storied, tile-roofed dwelling units. The house patterns were typically Korean, with heated floors, mud walls, and small courtyards formed by the coalescing of the L-shapes of the houses.

Even before the Japanese took control, modifications had been made in the pattern and character of the city. A new palace had been constructed; and when Korea cut its ties with China, a new Temple of Heaven, a symbol of independence, had been erected outside the city. But revolutionary changes took place under the Japanese. A railroad center, around which the Japanese population settled, was built south of the city between the gate and the Han River. This district soon expanded with large railroad workshops, a thermoelectric power plant, numerous industries, and, across the river, an airport. Within the city proper, houses were razed to make way for new, wide roads and large modern buildings soon housed the Government-General offices. Schools and hospitals, a French Catholic cathedral, and numerous hotels and office buildings drastically modified the skyline.

The population naturally boomed; the official census of 1925 gave Seoul a total population of 342,626, but by 1940 it was 935,464. Part of this increase was no doubt due to the incorporation of some suburbs as part of the city proper. The population continued to rise and jumped after the defeat of the Japanese, when Seoul became the seat of the American military government, and, subsequently, of the Republic of Korea. The importance of the city as an administrative, commercial, and cultural center caused the government to separate Seoul from Kyonggi Province in 1948 and give the city the same status as a province. Finally, when the Communists closed their grip on North Korea, Seoul was swollen by an influx of refugees. According to the 1949 census, the capital's population was 1,446,019, roughly one-twentieth of the population of all Korea.

Communist troops rolled into the city on June 28, 1950, three days after they had crossed the thirty-eighth parallel, forty miles to the north. But three months later they were driven out, following the Inchon landing and the northward surge of the United Nations troops. With the advent of the Chinese Communists into the war, Seoul was again lost on January 4, but it was retaken on March 14 and thereafter remained in the hands of United Nations forces. Despite its proximity to the front, the city was again made the seat of the Korean government, and more than ever before it stands as a supercharged symbol, evoking Korean aspirations for freedom and unity.

No matter what its fate as a national capital may be in the immediate future, Seoul will certainly continue to be the focal

geographic factor giving distinctness to the region of West
Central Korea. Although sectional differences may be distinguished within the region—the fishing economy along the
Yellow Sea, the agricultural economy of the hill lands and mountain slopes to the east, and the highly commercialized rice-
growing economy in the southern section of the region, which
merges with the region of Southwestern Korea—such considerations are of less importance than the dominance of Seoul in the
geography of this significant and highly-populated region of
West Central Korea.

## Southwestern Korea

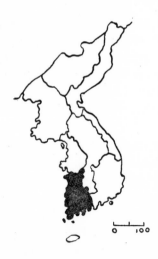

Of all the regions of the peninsula,
the one best suited by nature for the
cultivation of rice, the favorite crop
of Korean farmers, is Southwestern
Korea. Production has been so
abundant, especially in the areas of
commercialized farming, that sur-
pluses have been available for export.
Further, the combination of climate
and land forms makes double-
cropping possible. As might be
expected, the density of rural population in the region is the highest in
Korea.

Southwestern Korea cannot be divided from the adjoining
geographic regions on the basis of terrain alone. For instance,
the boundary between the southern mountains and Southwestern
Korea, though generally on a terrain basis, is specifically based
on differences in population densities; the Sobaek Range extends
into Southwestern Korea and an extension of the same range,

# SOUTH KOREA

The war has come to South Korea,

...though it has been the roads, cities, and industrial plants that
have felt the physical effect more than the countryside.

Along the East Central Coast, a narrow ribbon, the hills and valleys    73
stretch down to the sea.

Along this line the thirty-eighth parallel formed a rigid
barrier.

74

75          Quiet fishing villages with nets out to dry...

...or with boats drawn up
on shore characterize this
isolated region.

76

Much of the Central and Southern Mountains is rugged...

...and without much cover of vegetation.

In other areas dry fields and scrub forests cover the mountains and valleys.

78     ...though an occasional deposit, like this tungsten mine, gives variation to the landscape.

...this picture shows the commanding position of the Government-General building and the other modern buildings constructed by the Japanese.

In another direction the Catholic Cathedral dominates the view;
off in the distance are the University buildings.

81

Close up, the war damage is obvious,

...though even now buildings are being repaired and colorful buses chartered for wedding parties may be seen.

82

83

In the countryside, also, the effect of war can be seen,

...but the Korean farmers continue their work even in close proximity to the tents of Panmunjon.

84

85

Some country villages along strategic roads have been badly damaged,

... while the battle fronts moved quickly past others.

86

87  In Southeastern Korea paddy fields may be drained and planted with a winter crop of barley.


88  The villages may have clumps of bamboo as back-drops.

Newly reclaimed land is devoted to rice,                    89

...which in prewar days was milled and exported from busy ports such as Kunsan.

91

In Southeastern Korea the crowding of refugees has meant using even the flood plains of the rivers during the dry season for temporary camps...

and the building of shacks on the hill slopes around Pusan.

92

93        The old settled countryside with its tree-surrounded villages...

...and the large tiled-roofed houses of the *yangban*, or scholar-landlords, give an impression of permanence.      94

... capped by lofty Halla-san, has its settlement pattern in concentric rings of fishing villages, agricultural lands broken up into small, irregular fields, grasslands, and forest lands.

which marks the ancient provincial boundary, is used to separate the region from Southeastern Korea. In the north, where there is a gradual transition to West Central Korea, the provincial boundary is not utilized as the border of the geographic region, for part of the provincial border follows the Kum River. The town of Taejon and its surrounding area has been included in Southwestern Korea, although because of its character Taejon might be included with almost equal validity in West Central Korea. Instead, the county borders, marking differences in population densities, have been used for establishing the northern boundary. With the exception of a few counties in the north, the geographic region of Southwestern Korea lies within the political province of Cholla, historically a "makeweight" in Korean political life.

The cultivation of rice in Southwestern Korea is especially important on the numerous plains which border the sea and extend back into the mountain area. The most noteworthy one lies in the northern part of the region where the Mangyong River in the center, the Tongjin River in the south, and numerous short streams join with the Kum River, which flows from the northeast. The resulting plain—remarkably flat and favored with rich alluvium—is excellently suited to cultivation by modern agricultural techniques. The occasional eroded granitic hills in this area are no real handicap to production, for they provide a shelter to the villages and a base for the transportation lines. Similar alluvial plains, though less extensive, are found throughout the region.

In the southern part of the region the plains are down-faulted areas in the diverse hill structure. Here, one is never out of sight of hills and mountains, the offshoots of the Sobaek Range, which culminates in the southwest in massive Chiri-san. At almost cross angles to this range are east-west trending mountains, the so-called Han-San system, which are of more recent geologic formation than the Sobaek system. Consequently, the extreme southwestern section of the region is a veritable maze of peninsulas, hills, islands, and interior basins—such as the Namwon plain. Some of the stream valleys follow the structural lines for long distances; others are superimposed in winding courses.

The coast line at the end of the peninsula has been submerged, and the crenulation of peninsulas and islands is of the typical ria variety. The amount of arable land is limited, but catchment basins in the hill lands have been used to develop excellent irrigation systems for the profusion of paddy fields.

The climate of Southwestern Korea is one of its greatest assets. In the spring the weather is relatively mild, and a slight secondary maximum of rainfall in April affords sufficient water for the rice seedbeds and for preparing the paddy fields. In the early summer, after the rice has been transplanted, the rainfall is heavy. The temperatures are high, and humidity is great. This is fine weather for growing rice. The peak of the rainy season is reached in early August, and in September the relative dryness enables the farmers to drain the paddies, harvest their crops, and prepare the land for winter crops. This double-cropping is particularly important, since the farmers, or their landlords, usually sell the rice crop. Occasional typhoons upset the usual farming procedures by causing heavy rains and violent winds in the early fall, but the rice crop can usually be saved. Fortunately, the fall and winter seasons are mild, so that winter crops, commonly barley, provide a food crop for the farmer and his family.

The diverse topography of the region accounts for the wide range of climatic differences. The southward-facing slopes of the Sobaek Range receive heavy rainfall; Sunchon, for example, which is situated at the foot of the Chiri-san massif gets sixty inches of annual rainfall, of which thirty-two inches come in the three months of summer. However, Mokpo, also located on the coast, but not backed by high mountains, gets 42.5 inches.

Winter temperatures vary, the northern and interior parts of the region having temperatures two or three degrees below freezing for the January average, while along the coast the average January temperatures are two or three degrees above freezing. Summer temperatures throughout the region average between 79° and 81° F. in August.

Southwestern Korea's population has been increasing, though not so sharply as in some other parts of the peninsula. In 1925 the population for the 7,430 square miles making up the region was 3,404,283; in 1940 it was 4,175,838, making a density of 563.3 persons per square mile. Unlike West Central Korea, where Seoul is located, the region has no very large cities. Interior cities such as Kwangju (1940 population: 64,520) in the south, and Chonju (47,230) in the north, were the old-time economic and political centers. More recently, new cities have developed, but none of these can be classed as large urban centers. From the standpoint of densities of rural population the region ranks first in Korea. On the Kum River plain— the best rice-growing area—are four counties each having densities of more than 723 persons per square mile.

It was upon this region, with its fertile soil and high rural population, that the Japanese imposed their most extensive agricultural modernizations. They set about reclaiming land, building irrigation systems—some of which also served as sources of power—and breaking the Koreans from their centuries-old farm practices. Under the control of such organizations as the Oriental Development Company, the farmers were taught to select seed carefully, to transplant rice shoots in even rows, to fertilize their crops, and to cultivate and harvest with machines. Yields jumped tremendously, and rice warehouses—usually roofed with galvanized iron sheeting emblazoned with the trademark of a Japanese company—dotted the countryside along new truck highways and rail lines.

Caught in the rush and turmoil of this revolution, many of

the Korean farmers of the region lost their holdings. Unable to pay for assessments on irrigation projects, they became tenants or hired laborers. Korean living standards declined, particularly in those years when winter crops failed to produce a good yield of cereals. The tenancy became increasingly acute. The relatively benevolent practices of the semi-feudal days of old Korea, when the landlords had responsibilities for the well-being of their tenants, gave way to harsh practices of impersonal companies and rapacious agents. Many of the peasants became so destitute that despite their living in a land of plenty, "spring hunger" drove them to the hills to gather bark and roots in order to subsist until the grain harvest.

However, in many of the villages in the hill lands, and in the interior basins, traditional Oriental agriculture managed to resist the full tide of change. On the surface, at least, village life continued in the old pattern. The farm boys raked the hillsides for leaves and twigs, the girls fed mulberry leaves to silk worms, the women incessantly beat on the family's cotton clothing to keep it white, and the farmers toiled in their rice paddies and their other fields hoping that nature would be kind. Even there, however, ancient social lines were breached. The class of *yangban*'s—made up of scholars and landowners—who tried to segregate themselves and their fellow villagers from the shock of modern times and developments, slowly gave way. Many of them lost their lands; on the whole, class lines tended to disappear.

With the defeat of the Japanese and their expulsion, rice production in Southwestern Korea fell off drastically. Much of the production had been destined for export and these markets were not open because of the general postwar economic and political confusion in the Far East. However, two other reasons were also important: the Korean farmers were unable to obtain sufficient fertilizers, despite imports under aid programs from America; and the redistribution of lands held by Japanese companies, which took place, belatedly, in 1948, caused some of the large commercialized projects, well-irrigated and efficiently operated, to be cut up into small holdings owned by individual farmers. Though the redistribution did much to relieve the distress of the farm workers and set a good example for the redistribution of the land held by Korean landlords it meant a decided reduction in the amount of rice which reached the open market. Consequences of the reduced production and availability of rice became evident when hordes of hungry refugees crowded into the area following the invasion of South Korea.

Fortunately, Southwestern Korea was spared the great devastation to which other sections of the country were subjected during the Korean war. Spearheads of the Communist forces were unable to entrench themselves, and the farms and cities remained, on the whole, intact. Guerrilla warfare did a considerable amount of damage through sabotage and keeping the countryside in turmoil. The production situation, crucial to begin with, became even worse when the region's large reservoir of manpower was tapped to provide soldiers and laborers for the South Korean and United Nations forces. In recent years there has been a great increase in fertilizer imports, and the labor supply has been somewhat stabilized; the region is again becoming the rice bowl of Korea.

The two sections of Southwestern Korea that call for special comment because of their distinctive geographic character are the northern plains and the extreme southern coast. The first of these, Korea's largest plains, includes the highly productive flood plain of the Kum River and other similar river plains. Some of the land has been reclaimed from the sea. The plain is not continuous but is broken by remnants of old earth-folds that appear even more abrupt because of the flatness of the alluvial plains. The principal cities of the section are Taejon (1940 population: 45,541) and Kunsan (40,553). The former is important as a rice-milling center and as the junction point of the main north-south rail line and the line extending into the southwest; the latter has been a major port for exporting rice. Both cities show decided Japanese influence with their straight streets and Japanese-style buildings, particularly the large rice warehouses. Taejon was badly battered during the Communist advance and retreat, but it is fast being rebuilt because of its strategic supply location.

The extreme southern coast of the region is interesting because of its complex physiography, a confusion of plains, peninsulas, and islands, and its relatively mild winters influenced by its maritime position. The economy of the section is largely centered in rice production and fishing, though in the interior valleys the cultivation of cotton is increasing in importance. The Japanese developed two ports in this section—Mokpo (1940 population: 64,256), which is the terminus of the southwest rail line; and Yosu, a new port and also a rail terminus, located in the eastern part of the section. The constantly changing vistas which one sees as he travels along this coast are entrancing.

## Southeastern Korea

Southeastern Korea is most simply described as a basin of hills and valleys drained by the Naktong River and bordered, on the west and north, by the Central and Southern Mountains. Though the mountains are not extremely high, they serve as the boundary line of the region and tend to isolate it from the rest of the peninsula. The entire region lies within the confines of Kyongsang, long a distinct political unit, though in recent times for administrative convenience it was divided into a northern and a southern province.

The physiographic character of the region is marked by con-

siderable homogeneity. In distant geologic times it was a part of a basin in which a series of sedimentary strata (and in certain periods some lava and volcanic ash deposits) were laid. The basin was extensive, for these strata may be correlated with some of those found in southwestern Japan. Following this lengthy period of deposition, the strata were contorted by the warping and breaking of the earth's crust. The northern area, which now appears as an extension of the Taebaek Range, was subject to considerable faulting and bending, as was the western area adjacent to the present Sobaek Range. In addition, the whole basin was uplifted or warped upward. Subsequently, the Naktong River, its tributaries, and other streams cut down into this basin structure. Later, more uplift took place, so that the present river patterns are attributable to the streams following lines of structural weakness or to the entrenchment of the rivers in their previous channels. Some of the most ancient rocks of the region were arched up and are now exposed on the surface, but most of the surface strata are the sedimentaries, or the igneous rocks laid down in the basin.

The Naktong and the other rivers, as a glance at a map will show, follow winding channels, in some places cutting through structural ridges in steep-walled canyons. Along the rivers and in some valleys are ribbons of alluvial material, but most of the terrain is made up of hill slopes. Consequently, the amount of good agricultural land is limited; and terraced fields and dry fields are in higher proportion than in the western plains and hills of Korea.

Southeastern Korea's climate is well suited to intensive agricultural production. The summers are hot and very humid; heavy convectional and cyclonic rainfall accompany the indrifting monsoon air masses. The annual rainfall averages forty inches, with more than twenty-five inches in the four summer months. Temperatures in August average 80° F. in the interior plains. The winters are relatively mild; the 32° F. average isotherm for January runs closely parallel to the coast. Precipitation in the winter is light.

As early as 57 B.C. this temperate region, with its forested hills and fertile valleys, was the center of a flourishing culture. The Silla kingdom, one of three kingdoms in Korea at that time, had its capital at Kyongju, in the eastern part of the region. Following the introduction of Buddhism from China, it became a religious and art center as well. Even today the people of the region—who have a pronounced provincial loyalty—speak of the glory of the Silla kingdom which grew so powerful that between 668 and 918 A.D. it controlled almost all the peninsula.

But Silla had difficulty surviving. In 935 it was absorbed by the rival Koryo dynasty. For long periods of time the region was subject to attacks from Japanese pirates, who not only ravaged the coasts but on one occasion even sacked the capital city. The Japanese also had virtual control of a small kingdom, Karak, located on the southern fringe of the region, near the present city of Pusan. The Korean's powerful defensive measure was to build their towns back from the coast. The most devastating Japanese attack came when, from 1592 to 1598, under orders from Hideyoshi, the Japanese leader, they used the region as a beachhead for an abortive attack on Korea and China.

Between 1905 and 1945, when all of Korea was under Japanese control, the southeastern region was especially used by the Japanese. Pusan was the major transit point between Japan and the peninsula; this economic bridgehead soon widened to include much of the region, as Japanese developed commercial and transportation centers. The Japanese exerted a profound economic influence, developing irrigation works, fostering the production of rice, cotton, soy beans, mulberry, tobacco, fruits —in general commercializing the simple agricultural economy.

In this region, as is the case in Southwestern Korea, rice is the principal crop and double-cropping the general practice. Every available acre of tillable land is used to push production. The valley floors are covered with paddy fields, and on the hill slopes, where irrigation is impracticable, dry fields abound. Most of the fields are used for two or more crops a year. For example, in 1930 in North Kyongsang Province, the frequency of land utilized was 182 for paddy fields and 183 for dry fields; in South Kyongsang the figures were 208 and 184. (A figure of 200 would mean that the fields were used twice in the year.) In recent years there has been even greater intensification in the use of the crop land.

As might be expected in a region with only two large cities and with relatively few mines and industrial areas, the population is densely crowded in farming villages and towns along the river valleys. The average density per square mile in 1940 was 404.3 persons—this is an area of 10,798 square miles whose total population in 1940 numbered 4,365,894. The population explosion experienced in recent years by many other regions of the peninsula appeared not to have seriously affected the southeast; the population in 1925 numbered 4,028,193. However, these figures are slightly misleading since it was from this region especially that many Koreans migrated to Japan to work in industrial centers there.

A few cities are of more than local importance in this region. Kyongju has diminished greatly from its days of glory as the capital of the Silla kingdom and is now only a market town, surrounded by burial mounds, temples, and memorial stones which attest to its past greatness. The major city in the center of the region is Taegu (1940 population: 178,923), which has grown from its position as a rural center to become a commercial and manufacturing city, notable for textile and other consumer goods production. The largest city of the southern part of the region is Pusan, the doorway to Korea. In 1940 it had a population of 249,734 persons, of whom 57,281 were Japanese. In addition there are other fishing ports and one former naval base —Chinhae—along the southern and eastern coasts.

The principal transportation artery of the region is, of course, Korea's main north-south railroad, which begins at Pusan and runs northwest to Taegu, over the Sobaek Range to Taejon on the plains of western Korea, and from there to Seoul and on to the north. Important branch lines include one which follows roughly parallel to the coast to Chinju in the southwestern part of the region and another which goes east from Taegu to the port of Pohang on the Sea of Japan. The tracks on a line east from Kumchon (on the Pusan-Seoul line) to Andong were taken up during World War II to be used on a new line that was completed at that time north from Pusan through the Kyongju plain to Andong and from there west through the Central Mountains into the Han River basin to Seoul.

This region is predominantly agricultural. The venerable temples and pavilions, the stolid tiled-roofed *yangban*'s houses, and the innumerable closely-packed farm homes in the villages attest to the centuries of human occupance. Most of the farmers are still dependent upon the old-style irrigation systems. The water is caught from rainfall in small reservoirs with earthen dams in the side valleys. From these the water is diverted by gravity flow out on the alluvial slopes on the valley floors. The antiquity of some of these systems may be noted by the old gnarled trees which border the canals; more recently poplars have been planted along them. In many cases the channels have not been kept clear, rather the dikes have been built up; consequently, over the centuries, they may have been raised to six or eight feet above the levels of the fields. When the forests on the hill slopes have been overcut (as has been the case recently) the rush of water after a heavy rain will cause breaks in the canals and gravel will be washed out, ruining the fertile fields. As has been noted, the fields are intensively cultivated. This has only been possible through the use of large quantities of fertilizer. In this part of Korea human waste is often used as manure on the fields, a practice which is not very commonly followed in other parts of the peninsula. Commercial fertilizer was introduced and greatly used in the days of Japanese control. This practice has been continued with the help of American programs after Korea's liberation. In addition to the common crops grown in Korea, fruits—persimmons, pears, and apples— are produced. Bamboo groves are located around the villages and bamboo is used for many household articles. In some districts, especially where the soil is sandy, tobacco is a distinctive crop, and the tobacco drying sheds are seen in the villages.

Two sections of Southeastern Korea warrant special mention: the northeastern mountain section and the coastal fringe. The interior basin around Taegu and the Kyongju plain are unique in some ways, but, in general, they have the same characteristics as the rest of the region. The Taegu basin is noted for having the highest summer temperatures in Korea.

The northeastern mountains are a southward extension of the Taebaek Range of central Korea with elevations running from three thousand to five thousand feet. The population densities are relatively low, as much of the land is composed of forested mountains. Though the Japanese exploited the better stands of timber, what remains could provide an enduring and important resource if it were properly managed. Unfortunately, the second growths which are now found are not commercially valuable. Farming, of course, is handicapped by the short growing season. Double-cropping is carried on only in the lower elevations, and fast-maturing buckwheat is grown as a catch crop if the regular cereals are harmed by frost. The mineral resources in the complex mountain structure are of potential importance, though mining developments in the section hardly compare to those in the section to the immediate north in the central mountains.

Of much greater economic importance for the region is the section along the coast which, physiographically and climatically, is very similar to the southernmost section of Southwestern Korea. Complex lines of geologic structure and fluctuations of land levels have produced numerous bays and islands; the climate is mild, with January temperatures averaging above freezing. The pocketed plains, which are intensively cultivated, and the fishing waters along the coast support dense populations. Under the Japanese, fishing expanded into a major industry, as did also the gathering and processing of seaweed on the offshore islands. The seaweed had a large market as a supplement to the usual cereal diet in Korea and Japan.

But, above all, the section is noted for its excellent harbors—Masan, Chinhae, Ulsan, Pohang, and, especially, Pusan, Korea's leading port and one of its largest cities. Sheltered by islands, Pusan's deep natural harbor was early developed by the Japanese. It is a city of wharves, warehouses, and important factories for manufacturing consumer goods. Its industrial development has been handicapped, however, by a lack of power. It is almost wholly dependent on thermal power generated from coal in the Yongwol area in the central mountains, and brought in on high tension wires; or on a local plant which utilizes imported coal and, recently, as an emergency measure, on power from a Diesel plant on a barge.

If Pusan's docks and railroad facilities had been lost by the United Nations and South Korean troops to the North Korean Communist invaders in the summer of 1950, the history of the Korean war would be even more grim. During the early stages of the fighting the beachhead was reduced to a narrow crescent, but after men and supplies had poured in through the port the United Nations forces again took the initiative. Aided by the landing at Inchon in western Korea, they rolled back the invaders. The fighting along the Naktong River and in the hills and valleys of Southeastern Korea was severe; numerous villages were destroyed; abandoned tanks and trucks are rusted symbols of the fighting along the major transportation routes.

Though Pusan itself was not devastated by actual fighting, the effects of the hostilities on the city and its surrounding region were tremendous. Refugees crowd every possible shelter, and packing-case houses have become a new type of architecture. The fires that have broken out (or were set by saboteurs) on occasion have swept through parts of the city and created intense suffering. For a while the city became the temporary capital for the Republic and the offshore islands were turned into stockades for prisoners of war.

## Cheju

CHEJU

0   100

Cheju Island, lying some sixty miles off the southwestern coast, is Korea's largest island. It is an elliptical-shaped land mass, some 718 square miles in area. Because of an early account by a shipwrecked Dutch sailor, Cheju (or, as he called it, Quelpart) is not unknown in Western literature. In the last few years it has been used as a haven for tens of thousands of Koreans who have been forced from the mainland. The island is composed of two counties, the north and the south, designated in part according to differences in climate and economy on each side of the island. The major city and port, Cheju, on the north shore, had a population of 57,905 in 1949.

The island is composed of a core of volcanic material which rises in symmetrical form to the crest of Halla-san, 6,450 feet in height. Around this mountain mass lies a deep series of lava flows out of which numerous other volcanic cones have erupted. The volcanism which formed the island is of relatively recent geologic age; Halla-san itself was last active in 1007 A.D. The lava flows are covered with rocks and small amounts of ash. Because of the columnar structure and the prevalence of ash, water can soak rapidly in the volcanic material so that there are few surface streams. Except for a few patches of alluvial and uplifted alluvial materials near the coast, the land is relatively infertile.

Its maritime location in relatively low latitudes makes Cheju's climate extremely mild. It has the warmest winters of any region in Korea; the average January temperatures at the city of Cheju on the north coast are 40° F., and it is even warmer on the south coast. Summer temperatures are slightly modified by the maritime influence but are still hot; at Cheju August temperatures average 78° F. The average yearly rainfall at Cheju is fairly heavy, fifty-five inches, most of it occurring in the summer months.

Because of the symmetrical shape of the mountain mass, climate and vegetation vary according to a series of concentric zones. At the lowest elevation are sub-tropical plants; these give place to deciduous forests and then to conifers and finally, at the highest elevation, to alpine plants. The natural vegetation is luxurious where it can get a hold in the rocky soil. However, many of the forests were cut for shipbuilding timber at the time of the Mongol invasion of Japan in 1274 and have never been replaced; other forests were cut in more recent times to provide rotting wood for mushroom growing. Today much of the land is bare and grass-covered and not suitable for crops. Some of the cut-over upland areas were developed into pasture land, and the islanders became famous for breeding ponies and horses. This type of grazing economy was introduced by the Mongols and has remained as a dominant form of land use. When the Japanese gained control of the island, they supplied better breeds of horses and in recent decades over seventy per cent of Korea's horses were raised on the island. However, with the mechanization of transportation and the loss of markets, horse-raising in Cheju has declined. Cattle and goats are now raised on the upland pastures. Cheju is virtually the only region in Korea where grazing occupies an important place in the economy.

Agricultural possibilities are limited by the sterile soil; paddy fields cannot be developed except on a few tiny patches. On the lower mountain slopes, however, dry fields are quite extensive. Hardy cereals—like millet, barley, and buckwheat—and soy beans, and sweet potatoes are the usual crops. Specialty crops include oranges and winter vegetables.

In addition to the grazing and agricultural industries, fishing is of considerable importance, though in recent years most of the commercial fishing in the waters around Cheju has been carried on from bases on the peninsula and Japan. The island fishermen lack modern equipment and easy access to markets. However, some distinctive products are seaweed, shellfish, and pearl oysters, which are obtained by sea diving in the coastal waters. Much of the diving industry is virtually monopolized by organizations of skilled women divers.

This traditional feminine occupation gave rise to several interesting features of Cheju's social and political life. For many centuries Cheju was dominated by a matriarchal system. The women were described as Amazons and were the subject of many bizarre tales. Perhaps, too, because of this distinctive feature of its economy, the population of Cheju even in recent years numbers more women than men, the reverse of the situation on the Korean peninsula. Of the total population of 254,-589 persons in 1949, 139,830 were women and 114,759 were men. The density of population for the island as a whole in 1940 was 297.6 persons per square mile, a relatively high figure, considering the physical limitations of the economy. Most of the population is concentrated in a narrow belt along the coast. After the Korean war broke out there was a tremendous influx from the peninsula, particularly of women and children; this boosted the ratio of women to men even higher.

Another unique social and political feature of Cheju is that the island was long used by the Korean court as a place to which dissident political factions and their families were exiled from time to time, especially after periods of political upheaval. Some of these exiles settled permanently on the island, although they were slow in sinking their roots.

The landscapes of Cheju differ in many ways from those of the neighboring peninsula. The virtual absence of paddy fields is most striking. The walls of the houses are usually made of basaltic rock, and the eaves of the thatch roofs extend far out over the walls. The houses and villages are arranged in distinctive patterns, protected from the sea winds. Stone fences are common. The people traditionally wear colored clothing rather than white. Other differences may also be noted. For example, the ordinary diet emphasizes, not rice, but millet, other cereals, and fish. This food is eaten from bowls made of wood rather than brass or clay.

In recognition of its cultural and economic distinctness, Cheju was separated politically from South Cholla Province in 1948 and made into a province. Thus it again achieved a status somewhat similar to what it had possessed centuries before, when it was an independent matriarchy.

Cheju was considered as a possible base for resistance in the dark days of the war when the loss of the Pusan perimeter seemed imminent; yet the island would have made a poor base, as its only advantage is its isolation from the peninsula. However, military training bases and some large refugee camps have been established on the island.

## Ullung

Ullung Island—called Dagelet Island by early Western voyagers— is situated about eighty miles off the East Central Coast. Like Cheju, it is of volcanic origin. Though its area is only twenty-eight square miles and its population in 1940 was only 13,502, Ullung is considered a separate geographic region of Korea. A few miles east of Ullung is Tokto (or Takeshima), a rocky, uninhabited island which is the cause of a rather meaningless and irritating dispute between Japan and Korea over its possession and the use of the seaweed beds around it.

Geologically the island is a segment of an elongated zone of structural weakness and volcanism which starts in Paektu-san and trends southward through Ullung. From there the zone may be traced, with difficulty, to Japan. The island is not one symmetrical volcano but a series of lava flows which have been subjected to tilting and faulting. From time to time the volcanism has reoccurred. The most recent caldera is not the highest part of the island, for one of the edges of the tilted lava flows has the highest elevation, 3,200 feet. The terrain is mountainous and rocky, and the lava flows have a palisade structure. Obviously the amount of arable land is severely limited, and there are few harbors along the forbidding coast line.

Ullung has some distinctive climatic features, the most interesting being that the island has no dry season. The precipitation reaches one peak in July, which is normal for Korea. However, there is abundant winter precipitation and, in addition, the typhoon season causes heavy rainfall in September. The yearly rainfall averages fifty-nine inches.

For many centuries Ullung Island was a fishing base and a source of forest products, without much permanent settlement. The magnificent stands of deciduous and coniferous trees, however, were largely exhausted by ruthless cutting to provide ship and temple timbers and charcoal. With the clearing of forests, agricultural settlement of a permanent character took place. In 1949 the population numbered 14,688 persons.

Most of the residents live in small coastal villages or in the mountain valleys. Their houses are similar to those found in the forested lands in northern Korea, with heavy shingled roofs held down by rocks. In the isolated valleys of the mountainous interior some of the settlements are on a pioneer basis similar to those of the fire-field folk in the mountains of northern and central Korea. Farming is limited to dry-field cultivation. White potatoes, corn, and cereals, including winter barley, are the common food crops, and hemp and poor grades of cotton are grown for making cloth. The Japanese attempted to introduce sheep-grazing in the upland pastures, but this was not notably successful.

This isolated island has been by-passed, fortunately, by the Korean war, though a very small island nearby was practically wiped off the map when United Nations planes returning from an unsuccessful air raid in North Korea dumped their bombs inadvertently. The fact that the war has not had a direct influence on Ullung makes it distinctive among the regions of Korea, a distinction which doubtless the inhabitants of the other regions wish they could share.

# Chapter 11 | Conclusion

KOREA'S heritage—its geographical location and diversity —has been stressed throughout this book. It must not be concluded, however, that these factors are the only factors which affect Korea's future. In this day of dynamic changes in resource development, in cultural assimilations, in political and military tensions, in ideological conflicts, and in the many other features of daily life for the individual, nations, and the world, many factors will play a part in the solution of Korea's problems. It has not been the purpose of this book to treat all of these factors but rather to summarize the social geography, briefly to describe the geographic regions and to bring focus upon the geographic factors in Korea which are often neglected.

Three geographic realities are of paramount importance in Korea: its peninsular location in the heart of the Far East, its essential unity, and its geographic diversity. The last two items may seem to be contradictory, but they are not. The warp and woof of diverse physical and human features of the geography of Korea result in a colorful tapestry of landscapes but the total pattern has unity and differs decidedly from the geography of its neighbors in the Far East and the world. These realities naturally give rise to the conclusion that for peace and well-being to come to Korea the peninsula must have cordial relations with the other nations of the Far East, be independent and unified, and be able to profit from its regional resource pattern in building economic strength for all of its people. These possibilities seem remote today, though the avowed aim of all groups within Korea and the nations who play a role in Korean affairs is for "a unified, independent, and democratic Korea." Regrettably, these simple words have quite different interpretations to different people.

The impact of the Korean war on the lives of the Korean people, the sharpened cleavages between North and South Korea have brought about inestimable damage. With the influx of Chinese Communist armies into North Korea and subsequent political and military developments, North Korea is becoming less and less independent, more and more a satellite or "march," as part of it was centuries ago, on the border of Communist China and the Soviet Union. Economic ties are being tightly forged which seem to give temporary benefit to the North Koreans but in the long run will be of great value to Communist China, who has need of the resources of North Korea, especially its hydroelectric power. The South Korean economy is being bolstered by aid from the United Nations and particularly the United States, aid which cannot be given in great amounts and for long periods without repercussions.

The physical damage of the Korean war both in the north and south is being gradually repaired as the uneasy truce is maintained. But this is a slow process, for the havoc was tremendous. Measured in dollars, an inadequate measure, the destruction in North Korea, according to a Pyongyang radio broadcast, was over $1,000,000,000. In South Korea, according to an official report, it was over $3,000,000,000. A mere recital of figures of factories, bridges, locomotives, homes, and other physical facilities utterly or partially destroyed does not bring home so vividly the havoc as one trip through an industrial suburb of Seoul. Rubble, shells of factories, large empty holes where buildings once stood, mangled railroad locomotives, all overlaid with dust and dirt oppress a visitor.

But more than the physical damage have been the social and ideological shocks of the war on the Korean people. In the north "brain-washing" and regimentation have been the result of Communist control. In the south it is countered by a deep and soul-warping hatred. These intangibles cannot be easily measured, but they can be sensed and felt in conversations with people who have been in the north and are now in the south. Many people talk of loved ones who have died during the war or, almost worse from the standpoint of mental tensions, have simply disappeared or been taken into captivity. The horrors of war are very real to the Korean people.

Yet, as one gets out into the countryside the physical damage of the war is seldom seen, and the Korean farmers, the mainstay of the Korean economy, go on about their work. Their life is hard now, just as it has been throughout the past centuries. They do not have the tools or animals with which to work and yet with the increase of population they must feed many more people than they did in the past. One of the major exports of Korea before 1945 was rice; it furnished a means by which needed consumer and capital goods could be imported; it could do so again if production could be expanded and the channels of trade opened up. A real challenge in Korea lies in improving the agricultural life of the country—curtailment of the erosion of the barren hills, clothing them with trees which could furnish fuel and timber on a regulated basis, reclamation and improvement of agricultural lands, increased technical efficiency in agricultural production, establishment of fair rural credit practices, introduction of labor saving devices for peak seasonal work and of cottage industries for slack times, diversification and improvement of the diet through stress on new crops, rehabilitation of the fishing industry and development of animal husbandry —these and many other changes are possible. But such changes are difficult to achieve without widespread modification in the financial and governmental situations in Korea.

Along with agricultural improvement should go industrial rehabilitation. The resources of Korea are not limitless; there are many serious deficiencies for modern industrial life. The considerable potential which was developed under the aegis of the Japanese for their purposes could be redeveloped and expanded for peaceful objectives, for the improvement of living standards and for the absorption into productive work of the increasing population. Industrialization of Korea has many complexities. Of fundamental importance is the relation of Korea to its neighbors and the unification of the country. Again financial and governmental policies will play very large roles. Cultural change as a result of industrialization has taken place and will continue at an accelerated pace.

Both agricultural improvement and industrialization are possible in large part because of the nature of the Korean people. In fact, the human resources are the most valuable which Korea possesses. The Koreans have their faults, they are only human. But they also have their strengths—strengths which have enabled them to survive in difficult times in the past, as they are surviving today.

The future for Korea cannot with fairness be pictured in rosy hues. Life for the Koreans will be difficult. They will need all of the tenacity and the resilience they have evidenced in the past. But their heritage, as it causes problems, also opens up opportunities. The importance of that heritage is well known to every Korean; it should be known, as well, by all who are concerned with helping Korea to take its rightful place in a peaceful world.

# APPENDICES

# *Appendix A* | Bibliographical References and Notes

No attempt is made in this appendix to present extensive bibliographies on every facet of Korean geography. Rather, mention is only made of books and other materials, predominantly in Western languages, which are relatively easy to obtain in large libraries or through inter-library loans. I have purposely stressed my own publications to give the background of my research.

Something of great value to American scholars interested in Korea, a real milestone in Koreanology, is the *Korean Studies Guide*, University of California Press, Berkeley, 1954. This guide, prepared by students and members of the staff of the East Asiatic Institute of the University of California: Benjamin L. Hazard, Jr., James M. Hoyt, Warren M. Smith, and Kim Hai-tai, and edited by Richard Marcus, comprises a comprehensive annotated bibliography of published material on Korea. It understandably emphasizes Korean historical materials but gives a coverage of other materials, including bibliographies and reference works.

I prepared a brief and selected list of books about Korea in 1949 for classroom use and as a lead to students starting to learn about Korea. This was revised in March, 1950 and published with additions as : *Bibliography of Western Language Material on Korea*, International Secretariat, Institute of Pacific Relations, New York, 17 pages (mimeographed), September, 1950.

A very valuable series are the following bibliographies which were prepared in the summer of 1950 at the Library of Congress :

*Korea—An Annotated Bibliography of Publications in Western Languages*. Compiled by Helen Dudenbostel Jones and Robin L. Winkler, Reference Department, Library of Congress, Washington, ix, 155 pages, 753 items, August, 1950.

*Korea—An Annotated Bibliography of Publications in the Russian Language*. Compiled by Albert Parry, John T. Dorosh, and Elizabeth Gardner Dorosh, Reference Department, Library of Congress, Washington, xi, 84 pages, 436 items, August, 1950.

*Korea—An Annotated Bibliography of Publications in Far Eastern Languages*. Compiled under the direction of Edwin G. Beal, Jr., with the assistance of Robin L. Winkler, Reference Department, Library of Congress, Washington, viii, 167 pages, 528 items, August, 1950.

1. Almost all geographies of Korea have stressed the significance of the peninsular location of Korea. Five basic geographies which have been published recently are worthy of special mention. They have been used a great deal in the preparation of this book and I am much indebted to these works, particularly those of Hermann Lautensach. I reviewed some of these, plus some other

current geographic works, in a note : "Recent Geographical Works on Korea," *The Far Eastern Quarterly*, Vol. XII, No. 2, pages 222–25, February, 1953.

Herman Lautensach, *Korea, Eine Landeskunde auf Grund eigener Reisen und der Literatur*, K. F. Koehler Verlag, Leipzig, xv, 542 pages, 1945.

Hermann Lautensach, *Korea, Land, Volk, Schicksal*, K. F. Koehler Verlag, Stuttgart, 135 pages, 1950.

V. T. Zaichikov, *Koreia*, National Institute of Geographical Literature, Moscow, I Edition, 228 pages, 1947, II Edition, 480 pages, 1951.

*Geography of Korea*, by V. T. Zaichikov, translation of the first edition by Albert Parry, with an introduction and notes by Shannon McCune, International Secretariat, Institute of Pacific Relations, vii, 142 pages, (mimeographed), 1952.

*Korea, A Geographical Appreciation*, Foreign Geography Information Series No. 4, Geographical Branch, Department of Mines and Technical Surveys, Ottawa, vi, 84 pages, 1951.

Three geographical works, though not in Western languages and aimed at general audiences, are of value particularly for maps and pictures :

Pak No-sik, *Sin Choson Chiri* (New Geography of Korea), Tongjisa, Seoul, Korea, 2, 2, 3, 3, 130 pages, 1947 (In Korean).

*Nihon Chiri Taikei* (Outline of Japanese Geography), *Chosen-hen* (Volume on Korea), Kaizo-sha, Tokyo, Edited by Sansei Yamamoto, 416 pages, 1930 (In Japanese).

*Nihon Chiri Fuzoku Taikei* (Outline of Japanese Geography and Customs), *Chosen Chiho* (Korean area), Seibundo Shinkosha, Tokyo, 399 and 404 pages, 1937. (In Japanese).

2. Korea is a very well-mapped land. The whole peninsula was mapped topographically at a scale of 1 : 50,000 by the Japanese during their early days of control ; some 723 sheets were published; the only exceptions were of strategic areas. These maps were the base for a series at the same scale prepared by the United States Army Map Service ; these maps are constantly being revised and corrected on the basis of aerial photography and other information. In addition there are maps at other scales, such as 1 : 250,000 and 1 : 1,000,000 which are readily available. Other maps at scales of 1 : 25,000 and composite aerial photographic maps at scales of 1 : 12,500 and 1 : 25,000 are, unfortunately, not generally available.

For a fuller account of the map coverage of the peninsula see my note : "Maps of Korea," *The Far Eastern Quarterly*, Vol. V, No. 3, pages 326–29, May, 1946.

3. An interesting treatment of the concept of Korea as a Confucian state was given in M. Frederick Nelson's *Korea and the Old Orders in Eastern Asia*, Louisiana State University Press, Baton Rouge, xvi, 326 pages, 1945.

A cartographic presentation of this concept was in some old maps of the world prepared by Korean scholars in past centuries. I discussed these in an article : "Old Korean World Maps," *Korean Review*, Korean–American Cultural Association, Inc., Seattle, Washington, Vol. II, No. 1, pages 14–17, September, 1949.

4. Korea's geology has been well studied by Japanese and other geologists. I prepared a brief bibliography of some of these studies a few years ago : "Geomorphology of Korea : A Selected Bibliography," *Research Monographs on Korea*, Series C, No. 1, 7 pages, November 1, 1941. Early accounts, which are still of value, are those of Bunjiro Koto : "An Orographic Sketch of Korea,"

*Journal of the College of Science, Tokyo Imperial University,* Article 1, Vol. 19, Tokyo, 1903, and " Journeys through Korea...," Article 2, Vol. 20, Tokyo, 1904.

One of the most useful studies in English is that of Teiichi Kobayashi, " Sketch of Korean Geology," *American Journal of Science,* series 4, Vol. 26, pages 585–606, December, 1933. The same scholar has recently published a more detailed account of part of Korea: "Geology of South Korea," *Journal of the Faculty of Science, University of Tokyo,* Section II, Geology, Mineralogy, Geography, Geophysics, Vol. VIII, Part 4, pages 145–293, Tokyo, Japan, March 31, 1953. This has a very complete bibliography and sums up the work of many Japanese geologists.

A very brief account of Korea's stratigraphy is worth quoting in full ; it comes from *Mineral Resources of Southern Korea,* Report No. 84, Natural Resources Section, General Headquarters, Supreme Commander Allied Powers, Tokyo, 50 pages, 28 July, 1947, quotation on page 8 :

1. The Korean peninsula consists mainly of gneisses and granites that occupy more than half of the land area. Small blocks and wedges of Paleozoic and Mesozoic rocks are among the gneisses and granites, and Cenozoic rocks occur in some places.

2. Geologically, Korea is the top of a tremendous late Cretaceous batholith of granite, studded with roof pendants of older rocks. This granite, encountered in all parts of Korea, has not been previously named, except locally. The genesis of most ore deposits is attributed to it. It is here referred to as the " Young Granite " to distinguish it from the old pre-Cambrian granite of Korea.

3. The lithologic character and stratigraphic succession of the older rocks, from the Archean to the early Mesozoic, are similar to those of southern Manchuria and northern China. The lithology and stratigraphy of the younger rocks, from middle Mesozoic to Recent, resemble more closely those of the Japanese islands.

4. Korea may be divided geologically into two principal parts, called northern and southern Korea, along the tectonic line that trends north north-eastward from Seoul to Wonsan. Both areas contain abundant gneisses and granites. In the southern part of northern Korea is a large area of Paleozoic rocks, and in the southeast part of southern Korea is the chief area of Mesozoic rocks.

5. One of the most notable features of the geology of Korea is the hiatus in the middle of the Paleozoic. It is the same hiatus found in southern Manchuria and northern China.

6. Most of the Korean sedimentary rocks younger than the Permian are terrestrial or basin deposits ; post-Permian marine deposits are rare. The volcanic rocks erupted in Cenozoic times are chiefly alkalic rocks. Volcanic activity has ceased and earthquakes are almost nil.

5. A system of geomorphic provinces was developed after my field work in Korea and study of the literature in 1940 and 1941. A summary was published as an accompaniment to a physiographic diagram drawn by Arthur H. Robinson: " Notes on a Physiographic Diagram of Tyosen (Korea)," *Geographical Review,* Vol. XXXI, No. 4, pages 653–58, October, 1941.

Another classification of terrain regions is given in *Korean Environment,* Report No. 171, Environmental Protection Section, Research and Development Branch, Military Planning Division, Office of the Quartermaster-General, Depart-

ment of the Army, Washington, D. C., i, 25 pages, December, 1950. This classification includes seven regions in the peninsula :
    a.  South Coast
    b.  Southeastern Basin
    c.  East Coast
    d.  Southern Highlands
    e.  West Coast
    f.  North Central Highlands
    g.  Northern Mountains

A more intricate system was prepared by Frederick K. Morris and published in *Terrain and Climate of Korea and Adjacent Lands*, Arctic, Desert, Tropic Information Center, Research Studies Institute, Air University, Maxwell Field Air Force Base, Alabama, ADTIC Publication G–102, vii, 27 pages, January, 1952.

6.  The effect of the terrain on military operations is mentioned in all of the books dealing with the Korean war. The most detailed and interesting account of one area is that of S. P. A. Marshall : *The River and the Gauntlet*, William Morrow and Co., 385 pages, 1953. This is the graphic story of the defeat of the Eighth Army by the Chinese Communist forces, November, 1950, in the battle of the Chongchon River in northwestern Korea.

7.  In 1938 and 1939 I took the subject of the climatic regions of Korea for my Ph.D. thesis ; the major part of this study was presented in a series of monographs : *Research Monographs on Korea*, Series B, Nos. 1–4, "Climate of Korea," March–May, 1941, and Series E, Nos. 1–11, "Climatic Regions of Korea," June, 1945. These monographs include bibliography, climatic data, description of climatic elements and climatic regions. Much of this material was based on the meteorological data and publications of the Japanese-run meteorological service. The Meteorological Observatory of the Government-General of Tyosen (Korea), Zinsen (Inchon), Tyosen (Korea), published annual reports, monthly meteorological notes and statistics, and special publications, all of which are most useful.

The system of climatic regions I summarized in an article : "Climatic Regions of Korea and Their Economy," *Geographical Review*, Vol. XXI, No. 1, pages 95–99, January, 1941. A discussion and comparison of varied systems of climatic regions in Korea is discussed in "Climatic Regions : Delineation," *Research Monographs on Korea*, Series E, No. 1, June 1, 1945.

An interesting comparison of Korean climatic types with those in areas in the United States was published, along with comparable climatic data and notes on clothing requirements, in *Korean Environment*, Report No. 171, Environment Protection Section, Research and Development Branch, Military Planning Division, Office of the Quartermaster-General, Department of the Army, Washington, D.C., i, 25 pages, December, 1950. It may be of interest to quote :

> The biggest difference between the climates of places in Korea and those in the United States to which they are most comparable is in the amount of rainfall and snowfall, and in their distribution through the year. No place in the United States receives as much warm rain as most of southern Korea, especially the southeastern portion.
>
> For example, average July rainfall is 11 inches at Pusan, while at Baltimore, which it resembles closely in temperature, it is only 4 inches. The greatest average monthly rainfall anywhere in the United States (along the

Gulf coast) is about 8 inches—the July average for Mokpo, which in temperature is most like Evansville, Ind. However, Korean winters are drier than those of eastern United States, so that the total yearly precipitation is rather comparable: Pusan, 54 inches, Baltimore, 42; Mokpo, 41 inches, Evansville, 43....

In extreme northern Korea, the temperature variation from winter to summer is greater than anywhere in North America: Chunggangjin, on the center of the Manchurian border, in summer has mean monthly temperatures in the low seventies, similar to those of central New York, but in winter the average goes below zero (January: −6°F.), colder than any place south of Central Labrador or northern Alberta.

In selecting United States cities for comparison with those of Korea for which adequate climatic data are available, an attempt was made to maintain as great a degree of regional consistency and as much topographic similarity as possible. Consequently, climates of Korea, when compared to those of the United States, fall into three regions:

1. Korea's east coast is compared to that of the United States from Baltimore to central Maine.
2. Korea's mountains are compared to the Alleghanies and Adirondacks.
3. Korea's west coast is compared to the Mississippi Valley, from Evansville, Ind. to La Crosse, Wis.

8. Hermann Lautensach's study of Korean vegetation, though based on Japanese literature, particularly the works of Nakai, was also benefited by his extensive field observations in Korea in 1933. A classification of vegetation was summarized in his *Korea, Eine Landeskunde auf Grund eigener Reisen und die Literatur*, K. F. Koehler Verlag, Leipzig, xv, 542 pages, 1945, the map was opposite page 128; the discussion, pages 120–34. An early description of Korea's vegetation which can be read with profit is Ernest H. Wilson's "The Vegetation of Korea," *Transactions of the Korea Branch of the Royal Asiatic Society*, Vol. IX, 68 pages, Seoul, Korea, 1918. A summary of vegetation zones, which, however, are not too precisely described, was given by Homiki Uyeki: "The Regeneration of Conifers in Korea," *Proceedings of the Fifth Pan-Pacific Science Congress, Canada, 1933*, Vol. II, pages 973–79, Vancouver, 1933.

9. A brief summary of some Japanese soil studies was given in Hoon K. Lee's *Land Utilization and Rural Economy in Korea*, University of Chicago Press, Chicago, xi, 302 pages, 1936; material on soils on pages 23–28.

A discussion of some of the existing information on Korean soils and particularly the relation of soil fertility to fertilizer requirements is given in Section B, Chapter III, "Soils, Fertilizer and Manures," pages 92–115, *Rehabilitation and Development of Agriculture, Forestry, and Fisheries in South Korea*, a report prepared for the United Nations Korean Reconstruction Agency by a Mission selected by the Food and Agricultural Organization of the United Nations, Columbia University Press, New York, xviii, 428 pages, 1954.

10. The quotation comes from George M. McCune's *Korea Today*, Harvard University Press, Cambridge, xxi, 372 pages, 1950; his chapter on "The Historical Background," pages 8–21, is a very brief summary. Before his death in 1948 he had been working on a full-length history of Korea. Rough drafts of the first few chapters of this work were published posthumously in: "Notes on the History of Korea: Early Korea," *Research Monographs on Korea*, Series I,

No. 1, 25 pages, May 1, 1952. The *Korean Studies Guide*, University of California Press, Berkeley, 1954, has useful summaries of the various periods of Korean history as well as excellent bibliographies of historical materials. Especially useful are the chronology and the set of maps which are drawn on the same base as the maps in this book.

Two histories of Korea in English were written decades ago but are still useful, though, naturally, they do not benefit from the Korean and Japanese research of recent times. These are Homer B. Hulbert's *The History of Korea*, The Methodist Publishing House, Seoul, 2 volumes, 409 and 374 pages, 1905, and James S. Gale's *A History of the Korean People*, The Christian Literature Society of Korea, Seoul, varied pagination, 1927. Both of these appeared serially in publications of their respective periods. Unfortunately they are rather hard to obtain. One of the very real needs is for a modern history of Korea in English; the translation of a recent Korean or Japanese (of post-1945 date) history would be a real service to Korean studies as a temporary measure, though an original research work by some one such as L. George Paik would be preferable.

11.  There were a number of books written by Westerners about Korea in the decades when Korea was being opened to the outside world and as it was losing its independence. No attempt is made here to list these; reference can be made to bibliographies for the varied titles. However, it is worthwhile drawing attention to two journals which were published by a group of missionaries and Korean government employees at this time: *The Korean Repository*, 5 volumes, 1893, 1895–1898, The Trilingual Press, Seoul, monthly, and its successor, *The Korea Review*, 6 volumes, 1901–1906, The Methodist Publishing House, Seoul, monthly. The editor of *The Korea Review*, Homer B. Hulbert, was especially active. He was intimately associated with political affairs, so his basic work is most valuable for its picture of Korea of this period: *The Passing of Korea*, William Heinemann, London (Printed in New York), xii, 473 pages, 1905.

12.  A great many publications have dealt with the organization and character of the Japanese political and economic control of Korea. The *Annual Reports on Administration of Chosen*, published on an every-other-year basis at times and with slightly varying titles, by the Government-General of Chosen, Keijo (Seoul), Chosen (Korea), give the official viewpoint. An independent, but still pro-Japanese, view of the Japanese government in Korea was Alleyne Ireland's *The New Korea*, E. P. Dutton and Co., New York, xii, 352 pages, 1926. A critical view is given in Andrew J. Grajdanzev's *Modern Korea*, The John Day Co., New York, x, 330 pages, 1944.

13.  Since the attack across the thirty-eighth parallel, this artifical barrier has been much discussed, but there has been no very definitive statement as to its origin. Its character and an analysis of the danger involved in its existence were the themes of papers which I gave in 1947 and 1948 before different scholarly societies; these papers were summarized in an article: " The Thirty-Eighth Parallel in Korea," *World Politics*, Vol. I, No. 2, pages 223–32, January, 1949.

An analysis of the problems caused by the division of Korea and the development of two separate goverments was one of the themes of George M. McCune's *Korea Today* (With the collaboration of Arthur L. Grey, Jr.), Harvard University Press, Cambridge, xiii, 372 pages, July, 1950. This book was about nine-tenths completed before my brother's death in 1948. Though published just after the outbreak of the war, it was, thus, in reality written two years before.

There has been a veritable flood of journalistic and other accounts of political developments in Korea in the post-1945, and particularly the post-1950, period. The United States Department of State, the Republic of Korea, and organizations such as the Korean Affairs Institute (which publishes *The Voice of Korea*) and the Korean Pacific Press (which published a series entitled *Periscope on Asia* and now publishes *The Korean Survey*) have published a great mass of documentary and other material. Robert T. Oliver, who has acted as an advisor to Syngman Rhee, has written a number of pamphlets and books giving, generally, Dr. Rhee's viewpoint; a recent book is *Verdict in Korea*, Bald Eagle Press, State College, Pennsylvania, 207 pages, 1952. The references to the government publications and much of the other material may be found in bibliographic aids such as the *Public Affairs Index* or the *Reader's Guide*. Special attention does, however, need to be drawn to the *Reports of the United Nations Temporary Commission on Korea*, and its successor, the United Nations Commission for the Unification and Rehabilitation of Korea. These and other United Nations documents are listed in the *United Nations Documents Index*. A useful compilation of official statements and agreements was made by Donald G. Tewksbury: *Source Materials on Korean Politics and Ideologies*, International Secretariat, Institute of Pacific Relations, New York, 190 pages (mimeographed), 1950.

No attempt can be made to list all of the war books or the correspondents' dispatches from Korea. The *New York Times Index*, as well as other bibliographical aids listed above, is useful in tracing the various events during these unhappy but eventful years. To the numerous official publications which were prepared, some references have already been made. The *Voice of Korea* has been running a chronology of events, which is a useful tool in checking dates and official actions. A similar chronology, giving the Communist slant, is *A Chronicle of Principal Events relating to the Korean Question, 1945-1954*, Shihchieh Chihshih (World Culture) Peking, 1954, iv, 93 pages. A summary of the events and statements made at the Geneva Conference has been prepared: *The Korean Problem at the Geneva Conference, April 26-June 15, 1954*, Department of State Publication 5609, Washington, October, 1954, vi, 193 pages.

14. A description of the frontiers of Korea, as well as some of the internal political boundaries, is in my article: "Physical Basis for Boundaries in Korea," *The Far Eastern Quarterly*, Vol. V, No. 3, pages 272–88, May, 1946.

A brief but useful summary on the group of Koreans in the Soviet Union may be found in a section on "The 'Russian' Koreans," pages 32–42 in a book by Walter Kolarz, *The Peoples of the Soviet Far East*, Frederick A. Prager, New York, xii, 194 pages, 1954.

15. The population data for Korea which is used in this book is derived from censuses taken by the Japanese for all of Korea prior to 1945 and studies they made of earlier census material and by Koreans in South Korea after 1945. The reports are in Japanese or Korean, but the tables can be easily used with only a small amount of translation. Korean and Japanese scholars have been active in publication of articles and studies on Korean demographic problems.

In America, Dr. Irene Taeuber has made a number of studies of Korean population and has been in Korea to gather material. One of her earlier articles, but one which is still a basic study, is "The Population Potential of Postwar Korea," *The Far Eastern Quarterly*, Vol. V, No. 3, pages 289–307, May, 1946. Results of her recent research, including some materials which are to be published, have kindly been made available to me by Dr. Taeuber in manuscript form. A note on Korean demography which is a handy summary is Appendix B (pages 321–335) of George M. Mccune's *Korea Today*, Harvard University Press, Cambridge, xxi, 372 pages, 1950.

Using the available material, a very thorough geographic study of the Korean population with many maps has been prepared recently by Glenn T. Trewartha and Wilbur Zelinsky : " Population Distribution and Change in Korea, 1925–1945," *Geographical Review*, Vol. XLV, No. 1, January, 1955, pages 1–26.

16. Edward W. Wagner prepared a good summary report on *The Korean Minority in Japan, 1904–1950*, Institute of Pacific Relations, New York, 1951, v, 108 pages. There are a number of Japanese reports on this subject, also.

Dr. Hoon K. Lee made a study of the Korean migrants in Manchuria which was published in the Korean language by the Union Christian College Press, Pyongyang, Korea, 1930. An English-language article derived from this study is "Korean Migrants in Manchuria," *Geographical Review*, Vol. XXII, No. 2, April, 1932, pages 196–204. A recent propaganda piece which is interesting for some of the details and pictures it presents is by Sa Kung-liao : "China's Korean Minority," *China Reconstructs*, No. 6, November–December, 1953, pages 17–19. According to this newspaper reporter's information, of the 700,000 people in the Yenpien Korean Autonomous Region, more than three-quarters are Koreans.

17. An important phase of Christian missionary efforts in Korea was educational work. This was carried on under American and Western patterns for the Koreans for many decades. When Korea was under Japanese control there was conflict over such educational work, since Christian education was often at cross-purposes to that of the Japanese. A number of American missionaries and American-trained Koreans have written on the educational problems in Korea ; references to their works may be found in bibliographies.

The United Nations Educational, Scientific, and Cultural Organization and the United Nations Korean Reconstruction Agency sent an Educational Planning Mission to Korea in 1952. This Commission prepared two interesting reports on educational problems of South Korea : " Educational Conditions in the Republic of Korea," UNKRA/AG/22, Pusan, Korea, viii, 151 pages (mimeographed), 1 December, 1952, and " Rebuilding Education in the Republic of Korea," UNKRA/AG/23, Paris, France, x, 134 pages (mimeographed), February, 1953. The final report was in printed form : *Rebuilding Education in the Republic of Korea*, United Nations Educational, Scientific, and Cultural Organization, Paris, May, 1954, 221 pages.

The report on *An Economic Programme for Korean Reconstruction* prepared for the United Nations Korean Reconstruction Agency by the Robert R. Nathan Associates (Washington, D. C., xxvii, 459 pages, March, 1954) gives a very optimistic account of the potential of Korean manpower. Especially useful for the data on South Korea is Chapter 10—Manpower for Reconstruction, pages 195–209.

18. A valuable study of a Korean village on the island of Kanghwa is contained in Cornelius Osgood's *The Koreans and Their Culture*, The Ronald Press Company, New York, xv, 387 pages, 1951. This is a very thorough study by a well-qualified anthropologist, who was aided by a group of Korean investigators. Generalizations drawn from this village study and from other observations and study of the literature contained in his book need to be recognized as generalizations which do not take into sufficient account the regional diversities

in Korea. Another book which should be mentioned, though it is autobiographical in nature rather than a research study, is Younghill Kang's well-written account of his early years in Korea: *The Grass Roof*, Charles Scribner's Sons, New York, viii, 367 pages, 1931.

There are many Japanese research studies on the nature of Korean society and customs. A Korean scholar, Kim Too-hun, recently published " A Study on the Family System in Korea," *Korean Culture Series*, Vol. XII, Eul-yoo Publishing Co., Seoul, 771, 5 pages, June, 1949.

19. The differences in dialects in Korea are due mainly to differences in historical developments. As transportation and communications facilities have been established and, especially, with the violent movement of populations because of the war in the peninsula, these differences have diminished in recent years. The authoritative study of Korean dialects is by a Japanese scholar, Shimpei Ogura, *Chosengo Hogen no Kenkyu* (Studies in Korean Dialects), Iwanami Shoten, Tokyo, 2 volumes, 1, 7, 514 pages; 1, 7, 654 pages, 10 maps, 3, 2, 1944. The map of dialects (No. 10) has been reproduced; it is interesting to note that deviations from the provincial boundaries occur in only four places. Pak No-sik in his *Sin Choson Chiri* (New Geography of Korea), Seoul, Korea, 130 pages, 1947, reproduces this map and makes mention of these differences in drawing up geographic regions of Korea.

20. A brief summary of Korean religion and philosophical thought is in the *Korean Studies Guide*, University of California Press, Berkeley, 1954; this also has a selected bibliography of source materials. An interesting account of Confucianism, particularly in relation to the religions in Korea, is L. Eui Sou Youn's *Le Confucianisme en Coree*, Librairie Orientaliste Paul Guethner, Paris, x, 198 pages, 1939. An early French work on Catholic missions in Korea, but one which also includes a great deal of general information on Korea and its religions, is Charles Dallet's *Histoire de l'Eglise de Coree*, Librairie Victor Palme, Paris, 2 volumes, xii, cxcii, 383 and 595 pages, 1874. The best account of early Protestant missions, and one which also discusses other religions, is L. George Paik's *The History of Protestant Missions in Korea, 1832–1910*, Union Christian College Press, Pyeng Yang, Korea, v, 438 pages, xiii, 1929.

One of the first missionaries in Korea, Horace Grant Underwood, gave a series of lectures which were later published in book form : *The Religions of Eastern Asia*, The Macmillan Company, New York, ix, 267 pages, 1910. One of these lectures, Chapter III, " The Shamanism of Korea," pages 93–142, is very interesting because it gives a picture of religious beliefs and practices as of the time when Korea was still not too profoundly affected by Western impacts. One of Dr. Underwood's illustrations is worth quoting :

   The poetic name for the city of Seoul means a silkworm, and the native geomancers have traced a resemblance (to us foreigners fanciful) in the topographical contour of the region and find its head at the village of Han Kang, where an abrupt cliff touches the river. This silkworm must, of course, be properly waited upon and served, or in his anger he might ruffle his back, with sad, sad results ; and therefore not only are there regular sacrifices offered to the city, but on the further side of the river, which is from one-half to three-quarters of a mile wide, the authorities have planted and maintained for generations a mulberry grove. True, the leaves are now used for the feeding of real silkworms by the villagers on that side of the river, but

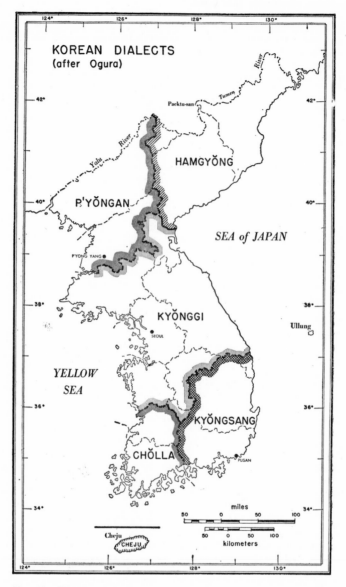

KOREAN DIALECTS
(after Ogura)

Paektu-san

Tumen River

HAMGYŎNG

Yalu River

P'YŎNGAN

SEA of JAPAN

PYONG YANG ●

KYŎNGGI

SEOUL ●

Ullung

YELLOW
SEA

KYŎNGSANG

CHŎLLA

PUSAN ●

miles
50    0    50    100

Cheju
CHEJU

50    0    50    100
kilometers

Fig. 21.—The distribution of the major dialects in Korea according to the studies of Ogura.

the reason for planting the grove and for its annual upkeep was the feeding and appeasing of the old mammoth silkworm, a ridge of whose back is the pine-covered south mountain of Seoul. (Page 137)

21. A good study of the impact of Communism was carried on under difficulties but with considerable success quickly after areas were freed from Communist control. The report of this study : *A Preliminary Study of the Impact of Communism upon Korea*, Human Resources Research Institute, Air University, United States Air Force, Maxwell Air Force Base, Alabama, vi, 324 pages (mimeographed), May, 1951, makes fascinating, and frightening, reading. Parts of this report were summarized (and supplemented by other materials translated from Korean sources) by two of the team who undertook the study : John W. Riley, Jr., and Wilbur Schramm, *The Reds Took a City*, Rutgers University Press, New Brunswick, New Jersey, viii, 210 pages, 1951.

22. The study of life in one Korean village by Cornelius Osgood and his Korean associates : *The Koreans and Their Culture*, The Ronald Press Co., New York, xv, 387 pages, 1951, is one of the few accounts in English on this important facet of Korean life ; it is a thorough and valuable account.

The villages of Korea are grouped together for administrative purposes into *myon*, or districts. The description of one *myon* in west central Korea which was given in the Air Force report : *A Preliminary Study of the Impact of Communism upon Korea*, Air University, Maxwell Air Force Base, Alabama, vi, 324 pages (mimeographed), May, 1951, is worth quoting. This village study was carried on by Dr. John Pelzel and Major Clarence N. Weems and includes a great deal of information on the Communist impact which, because of space limitations, cannot be quoted here in its entirety, though it is interesting :

Kumnam-myon, located about 15 miles NNW of Taejon, on the main Taejon-Seoul road...with a population of about 14,000, is divided among 23 settlements which, in turn, are divided administratively into 25 *ku*'s. Its settlements lie along the rather narrow (one to two miles wide) valley of the Kum River and in steep, short tributary valleys. The village area is characterized by high, deforested mountains and small valley floors. Most of the available flat land is used for farming, especially for irrigated rice farming, and settlements are built on the lowest slopes of the mountains. Certain settlements lie along the main road. The largest of these...and the largest in (Kumnam-myon)...is located in the approximate geographical center of the village, and contains the village office and most of the few non-agricultural installations of the village. Many other settlements, however, are a considerable distance (often two or three miles) from the road, from which they are separated by rough country. Before June, 1950 a bus plied regularly along the main road between Taejon and Chochiwon (10 miles north of Kumnam).... Except for the main road, all communication among settlements is over footpaths. Movement between the road and the more distant *li* is so tedious that representatives of the Communist civil government of the village are said to have penetrated to them infrequently and the more outlying portions of the *myon* were considered relatively safe places of refuge for all but the most persistently hunted anti-Communists.

The farm lands of Kumnam, though small, are quite productive in years of adequate rainfall, and the village is a large rice-producer. Small yeoman farmers predominate, and few owners have ever held much more than three *chungbo*'s (a *chungbo* is 2.45 acres) of paddy and field land together. (This is considered the holding desirable for complete support of the family by farming in this village.) Consequently, there has been little land to distribute under either the Communist or R.O.K. land reform programs. On the other hand, there are few families without any land of their own, though many have held too little for full farm support of the family and have had to send family members to other farmers as tenants or laborers, or seasonally, to the city for subsidiary work. The proportion of persons engaged in subsidiary work is said to have dropped sharply since the end of World War II, partly because of consistently good rice-growing years during the period, and partly because the tenants' rent, under the American Military Government and the R.O.K. government, was reduced from 40 or 50 per cent to 30 per cent of the main crop yield.

Almost no occupations other than agriculture are followed full time in Kumnam. The settlement in which the *myon* office is located contains a rice-cleaning mill, a small private hospital, a *kuksu* shop (restaurant), and a few tiny home shops selling sweets, stationery, tobacco, and spirits. In another settlement, a handicraft shop manufactures native rubber shoes. The establishments in the *myon* office area do not comprise a distinct shopping center, and most of the few purchases of goods not produced at home were formerly made in Taejon.... (Quoted from pages 105–109.)

In Kumnam, apparently the village as a whole was moderately conservative, politically, before the Communist occupation. There was apparently little pan-village solidarity under either a single informal leader or a group of closely cooperating informal leaders, while the mayor definitely held his position as a representative of the central government. So when the bureaucracy was changed after the occupation, there was no informal leadership to combat or leaven Communist control at the village-wide level.

The same situation existed even more markedly in the *ku* of the village that was most thoroughly studied. Members of all but one household in this *ku* belonged to a single clan and were descendants of a distinguished political refugee of the *yangban* class who had fled the court and settled here about 400 years ago. Although they belonged to the same kinship group, there was irreparable schism among the residents. In numbers, the households of the settlement were almost equally divided between those descended from the first wife and those descended from the second wife of the original founder. Traditionally, the descendants of the second wife are inferior in general status. They are forbidden to share as equals in local festivals ; they must hold themselves as subordinate in all personal contacts, working for the descendants of the first wife and considering themselves, in effect, the servants of the senior branch. The natural rifts this situation creates have apparently been widened very sharply in recent decades by the breakdown of traditional sanctions for the family system, and the settlement has long been sharply divided. Each of the two groups had its own leaders. Where the descendants of the first wife were conservative politically, those of the second wife were at least liberal. When the Communists came in, this division became irreparable. The leaders of the second wife clique became Communist functionaries and those of the first wife clique became hunted reactionaries.... (Quoted from pages 126–27.)

23. Books which deal with wider subjects have a considerable amount of tada

on Korean economy; two examples are: Andrew J. Grajdanzev's *Modern Korea*, The John Day Co., New York, x, 330 pages, 1944, and George M. McCune's *Korea Today*, Harvard University Press, Cambridge, xxi, 373 pages, 1950. Both of these books have selected bibliographies. A monthly publication, *Korea Economic Digest*, published by the Korean Economic Society, starting in June, 1944 was continued through Vol. III, No. 1, in January, 1946, but then was amalgamated with occasional publications of the Korean Chamber of Commerce in America and was changed in scope. However, it did contain a number of useful articles and it is to be regretted that it did not continue.

Korean economic data (including material on agriculture and varied other phases of Korean economy and life) are included in various Japanese statistical source materials and reports. The tables in these publications can be read with a minimum of translation and are most useful. The yearly *Chosen Sotoku-fu Tōkei Nempo* (Government-General of Chosen Statistical Annual) published by the Government-General of Chosen, Keijo (Seoul), Chosen (Korea) is a basic source. The volume for Showa 9th year (1934), for example, comprises 7 pages of index, a 42-page written summary, 510 tables on 544 pages, and a 6-page appendix devoted to the 1935 census. Other useful sources of economic data are the three issues of the *Chosen Keizai Nempo* (Economic Annual of Korea) published by the Zenkoku Keizai Chosa Kikan Rengo-kai, Chosen Shibu (Korea Branch, National Federation of Economic Research Organizations), Keijo (Seoul), Chosen Korea); the volume for 1941–1942, published in 1943, for example, has 2, 8, 326 pages and 78 pages of appendix devoted to a chronological account of events during the period.

These statistical materials were continued to be assembled and published after the Japanese left Korea, first by divisions of the American Military Government, by the Economic Cooperation Administration mission, and by various Republic of Korea and United Nations agencies. However, the best summary is *The Bank of Korea Economic Review*; that for 1949 was published by the Bank of Korea, Seoul, Korea, 12, 40, I:192, II:76, III:148, IV:435 pages; the fourth part of this volume, Statistics, has the captions to the many tables in both Korean and English, so that it may be easily used. These volumes, also, contain data for the years when Korea was under Japanese control, so that an easy transition may be made to the modern day for South Korea. The Bank of Korea also publishes a *Monthly Statistical Review*; this includes economic data and interpretative articles, some of which are translated or abstracted in English.

Recent data may be obtained from the *Korean Statistics Monthly Summation*, United Nations Korean Reconstruction Agency, Seoul, Korea.

In the programming of economic aid and planning for the future economy of Korea, United States and United Nations agencies, sometimes in cooperation with Republic of Korea organizations, have published a number of studies of South Korean economy. Some of these were brief non-technical analyses for public and Congressional presentation, in other cases they have been technical reports with a wealth of economic data. It is not possible to list all of these materials, but their titles may be found by consulting the normal bibliographic aids. A few need special mention for the background material they present:

*The South Korean Economy*, Korea Division, Economic Cooperation Administration, Washington, D. C., 40 pages, May, 1949.

*Report of the Agent General of the United Nations Korean Reconstruction Agency*, General Assembly, Official Records: Seventh Session, Supplement No. 19 (A/2222), New York, iii, 51 pages, October, 1952, and Addenda 1 and 2, v, 8 pages, February, 1953.

*Preliminary Report on Economic Reconstruction of Korea*, UNKRA/AG/13, Robert R. Nathan Associates. Inc., Washington, 193 pages (mimeographed), 15 December, 1952.

*An Economic Programme for Korean Reconstruction*, prepared for the United Nations Korean Reconstruction Agency by the Robert R. Nathan Associates, Washington, D. C., xxvii, 459 pages, March, 1954.

An independent study, though using a considerable amount of material from the Nathan Associates study is that of A. W. Zanzi : *Economic Reconstruction Problems in South Korea*, Secretariat Paper No. 2, Twelfth Conference, Institute of Pacific Relations, Kyoto, Japan, September, 1954, International Secretariat, Institute of Pacific Relations, New York, 75 pages (mimeographed), 1954.

24. One of the most useful books on Korean agriculture in English is Hoon K. Lee's *Land Utilization and Rural Economy in Korea*, University of Chicago Press, Chicago, xii, 289 pages, 1936. This was an independent study which was not based exclusively on government data but was supplemented by information gathered by teams of field investigators. A work on Korean agricultural conditions written decades ago, but which unfortunately had little use because of the iobscurity of its publication, was also based on field work and observation done n cooperation with American missionaries and Korean Christian leaders: Edmund de Schweinitz Brunner, " Rural Korea : A Preliminary Survey of Economic, Social and Religious Conditions," *The Christian Mission in Relation to Rural Problems,* Volume VI, The Jerusalem Meeting of the International Missionary Council, New York, Chapter IV, pages 84–172, 1928.

A handy summary volume on Korean agriculture is the Army Service Forces Manual, M370-7, *Civil Affairs Handbook, Korea, Section 7 : Agriculture,* Headquarters, Army Service Forces. Washington, D. C., x, 113 pages, 16 October, 1944. This was the only handbook which was published in the series ; it was prepared by the Office of Foreign Agricultural Relations, U. S. Department of Agriculture ; it was subsequently declassified from its restricted classification.

A post-World War II report on the southern part of the peninsula is *Present Agricultural Position of South Korea*, Headquarters, United States Military Government in Korea, Seoul, Korea, Report No. 2, 34 pages, April, 1947.

The United Nations Food and Agriculture Organization sent a survey mission to South Korea in 1952. They have prepared a voluminous report : *Rehabilitation and Development of Agriculture, Forestry, and Fisheries in South Korea,* Columbia University Press, New York, 1954, xviii, 428 pages. Though this is generally restricted to South Korea and to the present needs for rehabilitation and development, it includes a considerable amount of data on the general Korean agricultural economy.

25. A good treatment of the Japanese role in the agricultural economy is in Andrew J. Grajdanzev's *Modern Korea*, The John Day Company, New York, x, 330 pages, 1944 ; he makes a critical evaluation using Japanese source materials ; especially valuable is his Appendix II, " Reliability of Korean Agricultural Statistics," pages 296–99, in which he points out the change which was made in reporting on rice production in 1936.

26. The special problem of utilization of the uplands of Korea I examined in a study : " Utilization of Upland Areas in Korea," *The Development of Upland Areas in the Far East*, Vol. 2, International Secretariat, Institute of

Pacific Relations, New York, Part IV, pages 104–21 (mimeographed), 1951.

27. Land redistribution has been a common event after major political changes in Korea ; no exception to this historical phenomena was made in 1945 when in both North and South Korea land reform programs were put into operation. I described these briefly in an article and a postscript : "Land Redistribution in Korea," *Far Eastern Survey*, Vol. XVII, No. 2, pages 13–18, January 28, 1949, and "Land Distribution in Korea," *Far Eastern Survey*, Vol. XVII, No. 11, page 132, May 28, 1949. United States and United Nations documents discuss the tenancy problem very thoroughly ; one interesting account of the effects of land reform in North Korea was given in an Economic Cooperation Administration (Washington, D. C.) press release No. 2093, March 11, 1951, 3 pages (mimeographed) ; this summarized a report by Robert A. Kinney, who had headed a mission into North Korea to investigate the problem. An account of the operation of the largest Japanese landholding company by the American occupation authorities is C. Clyde Mitchell's *Final Report and History of the New Korea Company*, Headquarters, U. S. Army Military Government in Korea, National Land Administration, Seoul, Korea, 65 pages, 30 April, 1948. He described the sale of this land in an article : "Land Reform in South Korea," *Pacific Affairs*, Vol. XXII, No. 2, pages 144–54, June, 1949.

28. Hermann Lautensach summarized work by Japanese geographers and agricultural economists and studies he had done earlier in his *Korea, Eine Landeskunde auf Grund eigener Reisen und die Literatur*, K. F. Koehler Verlag, Leipzig, xv, 542 pages, 1945. He includes a selected bibliography in this work. The classification is given on page 183 and the map is Tafel 18, opposite page 129.

Robert B. Hall includes Korea within the Japanese Empire in an early and pioneer study : "Agricultural Regions of Asia, Part VII, The Japanese Empire," *Economic Geography*, Vol. 10, No. 4, October, 1934, pages 321–74, Vol. 11, No. 1, January, 1935, pages 33–52, and Vol. 11, No. 2, April, 1935, pages 130–47 ; Chosen (Korea) was taken up in detail in Vol. 11, No. 1, January, 1935, pages 44–52. Dr. Hall divided Korea into three major districts : Northern, Middle, and Southern.

Classifications of agricultural regions, generally using provincial boundaries and making distinctions on the basis of predominance of rice or double-cropping, are quite common in the literature on Korea ; agricultural statistics are often grouped into three divisions—north, central and south—by the simple device of spacing the data. A Japanese geographer, S. Sugai, in an article : "The Land Utilization in the Rural Districts of Chosen," *The Geographical Review of Japan*, Vol. 12, No. 12, December, 1936, pages 1081–1106, divided the peninsula into four regions : Central, North, West, and South.

The definitive work on the regionalization of Korean agriculture was done by Kenichi Hisama, *Chosen Nogyo Keiei-chitai no Kenkyu* (Research on the Agricultural Management Regions of Korea), Nogyo Sogokenkyu Kankokai, Tokyo, Japan, 20, 552 pages, July, 1951. During his days in Korea the author had written a number of articles and books ; one of these, because of its criticism of Japanese agrarian policy in Korea, had been the reason for his being forced out of his official position. In this work, completed after his return to Japan, the author reviews the various regional systems which have been presented in the past, takes up the regional characteristics in each province, and then presents his classification. This comprises five major zones, each of which is sub-

divided into regions and some regions into districts, so that 20 regions, 11 districts, and 1 district locality (the Konan rice-growing locality) emerge. The
final purpose of his study was to explain the characteristics each " agricultural
management " region had, how each region was related to the others, and how
these regions were composed as one geographical entity for the whole of Korea.

29.  The references which were given in Note 23 are also useful for material on
the mineral and power resources of Korea.  One report which deals specifically
with the subject is : *Mineral Resources of Southern Korea*, General Headquarters,
Supreme Commander Allied Powers, Natural Resources Section, Report No. 84,
50 pages, 28 July, 1947.  This report takes up the major minerals alphabetically
and includes maps of their distribution.  There are, of course, many Japanese
publications on these subjects.

30.  There has been a great deal of material and data published in Japanese, but
relatively little in Western languages which are easy of access, on the industrial
complex of Korea.  One of the few classifications of industrial regions is in
*Korea: A Geographical Appreciation*, Foreign Geography Information Series, No.
4, Geographical Branch, Department of Mines and Technical Surveys, Ottawa,
Canada, vi, 84 pages, 16 maps, 1951.  The regions are on Figure 11 and comprise : I–South Coast, II–Samchok, III–Wonsan-Hamhung, IV–Northeast Coast,
V–Northwest Coast, VI–Seoul-Inchon.

Appendix G gives a brief description of the major industrial regions as I
have conceived them to be.

31.  The various reports of the United States and United Nations agencies which
have been concerned with the rehabilitation of Korean economy all stress the
gigantic task which faces Korea in achieving economic reconstruction and development.  However, they are not completely discouraged by the prospect; for
example, the summary of the *Preliminary Report on Economic Reconstruction of
Korea*, UNKRA/AG/13, Robert R. Nathan Associates, Inc., Washington, D. C.,
15 December, 1952, on page 22, has this statement :

With good planning, adequate foreign aid, maximum efficiency in the use of
total available resources, and an all-out effort on the part of the Korean people, the reconstruction program can move ahead and the Republic of Korea,
within a few years, can become a self-supporting economy with a sound base
for further growth and development.

32.  Most of the books on the geography of Korea mentioned in Note 1 give
regional treatments of the peninsula.  The major classifications of regions I have
discussed in an article in the *Bulletin of the Institute of Geography, University
of Tokyo*, No. 3, Fall, 1954, pages 214–28.  In that article I have also given
in more detail the methodology I used in drawing up the classification of regions
which is used in this book.

Hermann Lautensach's latest contribution on the regions of Korea is contained
in his : " Der Geographische Formenwandel, Studien zur Landschaftssystema-
tik, " *Colloquium Geographicum*, Vortrage des Bonnes Geographischen Colloquium
zur Gedachtnis an Ferdinand von Richthofen, Band (Volume) 3, Ferd Dummlets
Verlag, Bonn, Germany, 191 pages, 1952.  In this monograph he attempts to
develop a system which is applicable to various parts of the world.  He uses
Korea as an example (Chapter V, pages 114–29) of his system.  Four major
factors are taken into account and for each of these categories are set up.

Therefore, Dr. Lautensach uses only these code letters to denote the regions which result. A map shows the 15 regions into which Korea is divided. The one big advantage that this system has is that it can be used for comparison of regions in Korea with regions in other countries of the Far East or of the world. The first basic criteria are winter temperatures, which are a reflection of the planetary (or latitudinal) position. Within these criteria subdivisions are made on the basis of finer gradations of winter temperatures associated with the character of natural vegetation and land utilization. The next criterion is the east-west relation to neighboring areas. Thus western Korea is thought to be closer to Manchuria than the rest of Korea; Ullung Island is the only part of Korea to be related to Japan in this scheme. The next criterion is central and peripheral location; the peripheral areas are subdivided on the basis of distribution of monthly precipitation. Finally, there is a criterion of elevation; the categories are varied according to the average height of the land and in some cases a combination of two categories is necessary.

33. On North Korea there are many books, though few of a geographic character. Two Korean language reference books which contain some data (and a great deal of propaganda) were reprinted in Tokyo: *Choson Chungang Nyongam* (Central Yearbook of Korea), *Home Edition, 1949*, 263 pages, reprinted in Tokyo without notice of publisher or date, and a later edition of the same work, 1951–1952, compiled by the Choson Chungang Tongshin-sa, Pyongyang, 1952, reprinted and published with a slightly different title on the cover and the date changed to 1953 by the Toko Shoin, Tokyo, 497 pages, 1953.

For a brief but reasoned summary of recent press releases and radio broadcasts on the North Korean ties with the Soviet Union and Communist China see the note by S. B. Thomas: "The Chinese Communists' Economic and Cultural Agreement with North Korea," *Pacific Affairs*, Vol. XXVII, No. 1, pages 61–65, March, 1954. Another summary of recent developments, also based on radio broadcasts, was published in *The Voice of Korea*, Vol. XII, Nos. 202 and 203, February 21, 1955, and March 14, 1955; these stressed the economic upsurge which the Communists had reported.

Harry Schwartz in an article in the *New York Times*, June 9, 1955, summarized "an unusually detailed article" from the Soviet newspaper *Izvestia*. According to this source, "...industrial reconstruction is progressing rapidly, but agricultural production is rising only slowly...inadequate coal production and a shortage of oxen for pulling farm implements are two of the most serious factors holding back recovery."

34. On South Korea there are many government reports and statistical materials available; many of these sources have already been noted. A recently published review in Korean, which it is hoped will be continued, has merit for its tables and other material: *Sonap Chung nam* (General Review of Industry), Series No. 1, Research Department, Bank of Korea, Seoul, 19, 1131 pages, 1954. An English language booklet, also published by the Bank of Korea, is very handy: *Economic Summation of Korea*, The Bank of Korea, Seoul, 21 tables, 17 pages, April, 1954. The Office of Public Information, The Republic of Korea, publishes in English the *Korean Report*. These summarize governmental activities and progress and reports from cabinet ministries. The latest report is Vol. III, issued by the Washington Bureau of the Korean Pacific Press, v, 108 pages, September, 1955.

## Appendix B | Notes on Place Names in Korea

Frequently, Korean place names give rise to confusion, particularly in the minds of Westerners who have no concept of their meaning. In reality the place names often have geographic implications which aid one in understanding the nature of the land which they name. A good example of this is the very word Korea. This is a European romanization, derived initially from the Chinese through the French and Italian to the English, for the name of a kingdom which flourished in the peninsula from 918 to 1392. The Korean words *ko* and *ryo* stand for "high" and "sparkling" and thus the name Korea may be poetically translated as "The Land of High Mountains and Sparkling Streams," a nice epitomization of Korea's geography. The name by which Koreans generally have called their land is Choson. This was the name designated for their country by the Yi dynasty, which started in 1392. It had been derived in turn from the name of a legendary kingdom which included much of the peninsula some 2,500 years before. This name, Choson, may be translated as "The Land of the Morning Calm (or Freshness)," again apt, though not so much so in these days.

The names of places within Korea are derived from many different sources. Some of them are named for famous individuals or families, or are derived from phrases in the classics. It is interesting to note, however, that many of them are geographic descriptions, using phenomena such as streams, rivers, mountains, passes, and plains. The names of cities in Korea usually are made up of two characters. These are often derived from the word for a physical feature plus a descriptive term. The names for the provinces, with one exception, were derived by combining one character of the name of a prominent city with one character of another prominent city's name. For example, in the northwest, the province name of Pyongan was derived from the *pyong* of Pyongyang and the *an* of Anju. The one exception was Kyonggi, the province which surrounds Seoul; its name literally means "capital," or home province. The provinces have for centuries been divided into districts and the district (or magistrate's) seat was called *ju*. Thus many of the city names, such as Anju, have *ju* as their last character. The names of places of less significance often denote local situations; for example, "the south bank of the river," or "the north side of the mountain." Prominent features, such as rocks, trees, temples, river-fordings, and so on, are often used in village place names. Family names are sometimes used, for example, Kumsong, the town or "castle" of the Kum (or Kim) family. Because of these local derivations there is considerable confusion and duplication in the names of smaller places.

The transliteration of Korean place names into other languages presents further difficulties for the Westerner. Though both Chinese and Japanese can read the characters which are used for Korean place names, they may have different meanings for some characters and, more commonly, have different pronunciations. Further complications arise from the varied ways in which Chinese, Japanese, and Korean pronunciations may be romanized.

The romanization of the Korean pronunciation of place names has been until recently largely a matter of improvisation. Different people worked out systems adaptable to their own alphabetical sounds. They sometimes used Japanese or Chinese pronunciations rather than Korean. Hermann Lautensach in reviewing this problem has compiled a list of fifty-six different ways in which the city of Pyongyang is romanized on maps and globes and in publications; this excludes the use of the Russian alphabet or of phonetic symbols which would add further variations. Actually, many maps published in Western languages are a weird jumble of Chinese, Japanese, and Korean romanizations of different types with some purely Western-derived place names.

In 1939 a romanization system based on *onmun*, the Korean alphabet, was devised by two American historians interested in Korean research, George M. McCune and Edwin O. Reischauer. This system was published in the Transactions of the Korea Branch of the Royal Asiatic Society, the leading organization of Western scholars in Korea. Using this system, anyone familiar with the Korean language can approximate the correct Korean pronunciation. The system was designed to meet the need for historical research and was a " compromise between scientific accuracy and practical simplicity." It utilized a number of diacritical marks, particularly for designating long or short vowels and for explosive sounds. (These diacritical marks have been omitted in this book.) The system also called for changes when some words ending in consonants were put together; an example of this change is the name of the southwestern province, Cholla; if the two characters were not together they would be pronounced *chon* and *na*. The Korean name of the Yalu River is made up of *ap* and *rok*, which when put together becomes Amnok.

Systems of romanizations have been developed by some Korean scholars. One of the best of them by Zong In-sob has many diacritical marks and some letters and letter combinations not commonly used, such as *z* and *cz*. It, therefore, results in romanizations such as *Zosen* for Choson and *Ogczon* for Okchon. A description of the system is given in an article : " The Unified System for the Romanization of Korean," *Chosen Gakuho*, Journal of the Academic Association of Koreanology in Japan, Tenri, No. 6, pages 171–98, August, 1954. It is worthwhile to note his comments in the Introduction to his recent book : *Folk Tales from Korea*, Routledge & Kegan Paul, Ltd., London, xxviii, 257 pages, 1952 :

> Now the Unified System of spelling is being adopted by schools and the Government, thanks to the untiring industry of the Korean Philological Association, established in 1921, with which I have been associated as a member of the committee, and the Korean Phonetic Association which I myself founded in 1935. The Romanization of proper names and Korean terms adopted in this book is based on the unified system which has been authorized by these two associations for general use. The original plan of this system was drafted by myself and introduced by me at the 4th International Congress of Linguists held at Copenhagen in 1936.

During World War II the United States Board on Geographic Names desired a standard system which could be used for romanizations of place names. Naturally they did not wish to sofues  aromanization of Japanesepronunciation

Korean place names. Since the McCune-Reischauer system was the only system which could be readily adopted for place names and because of its general usefulness, it was adopted as official. In view of the decision of the Board on Geographic Names, the United States Army Map Service series of maps used the McCune-Reischauer system. There are some place names which have become so standard in a form different from their McCune-Reischauer romanization that these established romanizations are used on maps. A good example is Seoul, rather than *Soul*, and Yalu, rather than Amnok. Western names for Korean places, like Quelpart for Cheju Island, or Dagelet for Ullung Island, have been decreasing in usage and this is a good development. It is doubtful, however, that the name of Korea will soon be replaced in Western usage by Choson or Taehan.

Some of the recent books and many of the early books in Korea in Western languages had lists of place names appended; often these were in Chinese or Japanese rather than Korean pronunciations. One of the earliest books devoted solely to the subject of Korean place names was by B. Koto and S. Kanazawa : *A Catalogue for the Romanized Geographical Names of Korea*, The University of Tokyo, Tokyo, Japan, vi, 88 pages, 1903; this system was not widely used. A brief and interesting discussion of Korean place names was given by Dr. Lautensach in his *Korea, Eine Landeskunde auf Grund eigener Reisen and die Literatur*, K. F. Koehler Verlag, Leipzig, xv, 542 pages, 1945. V. T. Zaichikov's geography : *Koreia*, 2nd Edition, Moscow, 480 pages, 1951, has a discussion on pages 80–86; he includes tables and lists as well as place name maps in Russian.

I discussed the problem in a note : " Romanization of Place Names in Korea," *Geographical Review*, Vol. XXXI, No. 1, January 1941, pages 150–52. This appendix in an expanded form was published recently in an article : " Names on the Land in Korea," *The Korean Survey*, Vol. 2, No. 1, pages 3–5, January, 1953.

The McCune-Reischauer system of romanization which is used here, but without the diacritical marks, was outlined in an article : " The Romanization of the Korean Language, Based upon its Phonetic Structure," *Transactions of the Korea Branch of the Royal Asiatic Society*, Vol. XXIX, pages 1–57, Seoul, Korea, 1939. Two Army Map Service publications have short introductions to the problem and lists of the place names which appear on printed maps : *Place Name Index for Korea* (*Chosen*), War Department, Army Map Service, Corps of Engineers, U. S. Army, Washington, D. C., xi, 63 pages, November, 1943, and *Gazetteer to Maps of Korea, Map Series AMS L 551, 1:250,000* (*First Edition*), War Department, Army Map Service, Corps of Engineers, U. S. Army, Washington, D. C., iv, 313 pages, September, 1944.

Rather than have a separate list of place names with their variations as an appendix to this book, in the index the Korean romanizations for the place names are followed by the standard Japanese romanization and any common alternatives.

# *Appendix* C | The Rivers and Drainage Basins of Korea

| *Listed in geographical order, starting in the northwest continuing around the peninsula to the northeast* | *Length in Miles* | *Drainage Basins in Sq. Miles* |
|---|---|---|
| Yalu (Amnok) | 491 | 24,185 |
| Chongchon | 123 | 3,655 |
| Taedong | 247 | 7,485 |
| Yesong | 108 | 1,563 |
| Han | 292 | 13,270 |
| Ansong | 47 | 665 |
| Muhan | 38 | 625 |
| Kum | 250 | 3,817 |
| Mangyong | 61 | 620 |
| Tongjin | 28 | 400 |
| Yongsan | 72 | 1,078 |
| Somjin | 132 | 1,891 |
| Naktong | 327 | 9,251 |
| Hyongsan | 39 | 450 |
| Ambyon | 51 | 448 |
| Yonghung | 84 | 1,285 |
| Kumjin | 56 | 352 |
| Songchon | 61 | 898 |
| Pukchong | 41 | 792 |
| Tanchon | 100 | 927 |
| Susong | 42 | 341 |
| Tumen (Tuman) | 324 | 15,880 |

*Appendix D* | **Population Statistics**

## Population Distribution by Provinces in Korea—1925-1949

| NORTH KOREA | 1925 | 1930 | *In Thousands* 1935 | 1940 | 1944 | 1949 |
|---|---|---|---|---|---|---|
| N. Hamgyong | 626 | 745 | 853 | 1102 | 1124 | |
| S. Hamgyong | 1413 | 1578 | 1722 | 1879 | 2014 | |
| N. Pyongan | 1417 | 1563 | 1710 | 1768 | 1881 | |
| S. Pyongan | 1242 | 1332 | 1470 | 1662 | 1827 | |
| Hwanghae | 1462 | 1524 | 1674 | 1813 | 2013 | |
| Total | 6160 | 6742 | 7429 | 8224 | 8859 | |
| SOUTH KOREA | | | | | | |
| Kyonggi | 2019 | 2157 | 2452 | 2864 | 3090 | 4187a |
| N. Chungchong | 847 | 900 | 959 | 945 | 980 | 1147 |
| S. Chungchong | 1282 | 1383 | 1527 | 1576 | 1673 | 2028 |
| N. Cholla | 1369 | 1504 | 1607 | 1599 | 1673 | 2050 |
| S. Cholla | 2159 | 2332 | 2508 | 2639 | 2748 | 3297b |
| N. Kyongsang | 2333 | 2417 | 2563 | 2472 | 2604 | 3206 |
| S. Kyongsang | 2022 | 2136 | 2248 | 2242 | 2416 | 3135 |
| Kangwon | 1332 | 1488 | 1605 | 1765 | 1857 | 1139c |
| Total | 13363 | 14317 | 15469 | 16102 | 17041 | 20189d |
| **Total Korea:** | **19523** | **21059** | **22898** | **24326** | **25900** | — |

Notes : a) This includes Seoul, though politically in 1949 it was separate; it also includes the parts of Hwanghae south of the 38th parallel, but excludes the part of Kyonggi north of the 38th parallel.

b) This includes Cheju Island, though in 1949 it had a separate political status.

c) This is only that part of Kangwon south of the 38th parallel.

d) This is only the area south of the 38th parallel.

Sources : Census Reports of the Government-General of Chosen for 1925-1944. Census Report of the Republic of Korea for 1949.

## Distribution of Korean Population by Age and Sex in 1944

| Age | Men | Women |
|---|---|---|
| 0— 5 | 2,540,256 | 2,487,719 |
| 6—10 | 1,771,158 | 1,702,728 |
| 11—15 | 1,483,725 | 1,392,808 |
| 16—20 | 1,092,099 | 1,126,058 |
| 21—25 | 856,074 | 947,291 |
| 26—30 | 813,083 | 852,325 |
| 31—35 | 753,666 | 780,490 |
| 36—40 | 640,693 | 645,742 |
| 41—45 | 579,668 | 564,162 |
| 46—50 | 530,884 | 507,337 |
| 51—55 | 446,223 | 451.061 |
| 56—60 | 341,634 | 353,568 |
| 61—65 | 290,508 | 311,854 |
| 66—70 | 176,672 | 201,857 |
| 71—75 | 126,079 | 157,014 |
| 76—80 | 50,357 | 68,514 |
| 81—85 | 20,070 | 31,611 |
| 86—90 | 5,645 | 10,747 |
| 91—95 | 1,638 | 3,452 |
| 96—over 100 | 1,541 | 2,663 |
| **Total** | **12,521,173** | **12,599,001** |

Source : Census of 1944.

Note : This includes only the Korean element in the population.

*Appendix E* | Statistics of Forestry

Character of Forest Land in Korea (*in chungbo; 1 chungbo=2.45 acres*)

|  | 1940 | 1943 |
|---|---|---|
| Standing Trees | 11,488,244 | 11,276,744 |
| Sparse Standing Trees | 2,164,818 | 2,316,870 |
| No Standing Trees | 1,129,554 | 1,198,047 |
| Fire-field Areas | 507,112 | 455,754 |
| Reclaimable for Forest | 163,401 | 199,593 |
| Useable for Pasture | 156,870 | 175,272 |
| Useable for Grass | 259,538 | 281,541 |
| Abandoned Forest Land | 403,108 | 370,402 |
| **Total** | **16,272,645 chungbo** | **16,274,223 chungbo** |

Quantities of Forest Products

|  | 1940 | 1943 | *Unit of Measure* |
|---|---|---|---|
| Cut Wood | 3,364,434 | 11,926,619 | Cubic Meters |
| Bamboo | 200,130 | 131,526 | Bundles |
| Firewood | 1,137,836 | 894,023 | 1000 Kwan or |
| Charcoal | 38,240 | 55,579 | 827 Lbs. |
| Branches and Leaves | 999,104 | 910,098 | " |
| Other Fuel Material | 1,492,068 | 1,254,271 | " |
| Green Cuttings | 208,943 | 263,612 | " |
| Compost Material | 1,257,739 | 1,816,260 | " |
| Animal Feed | 500,428 | 585,967 | " |

Source : The Bank of Korea, Economic Review, 1949, Seoul, Korea, 1950, Tables 44 and 47.

# Appendix F | Mineral and Hydroelectric Power Resources

### Production of Major Minerals in Korea (*in metric tons*)

|  | 1938 | 1944 |
|---|---|---|
| Anthracite Coal | 1,723,290 | 4,530,263 |
| Lignite Coal | 1,696,061 | 2,518,513 |
| Iron Ore | 768,000 | 3,331,814 |
| Gold (In Kilograms) | 27,788 | 598 |
| Copper | 5,828 | 5,193 |
| Amorphous Graphite | 44,815 | 74,879 |
| Crystalline Graphite | 12,503 | 28,427 |
| Tungsten Ore | 2,625 | 8,333 |
| Lead | 6,086 | 21,200 |
| Zinc Ore | 9,167 |  |
| Zinc (Metallic) |  | 20,011 |
| Manganese | 780 | 33,584 |
| Fluorspar | 37,391 | 75,227 |
| Magnesite | 31,937 | 157,745 |

Source: The Bank of Korea, Economic Review, 1949, Seoul, Korea, 1950, Table 51.

## Notes on Exploitation of Major Mineral Resources and Hydroelectric Power

**Coal.** Korea has large deposits of low-grade anthracite coal. In prewar years, production was increased very greatly, in part to provide an important export to Japan. The amount averaged over a million tons annually in the five years before the war. This anthracite coal export was matched by the import into Korea of bituminous coal or coking coal from Manchuria and north China, and of steam coals from Japan. In 1944, the export of anthracite coal totalled 1,423,802 metric tons, whereas the import of bituminous coal totalled more than 2,250,000 tons. In addition, northeast Korea possesses some low-grade bituminous coal deposits, termed more correctly lignite or brown coals. These deposits were developed largely to provide raw materials for coal liquefaction plants. The peak year of coal production was 1944, when 4,530,263 metric tons of anthracite coal and 2,518,513 tons of brown coal were mined.

In the postwar period the coal deposits were exploited extensively, particularly in South Korea, where the demands for fuel were very great. Production in South Korea increased from 463,153 metric tons in 1947 to 1,065,961 tons in 1949; however, because of the Korean war, production was only 128,871 tons in 1951, but increased to 575,906 tons in 1952 and 866,433 tons in 1953.

The major producing region in the south is in the Samchok region, which had been developed by the Japanese to the extent of producing 944,000 tons of anthracite in 1944. Near this field is another important coal mining area, the Yongwol field. This produced 275,000 tons in 1944; in previous years it had been a higher producer; for example, in 1941 it produced 441,000 tons. The coal in this area is an anthracite which disintegrates very easily because of its graphitic character. Both of these coal producing districts are isolated and transportation links have been difficult to construct. Nevertheless, production of coal was pushed, particularly in order to use the coal in the production of thermal power at the plant of Yongwol. Mining machinery and equipment were imported to develop and mechanize the fields. In 1952, the Samchok field produced 228,071 metric tons of anthracite, in 1953 production increased to 433,732 tons. The Yongwol field produced 126,377 tons in 1952 and 137,504 tons in 1953. One other major coal field in South Korea is in the Hwasun area in South Cholla Province, where two areas produced 254,000 tons of anthracite coal in 1944. The Hwasun field produced 41,679 metric tons in 1952 and 56,416 tons in 1953. The nearby Eunsung-Munkyung field produced 46,885 metric tons in 1952 and 54,946 tons in 1953. In addition, in recent years some peat has been hand-cut, mostly in the month of May from water-soaked lands. In 1952 peat production in South Korea was 80,677 metric tons; in 1953 it was 72,925 metric tons.

Most of the Korean coal exports were from northern Korea, the major anthracite coal fields being scattered in the northwestern section in the vicinity of Pyongyang. These deposits were exploited originally for the Japanese navy and for Japanese industries. Because this anthracite, like that of southern Korea, crumbles easily, it is most often formed into briquettes. The coal fields a few miles northeast of Pyongyang, along the Taedong River, are the most important producers. About fifty miles away, near Kaechon, in the basin of the Chongchon River, are other anthracite coal fields of less importance. The production of anthracite in northern Korea in 1944 is estimated to have been 2,986,000 tons; in 1946 it was reported to be 830,000 metric tons, but firm data on postwar production are not available.

In the extreme northeast of Korea along the Tumen River are fields which produce a low-grade lignite. Other lignite deposits occur in northeastern Korea near Kilchu. These coals which were used in coal liquefaction plants, supplied fuel to alleviate the petroleum shortages which Japan suffered. Production of lignite for all of Korea in 1944 was 2,518,513 tons, of which about 30,000 tons were produced in South Korea. North Korea lignite production in 1946 was estimated to be 433,000 metric tons.

Despite the scattered coal deposits Korea lacks one of the most important elements for modern industrialization—good-grade bituminous coal suitable for coking. Such coal, as well as steam coal for the railroads, has to be imported.

**Iron Ore.** At an early period of Korean history small scattered deposits of iron ore were mined. However, modern developments began when Japan exploited the deposits of northwestern Korea and developed the iron and steel industry which served them well in the 1920's. The big developments took place when the low-grade iron ore at Musan in extreme northeastern Korea was utilized for the purposes of war production. The production of iron ore in Korea in 1938 was 768,000 metric tons, but by 1944 it had increased to 3,331,814 tons, as shown on the accompanying table. The Musan area, whose ores accounted for the increased production, has a low-grade magnetite ore of about thirty-five per cent iron content; the reserves are estimated to amount to 1,200,000,000 tons.

The development of the Musan iron ore deposit in northeastern Korea was made possible only by the introduction of new methods of ore enrichment. American engineering firms aided in the development of the enterprise. The ore itself is mined from extensive open-cut deposits.

## Korean Iron Ore Production, 1944

| Deposit | Metric Tons | Per Cent |
|---|---|---|
| NORTHERN KOREA | | |
| Musan | 1,050,679 | 31.5 |
| Hasong | 568,419 | 17.1 |
| Kaechon | 473,253 | 14.2 |
| Yangyong | 289,513 | 8.7 |
| Iwon | 276,963 | 8.3 |
| Chaeryong | 216,195 | 6.5 |
| Others north of 38° | 346,035 | 10.4 |
| SOUTHERN KOREA | | |
| Total of all provinces | 110,757 | 3.3 |
| **Grand Total** | **3,331,814** | **100.0** |

Source : SCAP, Natural Resources Section Report No. 35. *Mineral Industry of Korea in 1944*, 14 May, 1946.

The processing carried on near Musan includes the milling of the ore, its separation by magnetic processes, and the sintering of the concentrate. In 1944 the mine produced over 1,000,000 tons, part of which was shipped to Japan. The rest was used in the iron and steel plants at Chongjin and Songjin where in 1944 electrical furnaces produced 25,000 tons of high-grade steel.

The largest production in northwestern Korea has normally come from the Kaechon mines, northeast of Pyongyang. The deposits south of Pyongyang in Hwanghae Province are mostly open-cut mines, exploiting small layers of hematite and bog iron. The iron ore from this area was used in the iron and steel plant built at Kyomipo during World War I. During World War II the Japanese developed batteries of small blast furnaces—which were believed to be more economical—in Pyongyang and elsewhere in northwestern Korea to utilize these iron ores.

South Korea has virtually no iron ore of any importance. The largest deposit is a low-grade iron ore, averaging thirty-seven per cent iron content, located at Samhwa, near Samchok. Production in 1953 for all of South Korea was only 18,971 tons of forty-five to sixty per cent enriched ore.

**Gold.** The gold deposits of Korea are scattered in almost every county. Most of the gold occurs in lode deposits in ancient schists and gneisses, often in combination with other minerals. Because of the weathering of the basic gold bearing veins, alluvial deposits occurred along the streams ; many of the small placer deposits have been exhausted.

In desperate need of foreign exchange, the Japanese exploited the remaining alluvial deposits as well as those in which the gold was a part of a complex ore. In 1938, 27,788 kilograms of gold were produced in Korea ; of this 8,240 kilograms were produced in southern Korea and 19,548 kilograms in northern Korea. After the outbreak of World War II gold production was virtually suspended in Korea except in those lode deposits where production of other minerals essential to war production was being exploited. Much of the equipment and the larger part of labor forces were diverted to the production of other minerals.

After the war, gold production was started again, particularly in the small alluvial deposits which Korean miners had been accustomed to working. In South Korea were two major producing areas, one o‘ them on the Ongjin peninsula just below the thirty-eighth parallel, where gold is found in association with lead and zinc, and the other in North Cholla Province, south of the town of Chongju. In South Korea production in 1948 was only 108 kilograms. Refinery production was increased to 807 kilograms in 1950 ; production fell to 237 kilograms in 1951, but increased to 573 kilograms in 1952 and 493 kilograms in 1953. The major gold mining areas in northern Korea were originally developed with American capital and technical skill. The most famous mines are the Unsan and Pukchin mines, located in the mountainous area northeast of the plains of North Pyongan Province. Scattered through northwestern Korea are alluvial workings, some of which were mined by large dredges. Little is known of postwar developments in North Korean gold mining.

**Copper.** Copper mining in Korea was often done in connection with gold mining. The sale of the gold which was found with the copper ore paid part of the mining expenses, and made possible the development of the poor-grade copper ores. Because of wartime demand, the production of copper was stimulated by government subsidies. However, much of the mining was on an uneconomic base, for the deposits were small and of low grade. Production reached a peak of 12,944 metric tons in 1940. The ore was smelted in Korea or exported to Japan. Most of the larger copper mines were in northern Korea, particularly in the northern interior, in Kapsan in South Hamgyong Province and in the Kanggye region of North Pyongan Province. In the postwar years a few copper mines were opened in South Korea but these did not begin to meet the minimum requirement for the rehabilitation of the electrical utilities in that part of the country. In the south the major production came from scattered deposits mostly located near the coast in South Kyongsang Province. 1949 production was 1,815 tons of four to twenty per cent concentrate copper ore, it then drastically decreased but increased in 1952 to 10,832 tons and in 1953 to 11,136 metric tons of concentrates.

**Graphite.** Korea has been one of the largest producers of graphite in the world. There are two types, amorphous and crystalline. The amorphous graphites are found in association with coal deposits, where folding, faulting, and igneous intrusions have changed the coal into graphite. Production was increased under the stimulus of the Japanese war economy and reached a peak in 1944, when 22,427 tons of crystalline graphite and 74,879 tons of amorphous graphite were produced. After World War II the industry declined, and in South Korea— where amorphous graphite was mined exclusively in the Sobaek Range between

North Chongchong and North Kyongsang Provinces—many of the mines and mills were looted. In 1949, after some of the mines were rehabilitated, 39,803 metric tons of amorphous and 808 tons of crystalline graphite were produced. 1953 production was 19,945 tons of amorphous and 648 tons of crystalline graphite.

**Tungsten.** Because of the demand for tungsten for the iron and steel industry, d:posits of scheelite-bearing tactite in Korea were greatly developed during the war years. In southern Korea, production increased from 700 metric tons in 1940 to 5,383 metric tons in 1944. The production for all of Korea in 1944 was 8,402 metric tons. The major deposit in southern Korea was at Songdong, on the border between Kangwon Province and North Kyongsang Province. The production from this area provided an important source of foreign exchange following the war. In 1949, 1,342 tons of sixty-four to eighty per cent tungsten ore was produced ; after a slump, production was increased to 3,789 tons in 1952 and in 1953 to 7,441 metric tons. This increase was possible because of an artificia'ly high price offered by the United States, but this contract lapsed in 1954 and production decreased.

**Minor Minerals.** Numerous deposits of minor minerals are scattered throughout Korea. Lead and zinc production was increased during the war ; as with copper, both of these minerals were exported to Japan in a raw or semi-refined state and the pure product was imported back from Japan. Production reached a peak during 1944 when 21,200 metric tons of lead and 20,113 tons of zinc metal were produced. Manganese production, which had been negligible before the war, increased to 33,584 tons in 1944 and magnesite production reached a peak of 157,745 tons. Numerous other minor mineral products were developed under the stimulus of war production—cobalt, molybdenite, barytes, fluorspar, mica, asbestos, and silica sand. Most of these came from small deposits which in normal times would not be economical to mine. Unsuccessful attempts were made to use the Korean alunite deposits, but in the end bauxite had to be imported. Finally, of importance in the human diet and for the chemical industry, salt was obtained by solar evaporation in salt pans along the coasts in northwestern and western Korea, and to a less extent in South Korea, where 1947 production was 5,877 tons. However, as a result of special efforts, production was raised in South Korea to 188,812 tons ot salt in 1949; it decreased in 1950 and 1951, but in 1952 production was 192,684 tons of salt.

**Hydroelectric Resources.** Under the Japanese great emphasis was placed upon the development of hydroelectric power resources, particularly in northern Korea. This, along with the mineral production, enabled the transformation of the economy of Korea. As of 1944, the total installed hydroelectric power capacity was 1,426,790 KW, and plants having an additional capacity of 1,169,750 KW were under construction. Another group of plants with a capacity of 904,220 KW was projected for construction. In addition, sites where 1,306,600 KW might be produced had been investigated. Finally, there were sites where 1,056,360 KW might be produced which were undergoing investigation. Thus a total of hydroelectric power developed or partially planned amounted to 5,863,720 KW. Of this 85.8 per cent was in North Korea.

The largest completed power plant was on the Yalu River, at Supung, where the Japanese had constructed one of the largest dams in the world, roughly qeuivalent to Boulder Dam in the United States. The plant which supplied an equal amount of power to southern Manchuria and northern Korea, had a generating capacity of 600,000 KW. It has been reported that three of the 100,000 KW generators, those designed to provide power for Manchuria, were taken away by the Russians in their period of occupancy. Under the original Japanese plan there were to be a series of seven hydroelectric projects along the Yalu and its tributaries. One of them, the Kanggye project, with a capacity of 340,000 KW, was reported to be well along in construction at the time of the Japanese collapse.

In northeastern Korea, some of the northward-flowing tributaries of the Yalu were dammed, forming large reservoirs; the water from these reservoirs was then taken by conduits over the drainage divide and down the escarpment to the lowlands along the Sea of Japan. Here hydroelectric power stations were developed, usually in a series. Three such systems, each with four stations, were developed on the Changjin (326,500 KW installed capacity), the Hochon (309,800 KW) and the Pujon Rivers (200,375 KW). These enterprises were of a gigantic nature. Numerous other smaller projects were developed. For example, a small plant on the upper Han River at Chongyang had a capacity of 39,600 KW, and another plant at Hwachun had a capacity of 81,000 KW.

In addition to these hydroelectric power plants there were several thermal power-generating plants which used coal or oil. At Pyongyang, in northwestern Korea, was a generating plant with a capacity of 10,000 KW. The largest plants in southern Korea were one near Seoul, with a capacity of 22,500 KW, one at Pusan with 14,000 KW, and a large one in the coal fields at Yongwol, with a capacity of 107,000 KW. In actual practice these plants were never utilized to their maximum extent; for example, the Yongwol plant averaged 35,000 KW production and had a capability of efficient production of 60,000 KW.

These hydroelectric power systems, with the small thermo-plants at the major cities and the one large plant at Yongwol, had a good inter-connecting transmission system and capabilities for great expansion. Unfortunately the imposition of the thirty-eighth parallel as a dividing line and the subsequent interruption in May, 1948 of electric power movement across the line negated this advantageous economic situation. The power supplies in South Korea were, as a consequence, in very short supply. In 1947, for instance, 274 million KW hours of power had been generated in the south but an additional 552 million KW hours had been drawn from North Korea. After the shut-off, power barges were brought to the ports of Inchon and Pusan to supply the major urban areas. In 1949 from all sources 655 million KW hours were generated in South Korea. The supply was, of course, curtailed during the hostilities, but by 1952 generation of power had reached 635 million KW hours and by 1953, 736 million KW hours; of this 394 million KWH were from hydroelectric plants, 131 million KWH from thermal power plants, and 211 million KWH from power barges. During the war, the power plants of North Korea were subjected to very heavy air raids and most of the installations were gutted. However, according to some reports, these plants are being rehabilitated with equipment from Eastern Europe and the Soviet Union.

## *Appendix  G*  |  The Industrial Pattern of Korea

### Nature and Growth of Industrial Establishments in Korea

| Category | 1938 Factories | 1938 Workers | 1944 Factories | 1944 Workers |
|---|---|---|---|---|
| Textiles | 608 | 47,384 | 2,082 | 81,441 |
| Metal Working | 295 | 13,612 | 619 | 61,523 |
| Machinery and Tools | 613 | 24,745 | 1,226 | 64,048 |
| Ceramics | 342 | 11,310 | 1,952 | 44,192 |
| Chemicals | 1,618 | 52,293 | 1,019 | 70,338 |
| Lumber & Woodworking | 360 | 7,485 | 1,799 | 30,682 |
| Printing & Binding | 313 | 6,905 | 586 | 10,121 |
| Food Processing | 2,348 | 35,547 | 1,990 | 36,006 |
| Gas & Electricity | 34 | 939 | 140 | 7,725 |
| Miscellaneous | 422 | 12,179 | 888 | 15,153 |
| **Total** | **6,953** | **212,459** | **12,301** | **421,229** |

### Size of Establishments in 1938 in Per Cent of Total

| | Number of Factories | Workers |
|---|---|---|
| 5— 30 Workers | 81.7 | 26.1 |
| 30— 100 ″ | 13.61 | 22.3 |
| 100— 200 ″ | 2.7 | 12.3 |
| 200—1000 ″ | 1.9 | 23.4 |
| Over 1000 ″ | 0.19 | 15.9 |

Sources :  Annual Economic Review of Chosen, 1941–1942, p. 154–155.
Census of Chosen, 1944.

### Industrial Regions of Korea

It is difficult to assess accurately the present industrial situation in Korea or to chart the future. Though some of the industries developed by 1944 were designed strictly for war production and were relatively uneconomic for times

225

of peace, it is still worthwhile to describe briefly the industrial areas which had been developed in Korea by that date, for it is upon these bases that future developments will depend.

The region along the coast in **Northeastern Korea** was developed in recent years into a large industrial area. In their attempt to raise war production, the Japanese took full advantage of the area's electric power potential—derived largely from the tributaries of the Yalu River—and of its mineral resources. Whole cities devoted almost entirely to manufacturing sprang up almost overnight as the Japanese industrialists moved towards their objectives. Where they did not build anew, they reconstructed, and ancient Korean commercial and administrative towns were transformed to meet their needs.

At Wonsan, in the southern part of the industrial area, where the Koreans had developed textile works and fish-processing and rice-milling plants, the Japanese constructed large oil refineries, storage depots, and shipping facilities. The city became the center for making and filling oil drums and cans for the distribution of kerosene. North of Wonsan in the Hamhung area, where for centuries the Koreans had processed agricultural products, a new port, Hungnam, was built at a former fishing village. The Japanese transformed the landscape with huge plants devoted to the manufacturing of copper, aluminum, and chemical products. The Hungnam chemical plant alone was one of the largest in the Far East.

Further north along the coast three smaller industrial towns, Tanchon, Songjin, and Kilchu, were expanded as workers poured in to man the newly introduced steel mills, copper refineries, and coal liquefaction plants. Finally at Chongjin, sprang up another industrial complex which utilized iron ore from Musan. Here, as in other ports along the coast, fish processing was stepped up. A number of minor industries, such as railroad workshops and construction equipment plants, which depended upon the iron and steel industry, were developed.

This industrial area of northeastern Korea suffered much as a consequence of the changing political control of the Far East. Because the industries had been built to expand Japanese war production, attempts were made, according to reports, to sabotage them when the Japanese were defeated. But in all probability, much more damage was done by neglect and mix-up following the exodus of the Japanese technicians. There are reports that the Russians dismantled many of the industrial plants for shipment to Siberia. Certainly North Korea did not need the tremendous productive capacity created by the Japanese. The dismantling may have been done on a calculated basis so that smaller and more efficient units could be operated. Specific knowledge of production in the postwar years is, of course, lacking, though there are reports that some industries were re-established and that Russian technicians replaced the Japanese. These plants were greatly damaged by air and ground action during the war in Korea. As for the future, it needs to be stressed that this industrial region could be converted to a peacetime economy; for example, the nitrogen-fixation plant at Hungnam, which produced TNT, also produced nitrogen fertilizer, which is needed by Korean farmers.

The second important industrial area in North Korea is located in and around **Pyongyang** in northwestern Korea. Included in this area is the port city of Chinnampo, the iron and steel center of Kyomipo, and the iron mines near Kaechon, northeast of Pyongyang. Nearby are productive anthracite coal mines and limestone, slate, gravel, and clay deposits. From the mountains to the east, minerals, such as gold and copper, were channeled into this region for refining and shipping. Power was supplied from the hydroelectric projects on the Yalu and its tributaries and there were, in addition, a small (10,000 KW) thermal power plant at Pyongyang and a few other very small plants at individual factories. The Taedong River has been used for rafting logs and for the movement of varied commodities from Pyongyang down to Chinnampo and upstream to and from rural areas and mines.

The Pyongyang area had long been an important manufacturing center for consumer goods and a processing center for agricultural commodities. However, it was not until the Japanese gained control that real industrial expansion took place. Rice milling was mechanized and new industries, such as a corn products plant, designed principally for the production of glucose and built with American capital and technical aid, were established. But the greatest development was in the exploitation of the iron ore deposits and coal fields. The blast furnaces built at Kyomipo which had the advantage of a tidewater location, were considerably expanded as Japan gained control of Manchuria and north China, important sources of coking coal. A large cement plant was built a few miles east of Pyongyang. Factories for manufacturing textiles, rubber shoes, and cigarettes were constructed in the industrial suburbs of the city. In the late thirties and during the war rayon mills and chemical and iron and steel plants were constructed and Pyongyang became more of a heavy-industry center. There had been an arsenal at Pyongyang for a number of years, but during World War II this was expanded, and new war production industries—aluminum and aircraft—were established. The copper refinery at Chinnampo was expanded, and a chemical plant was built north of Pyongyang at Sunchon.

The area as a whole was expected to have an even greater increase in industrial production when the hydroelectric power projects were more highly developed in the mountainous northern interior and when the industrial complex was closely integrated with the resource areas of north China and Manchuria. However, these intentions were frustrated with the collapse of Japan and with the imposition of the thirty-eighth parallel. Subsequently, the area's industrial facilities deteriorated and there was a reversion to the more simple manufacturing of consumer goods which had been early developed in this area. Finally, during the fighting in Korea, air raids on the industrial and transportation facilities wrecked the whole industrial complex of Pyongyang. According to recent reports from Communist sources, great reconstruction has taken place and the industries are flourishing. Close ties have been re-established with Manchuria and north China.

The last industrial area in North Korea centers in the town of **Sinuiju** at the mouth of the Yalu River, an important transit region between Korea and China. When the Japanese built a railroad line northward to connect with the Manchurian system, a railroad bridge was built about ten miles south of the old city of Uiju; thus a new city, Sinuiju (New Uiju) was developed. During World War II port developments were initiated on a promontory out in the Yellow Sea, but it is not clear how far this project was carried forward.

The industrial area of Sinuiju was initially important as a processing center for logs which were floated down the Yalu River. Later, new industries were established, using hydroelectric power generated at the large Supung Dam, located some sixty miles upstream. This power was utilized for the manufacturing of aluminum, chemicals, and aircraft parts. Because this region was so dependent upon war industries, it suffered greatly from deterioration and dismantling when hostilities ceased. The logging industry and the railroad work-shops have continued in operation, but the latter were hard hit during the recent fighting. Here, also, according to Communist reports, great re-development of industries has taken place.

In South Korea one major industrial area is located in and around the cities of **Seoul** and its port Inchon, some forty miles distant. Seoul has long been an administrative center and the home of advanced consumer goods industries, whose products were made by highly skilled craftsmen for the Korean court and the nobles. The city's fine textiles, delicate gold and silver work, brass-bound and pearl-inlaid furniture were famous throughout the Orient. The basic industries included plants for processing food products and for manufacturing textiles and paper products. In the early days of Japanese control large rice mills were erected at Inchon and at other towns in the region. On the whole, however, the Seoul area saw little heavy industrial development or war production con-struction. Rather its big developments were in the fields of consumer goods, particularly textiles, and transportation and communications equipment. Thus numerous small plants each producing a component part or manufacturing products such as rubber shoes, pottery, glassware, light bulbs, sprang up. Because the central government was located there, Seoul had a printing industry more highly developed than any other in Korea. At the end of World War II the Seoul industrial area did not deteriorate so greatly as some of the other industrial areas, through it suffered a shortage of managerial and labor skill. Further industrial rehabilitation was handicapped by inflation, which had the effect of driving capital into land investment. However, with the import of certain key commodities, such as cotton, industrial production picked up. But such progress was short-lived as a consequence of two events growing out of the conflict between North and South Korea ; first the region's industry was hard hit when electric power supplied from north of the thirty-eighth parallel was cut off in May, 1948. Second, the industrial plants themselves were devastated by general fighting and air raids early in the Korean war. The future of the industry in the Seoul area will be dependent upon the rehabilitation of the industrial plants and the stabilization of the Korean economy ; the prospects at the moment are bleak.

In **Southwestern Korea** are a number of scattered industrial centers which might be considered as making up an industrial area ; these include as major centers Taejon, a railroad center ; the port of Kunsan ; the inland city of Kwangju, important for its textile industry ; and the port of Mokpo. There are a number of other smaller industrial centers. This area is predominantly devoted to processing the relatively abundant agricultural products grown there. Densely populated, Southwestern Korea is an important market for consumer goods. There are numerous light industries, but few heavy ones. Consequently industrial rehabilitation was relatively rapid in the postwar period and after the area was liberated by UN forces.

A similar industrial area is located around the city of **Taegu** in southeastern Korea, where rice, cotton and tobacco, grown in the highly developed agricultural lands of the Naktong river basin, are processed.

A relatively small heavy-industry center, the only one in South Korea, is located in a rather isolated position in the area of **Yongwol** and **Samchok**. In-dustries here are based largely on the anthracite coal deposits found in the vicinity. A large (107,000 KW) thermal power plant and a chemical industry are located at Yongwol. A cement plant which, however, can supply only a fraction of the needs of South Korea, has been operating for a number of years at Samchok. This area suffered in the fighting which took place in Korea. In order to grow as an industrial area, transportation links need to be developed both within the region and from it to the other parts of southern Korea. Thermal power production is uneven at Yongwol because of the difficulty of transporting the coal and other raw materials in this mountainous terrain.

The city of **Pusan** in the southeastern corner of the peninsula has been the major Korean port since the days of Japanese occupation. Boat building and repair are important industries. Fishing equipment is also produced. Fish canning and fish-oil pressing are carried on. The factories in this densely populated region produce drugs and chemicals, rubber shoes, bicycles, bicycle tires, and other consumer goods. One recent noteworthy development was the expansion of the textile industry and its operation on a much more intensive basis. Because of the tremendous demand for clothing after the Korean war, the mills operate twenty-four hours a day, using, largely, imported raw materials. The impetus which has been given the industries in the Pusan area by this and other developments may continue to make it an important industrial area as well as a shipping point.

*Appendix H* | # Recent Economic Production in South Korea

| PRODUCT | 1947 | 1948 | 1949 | 1950 | 1951 | 1952 | 1953 |
|---|---|---|---|---|---|---|---|
| Rice *(1000 M.T.)* | 2111 | 2361 | 2284 | 2264 | 1759 | 1439 | 2191 |
| Wheat and Barley *(1000 M.T.)* | 520 | 548 | 708 | 731 | 426 | 611 | 721 |
| Other Grains *(1000 M.T.)* | 60 | 80 | 116 | 72 | 96 | 154 | 83 |
| Marine Products *(1000 M.T.)* | 302 | 287 | 300 | 219 | 277 | 278 | 259 |
| Power Generated *(Million KWH)* | 274 | 489 | 655 | 418 | 337 | 635 | 736 |
| Anthracite Coal *(1000 M.T.)* | 463 | 799 | 1066 | 456 | 129 | 576 | 866 |
| Lignite Coal *(1000 M.T.)* | 37 | 68 | 60 | 27 | 6 | 2 | 0 |
| Peat *(1000 M.T.)* | — | — | — | — | 319 | 80 | 73 |
| Gold *(Kilograms)* | 77 | 108 | 106 | 463 | 31 | 619 | 493 |
| Amor. Graphite *(1000 M.T.)* | 2.6 | 14.9 | 39.8 | 16.1 | 21.6 | 14.8 | 19.9 |
| Copper Ore Conc. *(4-20%) (1000 M.T.)* | 1.8 | 1.1 | 0.3 | 0.2 | 1.1 | 10.8 | 11.1 |
| Tungsten Ore *(64-80%) (1000 M.T.)* | 1.0 | 1.2 | 1.3 | 0.8 | 1.2 | 3.8 | 7.4 |
| Cotton Products: | | | | | | | |
| Weaving Yarn *(1000 lbs.)* | 11.2 | 10.5 | 23.6 | 17.7 | 10.4 | 15.1 | 20.0 |
| Sales Yarn *(1000 lbs.)* | 1.1 | 2.6 | 4.9 | 4.1 | 2.7 | 6.2 | 9.2 |
| Cotton Sheeting *(1000 yards)* | 30.6 | 28.1 | 63.7 | 53.9 | 29.9 | 43.2 | 60.4 |
| Woolen-Worsteds *(1000 yards)* | — | — | 47.4 | 716 | 336 | 431 | 581 |
| Rubber-Canvas Shoes *(1 Million pairs)* | — | 27 | 32 | 5 | 16 | 19 | 22 |
| Bicycle Tires *(1000's)* | — | 222 | 482 | — | 360 | 320 | 62 |
| Rice Rollers *(1000 pairs)* | — | 52 | 38 | 3 | 23 | 34 | 20 |
| Common Brick *(1000 M.T.)* | 3.4 | 39.5 | 112.8 | 84.0 | 65.6 | 91.4 | 42.0 |
| Cement *(1000 M.T.)* | 18.2 | 17.4 | 24.1 | 11.5 | 7.3 | 36.2 | 41.7 |

| PRODUCT | 1947 | 1948 | 1949 | 1950 | 1951 | 1952 | 1953 |
|---------|------|------|------|------|------|------|------|
| Coal Briquettes | 201 | 77 | 168 | 37 | 27 | 47 | 58 |
| (*1000 M.T.*) | | | | | | | |
| Tobacco Prod. | 8.9 | 11.1 | 13.6 | 10.5 | 11.5 | 17.5 | 15.5 |
| (*1000 M.T.*) | | | | | | | |
| Salt | 5.9 | 90.0 | 188.8 | 174.9 | 84.6 | 203.9 | 192.7 |
| (*1000 M.T.*) | | | | | | | |

Sources: United Nations, ECA, and Bank of Korea documents. Estimated from diverse data, though it may be noted that all of the economic data from South Korea during these years might be classed as gross estimates.

*Appendix I* | Notes on the Photographs

The photographs have purposely been arranged in four blocks and with limited, running captions. In these notes the sources of the pictures, unless I have taken them, the general location if known, and details of them are given. As I have noted in the preface to this book I am particularly grateful to the United States Army and Air Force Photographic Centers in Washington and to the United Nations Korean Reconstruction Agency in New York for their kindness in giving me an opportunity of going through thousands of pictures and furnishing me with copies of those selected for use in this book.

### The Land and People of Korea

1. Heartbreak Ridge is a steep rugged part of a mountain range which overlooks a passageway south toward Seoul. It had great strategic importance and was the scene of very bitter fighting. This picture taken in April, 1952 by the U. S. Air Force shows only the grandeur of the ridge, but the small "pock-marks" are caves, bunkers, and gun emplacements.

2. This photograph was taken in 1938 near Kanggye in the Northern Interior of Korea. The even skyline, as well as the narrow valley, is fairly characteristic of this region.

3. This was taken in 1938 near Sunchon in extreme Southwestern Korea. The paddy fields terraced up the valley slope have been prepared for a winter grain crop in this mild-wintered region.

4. This picture was taken by the U. S. Air Force early in the Korean war, August, 1950, when the UN forces were attempting to delay the North Korean advance. This shows a "run-off" at Kumchon, northwest of Taegu. The flat alluvial flood plain of the river laps up around the granite hills; at the junction point are the villages.

5. This and the following three pictures were taken on a flight on a small plane across Korea in May, 1954. The weather was clear but hazy for pictures. This first picture shows the weathered granite hills. The faint lines along the slopes—like contour lines on a map—are small trees or sod planted to try to stop erosion. The alluvial plain is used for winter crops and vegetables much in demand in nearby Seoul.

6. This picture shows the upper Han River entrenched in its course. This was taken north of Wonju.

7. The crest line of the Taebaek Range has an abrupt slope to the east, but a gentle slope to the west. The summit of the mountains are roughly concordant in level and are remarkably flat; they have been described as the uplifted and tilted former erosional levels. The small white patches seen in this

232

picture are snow fields which were still present in mid-May.

8. On the east coast the rivers coming down from the mountains have wide channels as they reach the coast in areas where the granite is easily weathered. In the upper right of the picture is the straight form of an artificial embankment to protect the land from the river in flood stage. This picture was taken near Kangnung, almost directly east of Seoul.

9, 10, 11, 12. These pictures of clouds and pavilions were all taken in Pyongyang in the 1930's by a skillful Japanese photographer, whose business name was Meijiya.

13. The stone observatory at Kyongju is shaped like a gigantic milk bottle. From a wooden structure (long gone) at its summit the royal astronomers during the Silla period took sightings on the stars. This picture was taken in 1939.

14. Kija, a Chinese sage, was reputed to have come into the area around Pyongyang in 1122 B. C. and brought Chinese civilization to Korea. There are a number of places in Korea which claim his tomb; this is the one at Pyongyang, photographed in 1938. The tomb is arranged in typical fashion with the name tablet before the mound and in front of it the ceremonial table of stone. Guarding the tomb are figures of warriors and horses.

15, 16. These two pictures of Korean people at work and leisure were taken in Pyongyang in the 1930's by Meijiya. They illustrate well the traditional clothing worn by the country people.

17. No location has been given for this picture, other than South Korea, by the U.S. Army, whose picture it is. Korean women pound clothes on rocks and like to wash them in fresh running water, if possible.

18. The carrying of burdens may be done on *chige*'s as the man in this UNKRA photo is doing; the double-tracked railroad going from Pusan to Seoul adds a contrasting item in the background of this picture.

19. Another way of carrying loads, like this trussed-up pig, is on ox-drawn sleds which are equally useful over the snow in winter or the muddy roads in summer in northern Korea. This picture was taken in 1938 in Kanggye in the Northern Interior. Actually most of the heavy loads are carried on wheeled carts, rather than sleds. Usually these are two-wheeled, but in the large city environs where the roads are better they may have four wheels.

20. Periodically, fresh thatch is laid on the roofs of the rural houses. This requires the cooperation of relatives and neighbors as this picture taken by the U. S. Army in December, 1950 shows. The latticed, wooden doors are hung on simple hinges; the relatively narrow eaves and the type of construction show that it was taken in southern Korea. The men on the roof are wearing hemp hats, denoting the fact that they are in mourning for some near male relative.

21. The farm villages in southern Korea are apt to be more widely spaced with more room between the houses. In the background, the long low building is probably a new school or public building. This is a U. S. Army photograph taken in July, 1950.

22. This Korean gentleman with the wispy beard and the *chige* on his back was photographed in an expressive mood by Meijiya in the 1930's in northern Korea.

23. The *mudang*, or female sorcerer, in a trance is very rarely photographed. This action picture during a dance was taken by Meijiya outside of Pyongyang in the 1930's.

24. Korean women have remarkable strength of character and ability to adjust to the problems of life. This elderly lady in the U. S. Army photograph taken in August, 1951 near Uijongbu close to the battle front sits beside the ruins of her home grinding grain in a discarded army helmet.

25. On certain days of the year, after offering ceremonial dishes to the spirits of their ancestors, a Korean family will enjoy a picnic at the family tomb, in this case with a new tombstone. The view out over the valley is picturesque; this is not happenstance, for tomb sites are picked for their pleasing vistas.

## The Economy of Korea

26. Alluvial material eroded from the hills and mountains washes down on the plains. On these gently sloping plains the paddy fields, diked with narrow embankments following the natural contours, make an intricate pattern. Some hill slopes may be cleared of their forest cover and used for crop land. In this U. S. Army photograph of June, 1951, UN troops can be seen going single file along the paths in a valley in North Korea.

27. The Korean plow is a simple bent wooden timber with an iron sheath pulled by an ox or cow. On this weathered granite hill slope near Taejon in Southwestern Korea the ground is being freshly plowed in the spring of 1954. One minor item is that this farmer under the guidance of an agricultural expert is plowing the field along the contour to curb the soil erosion—not in the straight rows used in previous years.

28. The seedbeds in the foreground of this picture (taken from a moving train south of Seoul in May, 1954) are just beginning to turn green with rice shoots. A farmer and his wife have flooded and are working over the earthen clumps in another field. In the distance is the village nestled against the hill slope.

29, 30, 31, 32. This sequence of pictures, taken by the U. S. Army in 1950, 52, shows some of the steps in rice cultivation:

29. Transplanting usually is done on a cooperative basis and cloudy, rainy days are advantageous.

30. Harvesting is done by cutting the grain with sickles close to the ground.

31. Thrashing may be done in the old-fashioned way of pulling the stalks of grain through the serrated edges of a board or

32. in modern ways by using a foot-treadle machine which revolves a drum with wire loops knocking off the grain.

33. Winnowing, measuring, and sacking the grain and stacking the straw are often carried on in the fields rather than in the farm courtyards, the more common practice. This is a U. S. Army photograph of November, 1950.

34. This family on a hill slope near Kwangju in Southwestern Korea in 1939 were winnowing chaff on a breezy day.

35. The communally-operated grinding wheel is moved by a patient cow urged on by a small girl while the women keep the grain spread beneath the stone. On the roof of the barn some gourds are growing. U. S. Army photograph, July, 1950.

36. *Kimchi*, the Korean pickle, is made in many ways. In this U. S. Army photograph taken in a rebuilt village in 1952, a group of women are cutting the turnips, shredding the cabbage, and washing them in brine before adding the red pepper and packing the mixture away in clay jars.

37. Though only a small number of the Korean fishing boats are motorized, the one in the foreground of this UNKRA photo is so equipped. Most of the boats depend on simple sails and oars for their power.

38. Usually the fish caught along the east coast (where this U. S. Army photograph was taken north of the thirty-eighth parallel) are salted and dried, though some are sold as fresh fish in the nearby farming areas.

39. Pottery jars for *kimchi* and for other uses are made of heavy clay and baked in simple kilns. This UNKRA photo shows the jars before they have been fired.

40. The farm women usually grind their grain in simple stone or wooden bowls or hollowed logs, but the rice which is sold commercially is usually sent to mechanized rice mills similar to that shown in this U. S. Army photograph taken in Wonju in August, 1951.

41, 42, 43. These market-place scenes were taken on market day at Kangnung on the east coast in May, 1954. They show the farm women who have brought in their vegetables, usually carried in wooden bowls perched on their heads. There is always a great deal of bargaining before a purchase is made and a crowd will collect to watch the process, particularly if it is a foreigner speaking Korean who is buying the item, like silk from a mountain village. On market days the permanent stalls will have many more customers than usual.

44. Molded-rubber shoes have become the standard footwear for the Korean people. This lively scene shown in this UNKRA photo is in the marketplace at Pusan. A small detail is the partly-used cigarette stuck behind the man's ear, something often seen.

45, 46. These two Air Force photos of the ruins of the nitrogen fertilizer plant at Hungnam in northeastern Korea show the effect of the air raids which demolished the plant early in the Korean war. The pictures give some idea of the size of this Japanese-built industrial plant which was a part of a big industrial complex.

47. This bridge across the Naktong River was subjected to aerial attack with obvious success as this U. S. Army photograph of August, 1950 shows.

48. This ferry across the Kum River, northeast of Taejon, was heavily loaded on this May afternoon in 1954. The bare hills in the background are typical of the eroded landscapes in the more densely populated parts of Korea.

49. At Songjin along the Northeastern Coast one well-placed bomb up-ended and twisted this freight car. Subsequently, in November, 1950 with the advance of the UN troops this U. S. Air Force ground photo could be taken showing American soldiers surveying the wreckage.

50. This U. S. Army photo of October, 1952 shows a new home which had been built for refugees in the area south of the battle line in central Korea. Around the house is rice straw and a man is carrying a bag of rice into the courtyard.

### North Korea.

51. This photograph of an old Korean gentleman outside Pyongyang was taken in the 1930's by Meijiya. However, it is likely that today persons like this may still be found in the countryside of North Korea.

52. A group of U. S. troops flank a road up which a tank is slowly moving toward Hyesanjin on the Yalu River in the U. S. Army photograph taken in

November of 1950. Snow has already fallen and the landscape is bleak.

53. Only the wreckage of a machine shop remained to be photographed by this U. S. Army photographer at Hyesanjin on November 26, 1950.

54. This photograph of a farmstead in the Northern Interior was taken in the fall of 1938. The main house, though made of logs, is plastered with mud. The work shed shows the log construction. Out in the yard on this sunny day the quilts were airing, giving a dash of color. The hollow log chimney is partially hidden by the climbing vines. High on the hill slope are dry fields; probably they were cleared by fire.

55. Settlement is sparse in the Northern Interior, and a settlement like this near the Yalu seems relatively large. The shingle roofs and the wooden fences to protect the houses from the cold winter winds and snows are typical and well shown in this U.S. Army photograph taken in November, 1950 as the UN troops advanced toward the Yalu.

56. In a valley near Kanggye the rice was being cut in the early fall of 1938 as this picture shows. The lower hill slopes are cultivated with dry crops and the steep slopes and mountain areas are forested.

57, 58. Old Korean cities, like Kanggye, grew without much pattern. Its strategic location between two tributaries joining a major river was enhanced by the building of a city wall. Within the wall, streets are narrow and crooked. Outside are some new industrial plants and housing areas with geometric designs. The air raids had already caused some damage as shown in the first picture, but the core of the city was wiped out by the severe raid which took place on November 5, 1950, shortly after which this U. S. Air Force picture was taken.

59. The magnitude of the Supung Dam is hard to visualize unless one studies a picture such as this Air Force photo taken in February, 1953. Note the doorways in some of the buildings to get an idea of the scale of the dam. The photograph looks to the northeast, up-river. It was taken by a jet pilot flying at a low altitude. On the right are the remains of the hydroelectric power installation on which repair work had started after the heavy air raids of the summer of 1952.

60. There were a number of hydroelectric plants along the Northeastern Coast. The plant shown in the U. S. Air Force photo of July 1952 is one in the series of four in the Pujon system. The air raids had not only gutted the power station but had dislodged the penstocks.

61. Wonsan was not only a harbor but also a railroad, industrial, and commercial center. This Air Force photo was taken on June 29, 1950 just before the first air raids of the Korean war. The marshalling yards and railroad workshops, the various factory buildings, and the harbor facilities show up clearly.

62. The oil refinery at Wonsan was devastated by air raids before the UN troops reached the city on their northward surge, as shown in this Air Force photo.

63. The top of the pass between South Pyongan and South Hamgyong Provinces is shown in this picture taken in 1938 when I walked this route. The pole at the right shows the political boundary. In the foreground is a pile of stones carried to the summit by travellers hoping for good luck. On the branches of the tree are tied pieces of clothing; these are remnants of clothing from sick children whose parents have brought the clothing to this remote spot in hope that the "evil spirits" affecting their children will stay with the clothing and leave the child.

64. These farmers on the way to market with rice bags fastened on frames on the backs of cows could be seen on this same route. Wheeled vehicles could not traverse this narrow mountain road, but a new railroad was being built through this area.

65. In the mountain area most of the farmhouses are dispersed rather than grouped in villages. A simple brush and sod bridge, which may be swept away by the stream when it is swollen by rain, connects the farmstead shown in this picture with the outside world.

66. Rocky fields for dry cereals, tobacco, and vegetables are found in the mountain lands of Northwestern Korea. In the small stream shown in this picture a farmer and his wife are trying to net fish with a wicker net.

67. The mountains and hills of Northwestern Korea have been etched into rounded forms where the bed rock is an easily disintegrating granite, as shown in this picture taken in 1938. Dry fields predominate, the roads are rocky, and the habitation is sparse.

68. A classic picture taken by Meijiya in the 1930's shows a farmer plowing his paddy field, ankle deep in the mud and water. In the background is a small village in the shadow of the hills.

69. In the courtyard of farmhouses in Northwestern Korea, as this picture taken in the 1930's by Meijiya shows, the farmer does a great deal of his work. Here a farmer and his wife are pictured beating the grain off the stalks of rice. The gourds are ripe on the thatch-roofed house at the right; to the left is the gabled tile roof of a larger house.

70. A market scene in Pyongyang in days gone by, taken by Meijiya in the 1930's. Country women with their clothes tied around their heads and the man with the horsehair hat are typical of those days. The jars for *kimchi* stand ready for purchasers to the left of the picture.

71. The plains and hills of Northwestern Korea stand out in this picture taken by the U. S. Air Force in July 1951. Most of the fields are for dry crops, but along the stream valleys are the square patterns of paddy fields. The effective bombardment of the twin railroad tunnels for the double-tracked Seoul-Sinuiju line is obvious in the foreground.

## South Korea

72. The United Nations air raids in Korea were aimed at military targets. This U. S. Air Force photo taken east of Kumchon in August, 1950 shows the the result of a hit on an enemy fuel truck. The picture shows clearly a small thatch-roofed farmstead, dry fields on the hill slopes, terraced paddy fields, poplars lining the road, eroded hill slopes which have only been partially re-forested—all items commonly found in South Korea.

73. This picture in a valley with paddy fields being used for seedbeds, or being prepared for the summer rice crop was taken in May, 1954 along the east coast near Kangnung. The scrub-covered hills with the grassy plots of grave mounds are typical.

74. The thirty-eighth parallel meets the east coast along the small valley shown in this picture taken in May, 1954. The small debris-laden stream is similar to those which come down from the mountains to the coast along this shore.

75. This UNKRA photo shows a quiet fishing village in a small valley, the type commonly seen along the East Central Coast. The nets are drying on the

beach, and the heaps of straw in the courtyards show that the people in the village carry on both fishing and agriculture.

76. This U. S. Army photograph was taken above the thirty-eighth parallel on the east coast in August, 1952. The boats have been brought up along the shore of this fishing village.

77. The crests of some of the ridges in the central mountains were bitterly contested during the Korean war. This ridge is pitted with foxholes and trenches and was subjected to strafing and napalm aerial attacks. An Air Force photo taken in April, 1951.

78. This small tungsten mine in the southern mountains near Taejon gives variation to an otherwise simple landscape of mountains covered with brush and scrub forest, and dry fields along the lower slopes. This U.S. Army photograph was taken in May, 1951 at the Chongdong mine.

79, 80. These two UNKRA pictures of Seoul are remarkably clear, for usually the dust is heavy over the city, creating a haze. The first looks toward the Capitol building, the former Japanese Government-General offices, the other looks toward the University over the spires of the Catholic Cathedral and the Young-nak Church. Looking closely at the buildings one can see that many of them are only shells and that there are wide gaps between buildings filled only with rubble.

81. The close-up view of destruction in Seoul is oppressive, like this photo of a wall of a former school near the West Gate of the city taken in May, 1954.

82. The Wha-sin department store on another corner of the intersection shown in this picture taken in May, 1954 has suffered even more destruction than the building shown here. The bus with its gay artifical flowers contained a merry wedding party and struck an incongruous note to this scene of destruction, but it did reveal the resiliency of the Koreans in times of trouble.

83. Korean villages which were used for shelter by military forces were attacked by aerial bombardment as this U. S. Army photograph of a village just north of the Han River taken in February, 1951 shows. The picture shows the types of houses which are common in West Central Korea and the variation between L- and U-shaped houses. Newer settlements like this are often strung out along the roads, rather than blocked together on the edges of the hills.

84. This rural scene—the plowing and leveling of a field after a period of non-use—is in nice contrast to the truce tents of Panmunjon visible in the background. The U. S. Army photograph taken in April, 1952 does show that " life goes on " in Korea.

85. This Air Force photo, taken near the same place as the first in this series, near Taejon in August, 1950 shows knocked-out tanks abandoned along the road. The village in the middle of the picture, at the curve of the road, has only one house left standing.

86. On the outskirts of the city of Chongju are some typical southern Korean farmhouses, thatched, open to the sun, and without high chimneys. This area seemed untouched by the fighting when I visited it in May, 1954.

87. In Southwestern Korea the winters are mild so that winter crops can be grown in the drained paddy fields, as this picture taken in the fall of 1938 on the outskirts of Kwangju shows.

88. A pine tree with its hacked branches frames this picture of a village near Sunchon along the southern coast of Korea taken in 1938. A farm boy

with his rake may be seen in the foreground. The village homes have clumps of green bamboo around them.

89. Newly reclaimed land along the indented southwestern coast of Korea is shown in the foreground of this UNKRA photograph taken near Kunsan. The regularly spaced fields are protected by a high dike and irrigated by water from the reservoir in the hills on the right side of the picture.

90. The port of Kunsan has many rice mills and storage warehouses. It is a relatively new harbor, and the streets are laid out in straight lines. Small boats shown in the foreground bring rice from the offshore islands. This is an UNKRA photo.

91. Refugees with tents and temporary shacks crowd the levees and flood banks of a river near Taegu in Southeastern Korea as shown in this U.S. Air Force picture of August, 1950. The river has built up its level between its artificial levees higher than the surrounding plain. Wells and ponds at the outer base of the levee provide some water for the paddy fields.

92. The temporary shacks along the slope of this hill in Pusan shown in this U. S. Army photograph of May, 1951 were later wiped out by a fire which raged through this part of the city.

93. The tile roofs of a *yangban*'s or scholar-landlord's house emerge above the surrounding thatch roofs of this village near Kyongju in Southeastern Korea, visited in 1938.

94. Looking down on the courtyard of a wealthy home at Kyongju, one can see the many rooms and courtyard, the polished wood veranda and even the servant carrying the tray of food.

95. This U. S. Air Force photo taken during World War II (and declassified for use in this book) shows in the foreground a Japanese-built airfield on Cheju Island. However, the picture strikingly shows the changes of land use with changes in elevation. Along the rocky coast are some fishing villages. The crazy-quilt pattern of the dry fields each surrounded by a stone wall shows up on the lower slopes. These merge into the grasslands which are used for grazing cattle and horses. Finally, the upper slopes of volcanic Halla-san are covered with forests or black ash and lava.

# INDEX

# Index

MAP OF KOREA: from a 15th-century geography published in Korea (see p. 32)